OCT 2 8 2009

D1737590

Soft Gold

Drawn from Nature by J W Audubon   Sea Otter   Lith Printed & Col.d by J T Bowen, Philad.a

Soft Gold

The Fur Trade
&
Cultural Exchange
on the
Northwest Coast of America

Oregon Historical Society
1982

COUNTY LIBRARY
TILLAMOOK, ORE.

Historical Introduction & Annotation
by
Thomas Vaughan

Ethnographic Annotation
by
Bill Holm

O/NW 979.01 SOFT 25 00
Soft gold

The exhibition, which was produced in conjunction with this publication, was presented jointly by the Oregon Historical Society and the Peabody Museum of Archaeology and Ethnology at Harvard University. All ethnographic artifacts are drawn from the holdings of the Peabody. Although many of these artifacts are among the finest of their kind in the world and well known to scholars and visitors to Harvard, few of them have been seen by the public at large. Through a nation-wide series of exhibitions, such as the one produced in conjunction with this publication, the Peabody is sharing its collection with the American people.

Other non-ethnographic objects shown in this volume and in the exhibition are drawn from the holdings of the Oregon Historical Society, and significant collections throughout North America and around the world.

This volume was conceived, designed and produced by the Oregon Historical Society.

Production of this volume was supported in part by the National Endowment for the Humanities and by funds provided by private and corporate associates of the Oregon Historical Society, specifically the S.S. Johnson Foundation for a gift without which this study, as here presented, could not have been produced.

Copyright © 1982 Oregon Historical Society
Library of Congress Catalog Number: 82-81739
ISBN 0-87595-107-4 (cloth); ISBN 0-87595-108-2 (paper)

All rights reserved. No part of this publication may be reproduced or transmitted in any form or by any means, electronic or mechanical including photocopying, recording or any information storage or retrieval system, without the permission in writing from the publisher, the Oregon Historical Society.

Printed in the United States of America

Contents

Frontis:

Glossy, closely packed sea otter pelts were prized throughout the world. But the Russian sea hunters, and, later, many other European traders gained wealth from the lucrative Chinese market where the heavy pelts were prized for their luxuriant ornamental qualities and durability. This great "soft gold" rush began in the eighteenth century when the Russians moved out of the Siberian taiga to the Pacific Ocean.

The rapid expansion of the hunters following, if not anticipating, Vitas Bering's investigation, caused international repercussions. To forestall expansion into *their* ocean the Spanish moved forces north from the Californias. But the great competitors for the magnificent pelts were British traders (following Cook) and especially the Americans out of New England and New York. The "Boston Men" eventually controlled the trade opened up between the Northwest Coast and the Chinese ports dominated by Canton.

Among many complications in the trade, the female sea otter produced only one pup a year and her pelt was preferred over the male. The statistics between 1740 and 1840 rose sharply, and fell as rapidly with the reduction of this golden harvest, pelts valued not so much for their warmth as the luxurious appearance so prized by the Manchu hierarchy in China. The Audubon print facing the title page is from the collections of the Oregon Historical Society. (OHS Library)

This work is dedicated to the contributors who have enriched the *Oregon Historical Quarterly* since its inception in 1900, and to all the other historical journals of the North American West; but in particular to Charles Carey, T.C. Elliott, Judge Frederic Howay, Edmund Hayes, Sr., and W. Kaye Lamb—scholar adventurers.

The title of this work, *Soft Gold,* is a direct translation from the Russian Мягкое Золото. During the seventeenth and eighteenth centuries, as Russian trappers moved eastward across the vast, forested taiga and throughout the North Pacific littoral, in search of the extraordinarily valuable sable and otter pelts. As a result, Siberia and the North Pacific were considered "gold mines" and the furs themselves, "soft gold."

Foreword

Founded in 1866, the Peabody Museum is the oldest institution in the United States devoted entirely to the collection, preservation and display of ethnological and archaeological artifacts. Today it houses one of the most significant collections of anthropology in the world. Objects gathered by Captain Cook during his voyages in the Pacific, American Indian artifacts collected by the Lewis and Clark Expedition, and more recently items from New Guinea assembled by Michael Rockefeller are but three expeditions that gathered ethnographic collections which form a part of the extraordinarily well-documented objects in the Peabody Museum. The majority of the collections at the Peabody Museum were gathered on scientific expeditions whose specific goal was the anthropological understanding of these now rapidly vanishing tribal peoples. Some of the objects exhibited in this publication were obtained on anthropological expeditions sponsored by the Peabody Museum. In certain instances they represent the finest available examples of the traditions of the tribal peoples on the Northwest Coast of America.

Before the turn of the century the Peabody sponsored pioneering expeditions to Mesoamerica and played a fundamental role in uncovering the earliest New World civilizations; the collections from these are among the best in the country.

The Peabody Museum tradition remains today much as it did in the past, a research and teaching institution devoted to anthropology. In comparison to the abundance of its collections, the Museum maintains only modest exhibition facilities and public programs. With support from the National Endowment for the Humanities and in an effort to place before a larger audience the great collections of the Peabody, the Museum has recently developed a "collection-sharing program." This program will bring to the public some of our finest artifacts which are presently being conserved, organized and photographed for exhibitions at art, history and science museums around the country.

The "collection-sharing program" is based on the assumption that the only way to preserve and do justice to our priceless ethnographic and archaeological treasures is to make them readily available for public viewing as well as for scholarly study. The public has shown more than a passing interest in these ethnographic and archaeological artifacts with an increasing appreciation that these items record the traditions and accomplishments of cultures that have all but vanished. They represent in many instances our only link of understanding with this past heritage.

The Peabody Museum is extraordinarily pleased to have a portion of its collection exhibited at the Oregon Historical Center. We greet with enthusiasm the extraordinary partnership which has linked our two institutions and look forward to further collaboration. Our heartiest congratulations are extended to the Oregon Historical Society for placing before the public in so attractive a format these rarely seen artifacts from the Northwest Coast of America.

C.C. Lamberg-Karlovsky
Director
The Peabody Museum of Archaeology and Ethnology
Harvard University

Soft Gold

Introduction

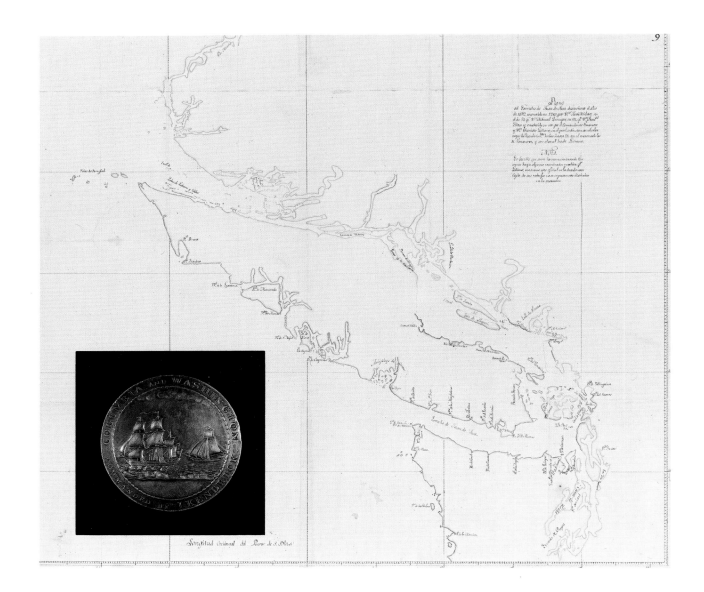

9

Introduction

Among the several purposes of any learned society, and especially historical societies great and small, is the preservation of information and worthy objects from the past, as historians attempt to gather knowledge and to diffuse it in interesting ways. Hence this book, for it is in thoughtfully composed exhibitions in cabinets and cases or in grand undertakings such as we record here that scattered treasures are seen with new eyes. Long hidden charts, carefully stored drawings, treasured artifacts and numinous objects are sometimes regarded with new perceptions.

The Oregon Historical Society has long wanted to bring together this rich and exotic gathering from around the world. Every member of our engrossed staff and the nearly 8,500 enrolled members will in some way participate in the pleasurable instruction about our unfinished past.

An essential reason for this vast undertaking resides in an observation made just over ten years ago, when this Society honored the centenary of the first British consulate established in the Pacific Northwest, an office but slightly older than the Society itself. From the never-ebbing sea of history, then Oregon Governor Tom McCall, in a vaunting flight, recalled for the honored dinner guest, British Consul, Sir James McDonald, KBE, British Consul, the mingled threads of ancestral ties, of "Viking, Celtic, Anglic, Saxon, Jutish . . . encompassing all hopes." Then the speaker of the evening, Aubrey N. Morgan, CMG, made a point now intimately linked to several aspects of our elaborate 1982 visual presentation.

The Spanish map of the Northwest Coast (shown on p. xiv) drawn perhaps by Galiano, is of supreme importance to the cartographic claims on the Northwest Coast.

The longitude of San Blas is established (at bottom left), which again points out the importance of this Spanish forwarding post. The particular interest about Vancouver Island is that it is still unnamed and not yet fully described, although the good work of captains Galiano and Valdez shows to advantage along with that of Vancouver's view. The map (82x71 cm) is color keyed (perhaps by Bodega y Quadra) to emphasize in gray all those discoveries made by Spanish explorers preceding Vancouver. His key emphasizes that Vancouver's exploration commenced in 1792, in association with Galiano, whose work is in blue. The red line indicates British discoveries along the continental shore. The small boat map made in Puget Sound is accurately depicted, and much else is there to describe the already monumental achievement of George Vancouver, RN.

The discoveries from 1592 (?) to that of Navarez in 1789, Quimper in 1790 and Francisco Eliza in 1791 are noted. Pointed reference is made to the early established Spanish claims by right of discovery. Cook made his landfall near Nootka which he entered and he missed the Straits, but he is not mentioned. (OHS Library)

It is no surprise that one of the finest holdings in the Society's museum collections is an elaborate Chinese willow ware dinner service brought back from Canton to Boston by merchant-skipper Robert Gray, from that first American circumnavigation in the late eighteenth century. In many ways China has since lain submerged, but in terms of world affairs Morgan that night stated with reference to the North Pacific:

> The recent emergence of China as a first class power has completely changed the scene. The straight hard line has given way to a much more fluid triangle . . . The triangle will soon change to a rectangle when Japan accepts her position as a fourth great power. . . . The United States, the Soviet Union, China and Japan all with great self interests in the North Pacific, will cause the fulcrum of power to move from the Atlantic to the Pacific, if it has not moved already. If the stresses and strains which are bound to occur in this rectangle are skillfully assessed . . . and if the economic opportunities are wisely judged, a great future can await Portland and Oregon in the coming developments in the Pacific Ocean.

How accurate our prescient speaker was. He was talking of course about international trade, which is what this publication is all about. As Thomas Jefferson was when in his instructions of 1804 he stated to government explorers Lewis and Clark: "The object of your mission is communication with the Pacific coast for the purpose of commerce."

In the Northwest today we must be out after our cargos as were those merchant sailors who came flocking to our coastline after the news of Cook's surprise windfall flooded European commercial centers. And we must include in the Aubrey Morgan equation the great needs and promises of another world partner, Canada, with emphasis on British Columbia.

But to better comprehend these looming possibilities we all need to better perceive what happened along the Northwest Coast in an era before our own, two centuries ago in a time more virgin than ours. Long dopples ran up from the uncharted seas toward as yet uncut headlands. Tree-covered capes plunged into waters aswarm with fish and fur clad animals known only to the tribes of Indian and Eskimo, peoples as yet unaware that they would ever barter or war except among themselves. They did not yet know that profitable trade is a universal interest.

The traders of New England had long transacted in furs. The records of the seventeenth and eighteenth centuries bear out the great activity of traders along the Hudson up to the St. Lawrence and to the Great Lakes. Trade in furs and in beaver and deer hides was a well-known and extensive activity from the time of the Dutch on Manhattan and the English dissenting colonies along the Massachusetts coast. The great spark however was the commercial news from Cook's third voyage. This combined with the pressing need for New England and New York merchants to pull themselves out of the moribund slough created by the victories of Washington's armies. In defeating the British the American colonies lost their old and valued trade associations with the Empire. Sheer necessity and dreams of quick fortunes drove the Yankee sailors around the Horn and up the west coast of the Americas. Their ships sailing on shares were of 100 and 250 tons burthen according to William Sturgis, a trader and historian. The crew might stay one season, which means a voyage of 22 to 24 months; but they usually stayed two summer seasons, making a three year voyage. Essentially they went to procure sea otter skins which were obtained from the natives by barter, "carried to Canton, and there exchanged for the productions of the Celestial Empire, to be brought home or taken to Europe, thus completing what may be called a *trading* voyage." The magnitude of these voyages can scarcely be understood.

In describing the elusive animal it is appropriate to quote Sturgis who with his first voyage in 1798 was close to the scene for 30 years. "A full grown prime skin which has been stretched before drying is about five feet long, and 24 to 30 inches wide, covered with very fine fur about ¾ of an inch in length, having a rich jet black glossy surface and exhibiting a silver color when blown open. Those are esteemed the finest skins which have some white hairs interspersed and scattered over the whole surface, and a perfectly white head." Mr. Sturgis, who may have been something of a character, said that he would rather look at a sea otter skin "than half the pictures stuck up for an exhibition, and

A superb numismatic piece (pp. xiv, 1) is "one of America's most famous early metalic rarities." (Some experts conjecture that this 4.1 cm medal was engraved by Paul Revere.) The medal was struck to honor the voyage of the *Columbia* and the *Lady Washington*. Several hundred pieces were cast in pewter and bronze, many of which were carried on the ships for trading. For the owners, about a dozen were cast in silver, one of which was sent to General Washington, who acknowledged it graciously. Only three are known to exist today.

This expedition, financed out of Boston, was of course stimulated by news of Cook's sea otter find and out of the desperate search for cargoes and markets among New England merchant traders, deprived of access to British-dominated ports.

An exceptional fact concerning this silver medal is that it was given to Hall Kelley, the famous Boston expansionist, and it is thought that he brought the medal to Oregon. The names of the merchant supporters (shown, p. 1), led by Joseph Barrell, provide special interest: Barrell, a prosperous and bold Boston merchant; Charles Bulfinch, the Harvard and European trained architect; Samuel Brown of merchant fame; John Darby, the Salem wharf owner; Captain Crowell Hatch of Cambridge; and New York merchant John Martin Pintard. (OHS Museum)

This 1800 surveying set (used for drawing at sea) includes a folding ivory ruler, friction dividers with adapters for instruments, the pen, compass and other pieces gathered together in a shagreen (fishskin) case. (OHS Museum)

puffed up by pretended connoisseurs." In fact, "excepting a beautiful woman and a lovely infant, he regarded them as among the most attractive natural objects that can be placed before him."

Actually the hair is about 1½ inches long, and the 80-pound animal is much larger than the 45-inch weasel-like land otter. Its feeding ground ran in a 6000-mile arc from the north Japanese islands through the Kuriles, the Commander and Aleutian islands down along the rocky inlets of the Northwest Coast, then the sloping capes of Washington and Oregon to the bays of California.

The emerging Russian hunters soon found the marine animal. The hunts were destructive. Andrei Tolstykh made three Pacific voyages, 1749, 1756 and 1760. The record suggests he took 10,218 sea otters including 821 cubs. Two Russian seafarers are reported by T. A. Rickard as taking 5000 otters their first year on St. Paul, the island discovered by Billing's officer. The second year Lukanov and Karekov killed another thousand. Soon the otters were gone. Quite naturally the hunters moved rapidly, following the pods toward the Northwest Coast.

We hardly know how long the several tribes and language groups had occupied the Northwest Coast from Coos Bay north. Legends of course had been passed down in oral traditions through generations. But a written language had not been devised by these peoples. The legends several generations or perhaps 300 or 250 years old could not encompass the great trek from northern Europe across Siberia and the bridge in the vicinity of Bering Strait. Our records suggest that could have been 30,000 to 35,000 years ago.

The last great ice age pressing down on the Northwest Coast began approximately 25,000 years ago, and lasted for 12,000. All was pulverized and destroyed under this massive weight. It was roughly 7500 years ago that native hunters began to move into the fastnesses of the coastal region first from the south and then the north, the earliest perhaps 10,000 years ago.

Here they found long narrow beaches running along the foot of hills interspersed with mountains and bluffs falling into the bays and ocean. The shores were bathed in fog, rain and warm temperatures stemming from a current rising somewhere off the Philippines and arching up around the islands of the Pacific Rim. All this being enclosed by the mountains rimming the edge of the continent.

Along with the beneficent climate and heavy plant cover there was abundant food, several kinds of salmon in different runs, cod, halibut, herring, smelt, pilchards, clams, oysters, mussels and crab. The fresh water abounded with food, as did the saltwater with whales, sharks, porpoises, sea lions and hair seals. The land sustained elk, deer, goats, varieties of bear including the Kodiak monsters. There were mink, marten, beaver and other animals in abundance and all the tribes down to Cape Mendocino in northern California had learned the basic necessity, how to store food. And many clever devices and constructions had been developed to capture food including weirs, salmon traps, baskets, nets, hooks, harpoons, as well as bows, arrows, javelins and boats. Because of the topography it was essentially a boat supported culture locked into hundreds of rivulets, river mouths, coves and bays.

The natives were, running from the north, the Aleuts, Kodiaks, the Chugach groups combined of Eskimos and Athabascans, (running back into the Yukon) and then the more fierce Tlingits, the Bella Coolas, Xaihais around the head of Queen Charlotte Strait, the Southern Kwakiutl and Nootka dominated what is now lower Vancouver Island and Cape Flattery. Far to the south were the Tillamooks, the Siuslaw, Alsea, Umpqua and the savage Coos. For all the centuries this great population had been left to themselves in a comparative Eden-like existence.

Perez was the first white to formally contact these many groups, at the head of Queen Charlotte Island in 1774. Along with warfare a preoccupation of both men and women was trade. It was instantly begun. But his monarch's claims were being contested by rival nations.

California scholars continue to vex the question of where Sir Francis Drake anchored along their fabled coast. But in the north we are convinced that for five days in June, 1579, preceding his lengthy stay in

Small terrestrial globe in a spherical case of laminated wood encased in shagreen made by J. Newton in 1800. The two halves have a brass hinge and clasps and paper constellation within shows the human and animal figures associated with the stars. The poles are fixed by two steel support pins. (OHS Museum)

lower New Albion, he anchored the *Golden Hind* and his Spanish capture in a "bad bay" directly south of a lowering Oregon headland later named Blanco. We like to think that "Red Beard" got men ashore to replenish drinking water if nothing else, but there is no record of a landing or any ceremony of possession. But the gleaming fact remains: before the Armada sailed, before *The Tempest* was written, Francis Drake was examining the coastal lands around Coos Bay.

Jumping the wide centuries we find another blue-water sailor raising the Oregon coastline under the English flag. James Cook, another legendary captain, left Hawaii (his just discovered Sandwich Islands) on 2 February, 1778. He was following Admiralty instructions and when, by design, he reached 45°N latitude he knew that he was in Drake's old waters, waters which were still thought by the Spanish to be theirs. In the 200 intervening years after Drake the Mediterranean naval empires had declined and those spawned on the Atlantic had flourished. But now in Cook's era Great Britain was girding to slowly grind and eradicate the once formidable Dutch, Spanish, Danish and French fleets. The same years had witnessed other dramatic changes, striking technical advances by nautical instrument makers such as Arnold, Kendall and Harrison, the watch maker. In making an accurate landfall Cook's genius and skill combined with that of the new scientific technicians.

After his seven week voyage Cook slowly moved north from his newly named capes of Perpetua and Gregory (now Cape Arago) to search out the water passage to Hudson Bay, that east road home that had earlier eluded Drake. Cook sailed with aplomb through Spanish waters naming headlands they considered their own, just as La Perouse would do. He found no landing places for his ships, which now needed watering. Darkness and foul weather cloaked harbors and important geographical points.

When at last Cook found that "inlet" to "recruit . . . Wood and Water and procure Refreshments," he was on the upper west shore of Vancouver Island. Since the season was early and blustery, he had encountered no natives along the coast, or sea hunters in their ocean-going boats. No nubile greeters swam out to clamber up the ship ropes, as in

Hawaii or as described in Tahiti in 1777 by the surgeon's mate, that "great number of Girls . . . who in symmetry and proportion might dispute the palm with any women under the Sun." The climate was different. And gallantry aside there was more to this local condition than a wan sun and distracting facial impedimenta. There seems little to compare with the local history and ardent customs of those southerly islands discovered by Cook, Wallis, Bougainville, La Perouse, Vancouver and others. Though Cook remained about Nootka Sound a month, he was never regarded as a god there or on any part of the Northwest Coast. A result, perhaps, of Spanish navigator Perez' brief offshore visit there in 1774. The novelty was gone.

Although the diarists with Perez left good accounts of Haida life from the Queen Charlotte Islands south, there are broad gaps in our knowledge of Indian culture and custom. It is generally accepted that great oceans serve to bring peoples together rather than to separate them. But the clans and tribes along the Northwest Coast estuaries were not travelers—except for hunting and warfare. We have little substantive knowledge of those remarkable people until Cook's observers began to pick up the "very pleasant and fertile" landscapes of our coast.

Whereas the Spanish commanders had come to the Northwest Coast almost directly from Iberian naval service via a crossing of Mexico, Cook's journey was a longer, a more exotic way. He had come into association with native life and custom at the beginning of his career in the maritime lanes of Newfoundland and Labrador. Indians were much in evidence on the broad St. Lawrence where he had done surveys and auspiciously advanced his naval career whilst serving Admiral Charles Saunders and General Wolfe at the siege of Quebec.

Cook had encountered countless tribes and cultures in his succeeding 20 years, yet his descriptions hold their freshness. His journal entries parallel Steller's on an earlier memorable one-day visit in 1741 to "the great land," when he left valuable objects in trade for those he carried away from a deserted Tlingit hut near Mount St. Elias. Cook, the supposedly taciturn Yorkshireman, later registers a sense of wonderment in King George's (Nootka) Sound, and a powerful vision. Having come

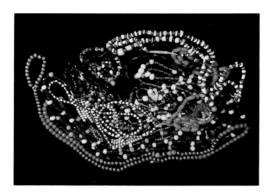

Perhaps 90 percent of the beads traded on the American continent came from the famous Murano glass producers at Venice. Smaller quantities of beads appeared from France, Belgium, The Netherlands, and later Bohemia and China itself. Three hundred years before Vancouver and Gray, Columbus in 1492 stated in his log: "Presented some of them with red caps and some strings of glass beads which they placed around their necks, and with other trifles of insignificant worth that delighted them, and by which we got a wonderful hold on their affections." Some Indians were so keen about beads they would trade horses, slaves and provisions for a small quantity—especially when the color was right.

As an example of trade, the U.S. Army traded six pounds of white beads for a Mohave captive, Alice Oatman. According to Oregon Historical Society Chief Curator Dale Archibald, Pimas at one time traded 30 sky blue "padre" beads for a good horse. On occasion Northwest Coast Indians traded for red and blue beads. (OHS Museum)

from "the pathless and wild seas", his command moves with relief toward a snug anchorage away from the ocean's immensity, coasting slowly toward a ceremonial reception,

> when a person [Maquinnah?] in one of the two last [canoes] stood up and made a long harangue, inviting us to land, as we guessed by his gestures. At the same time, he kept strewing handfuls of feathers toward us; and some of his companions threw handfuls of red dust or powder in the same manner. The person who played the orator wore the skin of some animal, and held in each hand something that rattled as he kept shaking it. . . .
>
> We observed that two or three had their hair quite strewed over with small feathers; and others had large ones stuck into different parts of the head. After the tumultuous noise had ceased they sat in a little distance from the ship and conversed with each other in a very easy manner. Some of them, now and then, got up, and said something after the manner of their first harangues; and one sung a very agreeable air with a degree of softness and melody which we could not have expected; the word haela being often repeated as the burden of the song . . . . One canoe was remarkable for a singular head, which had a bird's eye and a bill of an enormous size painted on it; and a person who was in the bow seemed to be a chief, was no less remarkable for his uncommon appearance; having many feathers hanging from his head, and being painted in an extraordinary manner.

This from Captain Cook who had by then greeted multitudes of exotically painted natives from Labrador, around the coasts of South America, Micronesia, Capetown and elsewhere: a perceptive observation forever notable.

The same leader "held in his hand a carved bird of wood, as large as a pigeon, with which he rattled as the first person had done; and was no less vociferous in his harangue." One wonders of course what those wonderful illustrators of Cook's achievement were doing at that moment—Ellis, Webber, Roberts and Clevely. Were they even then making their memorable sketches which enrich this volume? Cook would find that the broad faces painted ochre, red and black masked much beneath them, as the thick and hazy weather masked jutting points and wave-combed reefs. All was unpredictable.

Yet, how interesting that the power of song, of vocal music, is several times recorded as an important part of this remote culture. One might muse over who responded to the French horns and the fifes and drums of Cook's men, to the violins and accordians of the Russians, or much earlier to Drake's lutes and trumpets as he sailed this shore to the south. Later, the young American, Joseph Ingraham states the music was mostly sticks rhythmically striking boards that accompanied the Haidas' singing, "their music was not unpleasing." Perhaps Pope is right concerning the powers of music within the savage or civilized breast.

Much of this becomes a series of overpowering romantic reconstructions placed against the seadrift, the ravens and rock-piled shore and the dense, somber forests surmounted by cloud-capped mountains. But there the romance should end, for our theme again is discovery, trade and domination. While histories of this pursuit in the annals of the North Pacific Ocean are filled with exploits, broken ships and dreams also litter those waters; waters as remorseless and remote today as when the first European voyagers observed the sea endlessly breaking its back. Today, reports studded as ever with mysterious disappearances and chilling misadventures, convey the grand ferocity that hangs over every reach of the northern waters.

The Spaniards, in their long journey from Madrid, Mexico City, Acapulco and San Blas had come far out of their usual latitudes to make their North Pacific reconnaissance and to test the Russian presence. And it must be regarded as remarkable, even though the superb cartographer Henry Wagner said "the Northwest Coast is all that which extends from Cabo San Lucas (the tip of Lower California) indefinitely to the north." But they were in dilatory fashion exploring another part of their realm based on claims established 275 years earlier when Pope Alexander VI laid down the demarcation line between the Spanish and Portuguese at the Treaty of Tordesillas. A claim now being blithely ignored by all others as San Diego was hurriedly founded (1769), then Monterey (1770) and San Francisco (1776). The effort was too late.

Far to the north the more acclimatized Russian expeditions, official

Metal goods were always valued by Indians because they were items they most wanted and needed and often were beyond their technical skills. Copper was highly prized. On his second voyage Gray carried 143 sheets of it along with his 4,261 quarter-pound "chisulls." Brass pots and pails such as this were included in lists of gift distribution and trade items by the English and American traders on the coast. (OHS Museum)

The Marquesas were named Washington's Island by their discoverer Joseph Ingraham in 1791; four months later they were named by Marchand in the *Solide,* then in June 1792 by Hergest in *Daedalus,* and in March 1793 Josiah Roberts in the *Jefferson* again named them Washington's Islands. They are now in the Marquesa Group. These beautiful and exotic islands were occupied by a people van Langsdorff found to "excel in beauty and grandeur of form." The male he compared to the Apollo Belvedere, six feet two inches, Paris measure. Along with all else they were tatooed and almost hairless by choice.

On the von Krusenstern voyage von Langsdorff observed the "punctuation" and gave us a drawing engraved in London (1813) entitled "A young Nukahinvan not completely Tatooed." The painful *sittings* were undertaken at three to six month intervals and lasted from three to four weeks through 30 to 40 years. Important to their diet were fish, poultry and "man's and swine's flesh." (von Langsdorff, The Bancroft Library)

and otherwise, had in the 1720s begun their ocean hunts from Okhotsk and the stormy capes of Kamchatka. As with Perez, Heceta, Cook and La Perouse, these are extensions of endless quests guided from the imperial centers of St. Petersburg, Madrid, London and Paris. So, when romance intrudes distance too must be recalled to mind. The endless land trek of the Russians took many years simply to transport all the chains, anchors, rope, cannon, iron bars, hammers, anvils, axes and sailcloth across their vast country to the lonely Pacific shore. It was only then that Vitus Bering's first crude ships could be constructed. It was at last these same unremitting distances that sapped the Russian ardor for continuing expansion down America's North Pacific Coast. And in those days too one might more properly see the Russian traders as hardy and energetic adventurers rather than professional sailors. The sea swallowed many Russian enterprises before and after Bering, making available even more shattered planks and rusted nails to watchful natives.

One is reminded of Francis Beaufort who accomplished so much to make the seas safer for his fellow sailors. In 1789 the later famous hydrographer said, "On the whole I think being at sea when [I am] not sick in such a fine large ship and having pleasant Gents on Board is one of the most delightful places in the world."

But cruising, mapping or trading in northern waters does not match this youthful description. Consider Cook on his third voyage, who, while coasting here, was a worn, short-tempered man. Another who encountered problems of space, time and pure physical exertion also arrived on the Northwest Coast. George Vancouver (who was with Cook at Nootka as an observant young midshipman) returned in 1792 with official but cloudy instructions holding meager promise of fame or glory. It was almost a surety that his meticulous search for the Northwest Passage home would produce little but frustration. Brilliant and dedicated as he was, Vancouver's time and temperament were with the neap tide, but his mapping triumph lives forever.

And how very lucky we are today to have such a vivid pictorial record. As Rüdiger Joppien points out, Bligh had no artists for his exceptional voyages, nor did the great Alexander von Humboldt. Painters later had to work up the latter's very rudimentary sketches, but Vancouver

10

had much better artists than he first realized in Humphrys, Heddington, Sykes and Lt. Zachariah Mudge. He noted in 1791 as A.C.F. David reminds us, "It was with infinite satisfaction that I saw amongst those officers and young gentlemen on the quarter deck, some who with little instruction would soon be enabled to construct charts, take plans of bays and harbours, draw landscapes, and make faithfully portraits of the several headlands, coast and countries, which we might discover." Just a hint of the martinet there perhaps, but we do have the wonderful drawings now on record; and for special pleasure, the skillful *Discovery* drawing from Mudge.

And as in Cook's case, Lt. Commander A.C.F. David observes, some of the finest engravers in Britain prepared the Vancouver plates. "These included John Landseer, father of the painter Edwin Landseer, James Vittler, James Heath and Benjamin Pouncy." They were to do a lot with the "pleasing diversity and sublime desolation" of the Northwest Coast with its "pleasingly . . . cloathed eminences" and "chequered . . . vallies; presenting, in many directions, extensive spaces that wore the appearance of having been cleared by art." Edmund Burke and other romantics would have liked that very much. And John Sykes certainly improved as we see in his bold and strategically important views of San Carlos Mission near Monterey and Valparaiso in two strategic views useful to later fleet commanders.

Over 60 years later one again sees the engravers' art and some of their imagination prevail in the plates made from Henry Warre's fine field sketches, not to mention those of Paul Kane and several members of the Wilkes Expedition, represented here by the plain artistry of Joseph Drayton at the estuarine boundary of Willamette Falls.

Aside from the problems of interpreting the accuracy of trained artists and delineators who were on the spot versus deskbound engravers improving on nature, there is the matter of degrees of experience. Men with Vancouver and Cook, with Krusenstern, von Langsdorff, Lisianskii and Belcher had traveled many strange seas, as had some of Malaspina's illustrators. The comparative sense is introduced in varieties of wondrous decoration in von Langsdorff's emblazoned Marquesan as opposed to "old world conventions of the picturesque" containing notions and

This charming mirror with its original French glass was carried in the sea chest of Robert Gray, and was in his cabins on the *Lady Washington* and the *Columbia Rediviva*. One might ponder looking into this mirror on the wall. It has traveled far and been witness to all that it has seen with Robert Gray, the Plymouth Colony descendant.

On the second voyage this mirror traveled the 41,899 miles logged by the *Columbia*. (OHS Museum)

dreams beyond reality. As Joppien observes of the post-Cook era, "a flood of engravings, etchings, woodcuts and aquatints were produced; they were pirated from illustrations of Cook's narrations and often inaccurately altered and badly distorted." Which is not to deny some are most enchanting in their enhancements.

From these observations we can easily go to something so simple and useful as the drawings George Davidson made while serving on the ship *Columbia Rediviva*. There, in Robert Gray's complement he is listed as the ship's painter, actually the person who kept fit the *Columbia*'s paintwork. Happily he extended his skills to give us an important visual record for the anthropologist as well as the maritime historian.

More important to the ethnographer-anthropologist are the altogether remarkable drawings of German-born Sigismund Bacstrom. As Douglas Cole aptly states, contrary to Webber's treatment 14 years earlier, "He is not concerned with the representative scene or the typical specimen." Of his 1 March 1793 portrait of the natives aboard *The Three Brothers* off Port Rose at the south end of the Queen Charlotte Islands, Cole states: "The strong features are neither flattered nor romanticized, and while the picture may not be 'beautiful,' it possesses a documentary value far surpassing the majority of eighteenth century drawings of these New World natives." As with Tikhonov, Voznesenskii and Davidson, and Vancouver's young gentlemen, Bacstrom's careful, sometimes impetuous on-the-spot drawings in their fresh exuberance transcend the static skills of portraiture as portrayed for example in Kane's studio-hardened works. There is no doubt of the value of drawings done on location, even by those unskilled.

In his arresting account of "hard luck" Bacstrom's astonishing voyages about the world, Douglas Cole provides grand insights into a rediscovered, magnificent visual record of the Northwest Coast of America. Bacstrom's drawings are as important as any to be seen, for they appear to be meticulous delineations. As with many other scientifically minded men, Bacstrom came to the Pacific through the offices of the indefatigable Joseph Banks. He seems to have applied for a naturalist's post on Cook's second Pacific voyage, but this did not materialize. Until 1791 his life is an incredible tale of woe on both land and sea, reminiscent of Daniel

Defoe's most fervid imaginings—then it gets worse. That his drawings would survive such a turbulent career is miraculous.

In the summer of 1792 (shortly after Gray's discovery of the Columbia River) Bacstrom is with invidious Captain William Brown on the *Butterworth*, accompanied by two lesser vessels, the schooner *Jackal* and the sloop *Prince Lee Boo*. As too often happened with adventurers, they were cheating and robbing the natives. Ingraham reports on them in his personal account, and although he was anti-British (an understandable emotion at the time), his is probably an understatement.

Fortunately Bacstrom was able to leave Brown's service, seeking asylum at Nootka, where he drew some early and accurate autumn scenes. In subsequent voyages on *The Three Brothers* (Captain William Alder) he provides us with exceptional views of the natives, their family and village life, not only in our archipelago, but in the Hawaiian Islands too. They are of extreme importance. From his accompanying notes one perceives Bacstrom's scientific drive for accuracy combined with an apparent lustiness.

His account as well brings to the surface one other problem of the time—slavery. He mentions the *Jenny*, a former slaver. She would certainly be recognized for what she was. Among other matters her captain's actions along the coast (shooting natives whose canoes had been tipped over) suggest a hardbitten crowd. Regrettably, slavery was an accepted fact of life, certainly in Russia, in the new United States, in the Spanish colonies (until 1810), not to mention plain economic servitude among French and Spanish peasants—and others. To complete the picture, we now should regard the enslaved Indians. From their first contact, Russian hunters held Aleut hunters hostage, and among the Indians the Tlingits in particular had a more than modest holding of slaves, some parts of whom may have ended up as a ceremonial meal, or an occasional sacrifice. The Tlingits had something else—the Russians must have recognized it as something in their own nature, a special quality, the ability to endure, to last things out. Ever present, available for trade and to act as middlemen between the Europeans and the interior tribes (from whom slaves were traditionally taken), the Tlingits (Kolosh) never lost their ferocity. Commerce did not mellow them, especially since they left so

The 59 pieces of Cantonware in OHS collections were secured as much neeeded cargo by Captain Robert Gray during the first American circumnavigation, 1787-90. Named for the Chinese port city, "the Forbidden City of the Rams," whence came these precursors of English willow pattern, these dishes were heavy, irregularly shaped ware featuring hand-painted oriental scenes such as rivers, temples, birds, bees, butterflies and other embellishments. The first pieces were given to OHS in 1917 and the remainder (belonging to Martha Gray) were donated in 1941 by Miss Amelia Peabody, a great-great-granddaughter of the merchant-explorer.

Gray left Boston in 1787 in the *Lady Washington* but returned as captain of the larger *Columbia Redeviva*. (OHS Museum)

Robert Gray's sea chest. With its red fabric-covered rope handles and its dove-tailed construction, it is faithful to the period. Its size (128x44x46.5 cm) provided commodious space for the storage of the Captain's valuables, collected from the Pearl River estuary in China, the tribes of the Northwest Coast and from Tillamook Bay Indians. When he returned home in 1790 from his great voyage around the globe, this chest was packed with treasurers. It was in his cabin on the second voyage, a voyage that started a few weeks after his return from the first; a voyage 190 years ago during which Gray discovered the Columbia River. This valuable artifact from an illustrious era of American exploration was given to the Society in 1908. (OHS Museum)

much of that to their women whom they considered more skilled at trade.

We should remember that the coastal natives wanted very much to barter and trade; after all, they had been at it centuries before the white men arrived. They were, as was so often bitterly observed, as skilled in trade fair or foul as they were at war and feasting. And they easily managed to corner markets in certain regions while enjoying 100 to 500 percent markups on trade with the interior tribes who found most new goods irresistible. And the women were more skilled at trade than the men. From beginning to end they appear to have been more successful in all transactions. It was a hard time and no innocents lasted long in the trade. Even the Spanish when they came north with their priests were by engrained habit searching for silver and gold as they traded abalone shells for furs.

In noting the peculiarities and hazard of trade endured by old hands and young Boston men on the make, their financial backers must be mentioned. Whoever was really at the bottom of those first fur ventures out of China, the voyages of 1786 were essentially spurred by the British East Indian monopoly. When anomalous John Meares for example arrived on the coast in the *Felice* he was energetically seeking the Company's gain. C.J. Dewey points out that the British East India Company he represented was "in many ways the most successful 'multinational' company of all time. The perfect embodiment of the spirit of mercantilism dependent on power." When we think then about aspects of the Nootka Controversy stimulated by Meares, we must keep in mind that Company's special relationship to British government. It far exceeds that with which we are in this hemisphere more familiar, the association between British government and Hudson's Bay Company interests. Hydrographer Alexander Dalrymple had in fact expressed in one of his less eccentric moments the hope that the two companies might together coordinate their trading monopolies in North America. It was Meares in pursuit of his haphazard second colonizing voyage who sparked the controversy with Spaniards. Some of the Dons continued to unrealistically presume that not only the Pacific Ocean but the lands whose waters it lapped were theirs until a Russian barrier or an icefield blocked them.

14

Let us examine again the particulars of trade as seen through the eyes of enterprising Boston traders. John Boit, Jr., who was with Gray in 1792 returned in 1795 as Captain of the *Union*, 89 tons and 10 carriage guns. May 10 at Clayoquot the 20-year-old reports, "Capt. Hannah Hatswrak principle chief of the place came alongside, followed by a vast many canoes full of Indians. They all appeared happy to see me again & inquired insistently after the Columbia [and] purchased many valuable furs & plenty of fish." Five days later, having safely sailed through migrating whales, near Uker's village, "At 9 AM the Chief came attended by a number of canoes & a fine lot of Sea Otter furs was purchased for blue cloth, for Iron they wont take as presents & Copper is not much better." On June 7, "These natives [at Tadent's village S.E. point of Lagara Island] inform'd me that a Portugueze Brig had been here & carried away two of the king's daughters to Macao in China by consent, that he was to return them in 6 moons." June 9, 1795, "Some Small Canoes from Cunniah's [*sic*] with fish. Iron & cloth most in demand but furs are at least 100 P cent dearer than then the *Columbia* was to the coast." On June 21 the youthful crew is attacked by 40 canoes with at least 30 men in each.

William Sturgis records his bartering problems as a captain for the famous trading house of J. and T.H. Perkins, descendants of Thomas Perkins, an early Massachusetts fur explorer. Knowing the Northwest natives' desire for ermine, Sturgis bought 5000 skins cheap at the Leipzig fair. In one 1804 forenoon he traded the German skins at 5 for 1 sea otter—500 of them. Sea otter skins sold that year for 50 dollars in Canton, and the ermines were purchased in Boston for 30 cents each. Of course such markets did not hold. Taste was fickle.

Joseph Ingraham, formerly a mate on Gray's *Columbia*, returned to the Northwest Coast in 1791 in the 70 ton *Hope*. After careening at Washington Islands (now the Queen Charlottes) the young captain began to trade. But an area which had yielded so profitably to Gray produced nothing. Two British ships, crafty Douglas in the *Grace* and Barnett in the *Gustavus III* (formerly *Mercury*), had beat him on the ground. But Ingraham reflected, and with some Yankee ingenuity had his blacksmith turn untradeable iron rods into iron necklaces. The

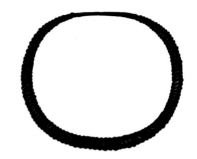

The iron collar drawn by Sigismund Bacstrom has peculiar immediacy, for in July 1791 Joseph Ingraham began to make iron collars for the Northwest Coast trade, because his other goods were not interesting. His were made of three pieces twisted together, weighed five to seven pounds, and were highly prized in a wide area. Native necklaces were made of copper, but this 13-inch collar is of twisted iron undoubtedly from the *Hope*'s forge.

While Ingraham imitated the native metal workers, other traders began to imitate him, producing (according to Douglas and Gunther) even heavier neckware and bracelets. (S. Bacstrom, Private collection)

resultant three-strand polished neck rings weighed five to seven pounds each! They were a great hit that season and something different from the rum, guns, ammunition, blankets, rice and molasses which were eventually brought to the trade sessions. Some were found on totem poles and at grave sites by later travelers.

Ingraham also gives us our first full description of totem poles. He was altogether a remarkable person, with the energy and insights Cook and his best officers commanded. His earlier account written as a narrative report for Don Esteban Jose Martinez in 1789 should be included here. Now in the Archivo General de la Nacion in Mexico City, his account written at Nootka states:

> Of trees I have seen white pine, pitch pine, red and white cedar, cypress, double and single spruce, wild cherry, elder, black and white alder, crabapple, birch, hemlock, maple, willow, poplar and some kind of dyewood . . . .
>
> Among the quadrupeds are bears, wolves, foxes, deer (both moose and fallow), racoons, brown squirrels, brown mink, sea otters, dogs, martens, beaver, wild cats, gray rabbits and mice.

He names in his densely packed account the birds and fish and the habits and vagaries of various tribes. The description of fishing for whales is especially interesting, essentially a middle Vancouver Island activity:

> The young men who are most expert in striking the whales are kept at some distance from the shore, but not so far that they may not be seen distinctly by a person who is always appointed to observe their motions. As soon as the whale is struck the one looking out gives notice by a shout. Then they seldom exceed a minute in preparing and launching from thirty to forty-five canoes which with great speed repair to his assistance. As each canoe comes up they strike the fish. As soon as the harpoon is in, the staff draws out of the socket and leaves the bladder floating, which buoys the animal up near the surface.

This is the manner in which Maquinnah and his villagers hunted. Mate Ingraham noted all these details in a 1778 letter to Martinez written when aboard Gray's *Columbia*, to our knowledge the first trading vessel to winter on the Northwest Coast.

He too notes the great fondness for music. "Singing and dancing they are extravagantly fond of. The music is altogether vocal except drumming on a board, which always accompanies their singing." Perhaps some of these tribes heard the harpsichord player aboard Malaspina's *Descubierta* playing through the endless summer nights (Scarlatti, no doubt) beneath Mount St. Elias, or as the Spanish commander's flotilla slowly progressed toward the as yet undiscovered Columbia River (which would be fog blanketed), and south to Monterey and on to the Philippines.

But for now let us return to Cook and the *Resolution* and *Discovery*. Having spent almost a month in King George's Sound, his party is ready to leave Nootka. As Beaglehole noted in his masterwork, *Captain James Cook,* "all the nearby canoes assembled and their occupants sang a parting song, flourishing the more valuable goods they had acquired, while one man mounted on a platform, danced to the singing in a succession of masks." The arrival and departure were obviously attended by a colorful, Northwest Coast version of a European water festival. And, as we know, for many favors of the night and pleasures rendered in other hours, many British pewter plates were missing. Clothes too were less intact since the increasingly less unattractive ladies had come to covet brass buttons. Cook had noted too that the high culture to which he and his men had been witness in the bays·and estuaries were essentially born of an "untouched civilization" that had largely resolved the problem of regular food supplies, of clothing and shelter—although not intertribal warfare.

As the ships moved cautiously north, feeling their way along the rocky coastline toward ever frostier seas, Cook approached what he eventually named Prince William Sound. He was consulting the Russian experience—the somewhat rough-and-ready but available maps of Müller and Stählin. As per Admiralty instruction he was working toward latitude 65°N while acknowledging "the late Russian discoveries." He was also moving against two human imponderables—wary natives and secretive Russians. It is in this general area that Russian hunters had been stalled by the stubborn obstinancy of the Chugach tribes. These Eskimo-Athapascan hunters could not be subdued as had been the Aleuts a generation

This Northwest Company brass trade token (opposite) is a great rarity; it may be the unique exemplar. George IV is shown laureated between "token" and "1820." The reverse of this 2.9 cm coin is even more interesting, for it has a beaver in the center and the North West Company name encircling the rim. The tokens were issued for many years, but, as with Hudson's Bay Company, beaver skins were always preferred. Furs were the currency of the fur trade, but the need for a more portable form led to trade tokens issued in the denomination of skins. The beaver skin was the preferred standard of value for 200 years. Prior to 1700, the Hudson's Bay Company was listing its returns as "made beaver" and published standards of trade, as did many colonial governments, with the prices listed in beaver pelts. (OHS Museum)

The sophisticated Northwest Coast artisans learned quickly, and were imitative. They were also taught, especially in Kodiak and Sitka, how to work metal. Among many training programs in Sitka the apprentice metal workers could have learned to make this copper kettle; perhaps from shipyard carpenters and coopers who often worked a forge to make repairs.

Aleuts had become great tea drinkers as well as tobacco chewers. Copper and iron kettles were also bartered for furs. The Indians "gave as many . . . pelts for one iron cauldron as it could hold." In 1822, a 25-pound iron cauldron traded in Sitka cost the Indians two black bear skins or the equivalent. (Peabody Museum, Harvard University)

earlier. As an example, the St. Constantine Redoubt was not established on Nuchek (Hinchinbrook) Island in Chugach until 1793. At the same time the Russians began to consider occupying Nootka—a decision they and eventually everyone else abandoned. But, they had come a great distance from Kamchatka, and they would travel a much longer distance down the coast in their search for furs and food.

We regularly note the scientific aspects of all of Cook's voyages. And some assume that his were the first. His luster is in no way diminished by pointing out that the Dane Vitus Bering's voyages at the command of Peter the Great were highly organized scientific voyages of exploration and inquiry. They commenced fifty years earlier in 1725, and were preceded by Evreinov and Luzhin in 1718. The Tsar's instructions were formalized and detailed and in time the historical record returned was substantial and impressive. The several scientific advances were great— and so was the output of certain geographical information. Hence, the Spanish response to what looked like territorial encroachment in their waters. Such an expensive undertaking would never have been undertaken by Madrid were it not for the increasing exhortations from the Spanish ambassador in St. Petersburg concerning the inexorable penetration of mare nostrum.

When the Russians at last reached the Sea of Okhotsk and the Kamchatka Peninsula in the first half of the seventeenth century, basic changes occurred in order to adapt to the new landscape. They moved from a forest-taiga atmosphere to an open unpredictable sea where they had little experience, and that mostly on the shallow Baltic and broad Russian rivers. In the forest sable was king, and although sables gave birth to five or six pups a year, trapping had depleted the supply. Along the North Pacific island chain swarmed the sea otters so prized by the Chinese nobility. But the sea otter female generally gave birth to only one pup per year. Worse yet, the female pelt was more highly prized than that of the male.

As James Gibson, E.A.P. Crownhart-Vaughan and Basil Dmytryshyn have brought into focus, there were other marked changes. The Russian forest hunters never learned how to take sea otter. What they captured were the native men (with their families) who would hunt for them. Aleuts and eventually Kodiaks came under the yoke. Because of harsh treatment, accidents, sickness and storms at sea, in the last half of the eighteenth century the native populations plummeted, even as the sea otter vanished. While Russian officials quaintly reported that the Aleut would happily sit in his baidarka for 10 to 12 hours waiting to spear an elusive sea otter, it was arduous labor. Land has its attractions too. Ivan Veniaminov, the great missionary priest, asserted that an Aleut baidarka is so perfect in its type that "not even a mathematician could add very much or scarcely anything to the perfection of its nautical qualities." But a baidarka did not come easily, for it originally required over a year for a hunter to construct his finely crafted 37-pound vessel. The reports also reveal that an Aleut hunter could paddle his craft 10 miles per hour in a moderate sea (Gibson). Whatever their skills, by the time Cook reached the northern waters the captive hunters were stretched out very far along the archipelago. And their usually scurvy-weakened Russian masters were not in shape for "the very toilsome and sometimes dangerous hunts." Baron Von Wrangell notes that fur seals, sea lions and walruses were more easily taken.

Gibson's finding is that with the establishment of the official coordinating Russian American Company in 1799, "half of all [Aleut] males more than eighteen or less than fifty years of age had to labour for the Russian American Company." The resultant toll was appalling, but not surprising. At least 80 percent of the Aleut population was lost during the first and second generations of Russian contact. This before the Russians moved south to Sitka (New Arkhangel) and their permanent Tlingit confrontation.

The needs that prompted such harsh exploitation in an unrelenting geographical landscape are interesting. Sables and other Siberian furs had been supplied through Moscow to a European market (recall those favored persons whose portraits we examine in their high renaissance cloaks and gowns—the Dutch, the English, French and German princelings and their thin-blooded dukes, margraves and earls). The sea otter (or "sea beaver") was not so warm, but its dense, durable fur was

This Cantonware teapot would provide special charm in any location but its interest is much enhanced by its historical associations with Captain and Mrs. Robert Gray. Tradition states that it was among the pieces brought back from Canton by the Boston trader. From the more than 14 shares valued at $3,500 each came bountiful returns associated with some American fortunes and business concerns of the twentieth century. Gray may have had some great memories during the tea hours. (Private collection)

Camphorwood Chinese chests were covered with pigskin, and ornamented with brass tabs and floral painted borders. When Americans entered the China Trade in 1785 they naturally brought home these colorful chests, packed one inside the other. The smallest chest would be lined with tea paper and filled with choice tea. The set of chests might include sizes from five feet down to two feet. The Chinese locks and handles were adopted from English chests.

We might assume Gray brought some of these home with their special stash tucked away for the home treat. (OHS Museum)

more attractive to the Chinese rulers. In return their hard-bitten traders exchanged tea, silk and porcelain—but most of all the tea, which fed samovars from the Baltic down to Samarkand to far off Norfolk Sound. The importance of Chinese tea had extended to the Russian areas of North America. In 1865 this was noted by Frederick Whymper at the inland Russian post of Nulato, Alaska, "a few minutes later we were lunching at the 'bidershik's' [supervisor's] table on raw salt fish and bread. It need not be said that the 'samovar' had been prepared as soon as they sighted us in the distance." Tea along with snuff became an Aleut habit. They and other natives and "creoles" fashioned their own tea kettles and samovars.

The Chinese however were difficult—unpredictable. The Russians were allowed to trade in one place only—the Chinese border town of Kiakhta. In some years a sea otter pelt might be worth 40 times more than a sable pelt. But the Chinese traders might decide not to trade at all, or only fitfully. Hence, although the Russians were in command as middle men, they were at the mercy of their shrewd Chinese buyers and their native suppliers; the latter increasingly began to provide basic food as well as furs and sexual arrangements of an ever broader nature. Along with all these vexations, Chinese officials had forbidden the Russians any entry into their ocean ports. As other nations began to take otter this exclusion naturally rankled, for the British, American, French, Portuguese, etcetera, had access through the Pearl River and later other Treaty Ports.

This was the general and highly complex situation Cook encountered as he met his first scattered Russian hunters. However, he was hardly in a position to analyze their strengths and weaknesses. And he was on those "pathless and wild seas" for more basic reasons. There must have been a bit of irony and compassion mixed as he encountered the Russian colonists—especially in the Aleutians—and noted the scurvy problems This problem haunted the Russians to the end of their days in North America. Despite all their farming attempts their agriculture never prospered—not even in California. This inadequate food supply combined with excessive drinking among Company employees produced serious problems of health, morale and leadership. Even in later years a former Chief Administrator, Tebenkov, said in 1852 of Alaska,"—a good worker can only get there accidentally." Most comments were even more negative.

During the time of Alexander Baranov (1799-1819), the Russian hunting groups moved south. They established themselves at New Arkhangel where, with the Tsar's approval, "the Gibralter of the North" was established by the Company's vigorous chief administrator. Here they hoped to improve their trade, build ships and sturdy shelters while resisting pressure from British and American factors. Gibson states that in 1800 New Arkhangel accounted for three-quarters of all the sea otters taken in Russian America. The lofty site chosen by Baranov must be

Meares brought Chinese laborers with him to construct his "hut" at Nootka and to work on his vessel the *Northwest Adventure*. This is the kind of storage jar (a rather elaborate version) brought to the Northwest Coast by Chinese workers and settlers. The jar and cover are buff colored earthenware with a dark brown interior and an exterior glaze of glossy green-blue shading to variegated greens and blues. This was returned from New England to the West Coast by a wagon train family via the Oregon Trail. (OHS Museum)

viewed with mixed feelings. It was sited next to an expanding Tlingit village that threatened the company "fortress" day and night until the Russians departed almost 70 years later.

The Russians described the Tlingits as "completely independent." A neat understatement. In 1802 they seized New Arkhangel, and they threatened the capital in 1809 and 1813. They destroyed the Ozersk Redoubt and besieged Sitka (New Arkhangel) in 1855 when many were killed and wounded on both sides. The aggressive Tlingits possessed falconets and cannons as well as rifles and muskets. Their suppliers quite naturally were Americans and to some extent the British.

The Aleuts who had also been necessarily relocated at Sitka were meanwhile hunting down the shores of Washington and Oregon and on into Trinidad and San Francisco bays. The American Jonathan Winship with the (*Joseph*) *O'Cain* related that,

> from five to fifteen bidarkas usually went forth to hunt together. The moment an otter was seen floating on the water the alert Indians fixed their eyes upon it, and trembled like the eager dog at the sight of game! Swiftly but very silently the canoes approached from the windward. When within shooting distance, while the man at the stern guided the boar, the nearest bowman raised his dart, and with sure aim threw his pronged bone spear with incredible accuracy. For twenty minutes or so the otter submerged, his course being marked by a bladder attached to a long cord. When the animal arose to the surface for air a screaming hunter was on hand to finish him.

The *O'Cain* was moored at San Quentin. On 4 March 1804 Alta California Governor José Arrillaga reported to the Spanish viceroy that "there is not an otter left from Mission Rosario to Santo Domingo." The governor stated that Jonathan Winship simply would not respond to repeated orders to cease and desist and to leave. When the Yankee returned to visit Baranov at the end of the season he split 1100 skins with the Russian administrator. He was also carrying 700 additional sea otter skins he had purchased personally from various Spanish officials and missionaries. Naturally he returned south for a second season taking over 100 Kodiak hunters and 50 baidarkas. They often used two-man crafts. Winship spread them about the various islands and bays to frustrate Spanish guards and custom agents. During the summer, skins were taken that were worth $60,000 in the Canton hongs. The southern skins however did not have the quality of those from the Kuriles, the Aleutians and other cold water areas. Winship had also attempted to colonize the Columbia River near Puget Island, as always, in search of food.

It was this somewhat extended and disorderly situation that Captain John D'Wolf encountered when, early in 1805, he brought the 250-ton *Juno* from New England to New Arkhangel—more furs than food, and a shortage of ships and men. It was here that he met Baranov. He was "agreeably disappointed as I had been led to believe that they had scarcely emerged from the savage state." Later he met Nikolai Rezanov, a frustrated ambassador who was evaluating Russian American Company posts on behalf of his Petersburg partners. Among others in Rezanov's party was a distinguished German scientist in Russian service, Dr. George von Langsdorff. Two naval lieutenants of the Russian fleet, Nikolai Khvostov and Ivan Davydov, became friends of John D'Wolf. With the assistance of Langsdorff, the *Juno* was sold to the Russian American Company. Von Langsdorff took some time to make an important visual record, which we value today, and so did Bristol sailor D'Wolf.

Equally important, D'Wolf crossed the North Pacific in a small boat, with a vast profit from the *Juno* sale. At 26, he took along a former crew member to serve as valet, and to occasionally play his clarinet or violin as they sailed through the herds of barking seals in the enfogged Aleutian archipelago. The first American to become a transcontinental Russian traveler, D'Wolf also described Siberia, as well as Moscow before Napoleon's invasion.

It was men such as D'Wolf who were the extension of long established New England traffic in furs and sandalwood, who became as much at home in the floral boats and hongs of China as they were the quays of St. Petersburg or Cronstadt, and the wharves of Lisbon, Naples and Havana. When the fur trade eventually declined Yankees continued to trade with and feed the Russians. When the Russians departed, so did

This flintlock pistol features a box lock with a screw barrel. According to OHS firearm consultant, the Hon. Victor Atiyeh, who restored this piece given to the Society by John Leach, the center-hung hammer is boxed inside the frame rather than fastened to the side.

To load this trade piece, the barrel was unscrewed and powder and ball dropped into the upended chamber. The barrel was rescrewed, and (with good luck) fired. This piece (16.2 cm long) from the Leach Estate was also used on the Oregon Trail in the Leach wagon train. (OHS Museum)

the men of New England. Let us remember that right on their heels came the great new whaling fleets and the sealers, with new demands and problems born of hunts on the ocean deeps.

The American traders had, until the British agreements, dominated the trade in the first 40 years of the nineteenth century. Gibson notes their staggering success. Tied to this are Kenneth Latourette's statistics for the Chinese trade. Between 1805 and 1809 the imports and exports were a trade-off at $3,900,000. Balance was almost achieved in the 1820s with $6,200,000 with $100,000 less in imports. Between 1840 and 1844 the balance changes with $1,700,000 in exports as opposed to $4,600,000 in imports. Three or four firms now dominated the trade based in Boston and New York; and of course they had among other dodges begun to trade contraband in all the Spanish ports from Valparaiso north. Gibson states that the American ships annually numbered around 250 after the revolutions of the 1810 era, and the profits were "enormous."

In this same era as Barry Gough records, we see the dramatic fall off of British traders hamstrung by the East India Company, whose restrictive charter had been renewed by London in 1793. Between 1797 and 1820, the time of Great Britain's Napoleonic entanglements on the Continent, only 26 British vessels came to the Northwest Coast compared to 238 American ships.

As the imperial interests waned, certain competitions intensified. The French made no lodgements, and the Spanish entries vaporized, the Americans through clever and aggressive diplomacy took full advantage of a cloudy situation. They took much more than a share in the Spanish Treaty of 1819. First of all there was much talk about sovereignty along the west coast between Spanish, British and French flag planters; but the fledgling United States in effect had no traditions of sovereignty. The basic and early key is that Heceta had noted and marked the great river of the West in 1775 (the year of Lexington, Concord and Bunker Hill, where Broughton fought). Gray's coup was followed by the Lewis and Clark trek to the Pacific Coast. Then the Americans founded Astoria, beating British interests out by a whisper, as a prelude to settlements in the Willamette Valley. When President Monroe directed affairs he

24

advised his agents that his negotiators at the Treaty of Ghent to conclude the hostilities of 1812 should accept nothing below the 49th parallel as the boundary line between the two national interests.

In 1819 the Adams-Onis Treaty with Spain contained a detail of profound importance. Spain conceded all her unenforceable and centuries-old rights north of the 42nd parallel to young America. A very neat trick at the time, for it more than clarified hazy aspects of the Louisiana Purchase boundaries.

As time went on the British fleet, linked to commercial interests including the transcontinental fur trade, moved into the vacuum created by the retreat of Spanish and Russian interests. The Americans gradually came to dominate the Columbia River interior and through immigration, the land mass around Puget Sound, until the final boundary line was determined at 49°N. The Bay Company men continued to thread the northern passes from the interior river systems in the north down to salt water rendezvous.

Until the 1840s most of the ships were small and sometimes unacceptable. Consider Vancouver's low opinion of the *Sutil* and the *Mexicana*. Sometimes their sailing qualities were simply bad, as with the British ship HMS *Chatham*. Often by the time crews reached the Northwest Coast they and their captains were worn out and sometimes were too old and exhausted for such perils, physical vicissitudes and the unceasing need for command decisions. Fatigue is always an obvious factor. Russian shipbuilding in Petropavlovsk and the Alaskan fjords must be thought of as a tour de force, equal to the malaria-wasted activities at San Blas which were a genuine Spanish accomplishment; but both were short lived.

While we read of the Hudson's Bay Company vessels *Cadboro*, *Cowlitz*, *Dryad*, *Vancouver*, and *William and Ann*, a strong new element appears on the coast. Enter then the British navy with its increasingly elaborate structure and its far flung naval-commercial stations. It is in this interim period that the long arm of the British navy is again extended, with considerable strength, whether it be the *Racoon*, *Modeste*, *America*, *Blossom*, *Sulphur*, *Cormorant*, *Fisgard*, *Herald* or *Pandora*. The list is almost endless. For the United States, the famous *Ontario* and Captain

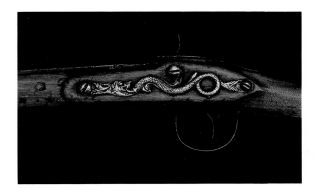

This is a fine example of the famous Hudson's Bay Company trade gun showing its distinctive dragon or sea serpent side piece. In the seventeenth century English gunsmiths borrowed this ornamentation from the Dutch. This attractive design is very often missing from the few surviving trade guns.

George Himes reported that before a Hudson's Bay Company trader would exchange with a bartering Indian, beaver skins had to be piled up to the length of the long-barreled flintlock barrel. Indians would later cut the barrel down for more convenient transport by horse or canoe. The coast traders' lives became even more at hazard when Indian canoes, sometimes carrying 30 or more persons, arrived with firearms rather than spears, bows and clubs. (OHS Museum)

The Indians of Norfolk Sound, Sitka area, carved with exceptional skill and for small objects had access to such materials as whale bone. When handled in full round, in combinations, even small pieces such as these combining large and much reduced figures in complex contortions reveal bodies of birds, animals and humans intimately associated.

Those judged best of all were made by the Coast Tsimshian, but these which must be of Tlingit are very strong and of dexterous and imaginative design. (S. Bacstrom, Private collection)

James Biddle, USN come to mind, as well as Commodore Wilkes, the imperial scout in the *Vincennes,* with *Porpoise* and *Peacock.* Although McLoughlin despised it, in several ways it is Simpson's steamer *Beaver* that turns the tides of commerce, but it is the British fleet organization that stabilizes the boundaries at the 49th parallel. Within a few years the argonauts of California surge north toward the gold strikes on the Fraser River. The force of the fleet in company with James Douglas and the Bay Company holds the border secure. Thousands of gold seekers swarmed over Vancouver and the Queen Charlotte Islands and into the Fraser River. They were an occupying force, but their energy was neutralized.

The shallow gold strikes gave way to other interests as time went by; the more thought was given to the fisheries, the timber and lands available around Puget Sound. As the valleys of Oregon and then the Washington Territory were occupied so also was the Crown Colony of Vancouver Island.

With the signing of an agreement between Hudson's Bay Company and the Russian American Company in 1839, the Russians slowly withdrew from California and then eventually (as the unsuccessful Crimean War wound down) inside themselves. Psychologically, and then at last physically, withdrawing to the Kamchatka Peninsula and behind it, the Russian government concentrated its interests on the Amur Valley and related Chinese questions. The British, Americans and mostly enfeebled tribes remained, and their imperial interests were centered on the newly acquired lands and sheltered waters around them.

These waters of special commercial interest again concern us in this brief overview as the sea otter trade disappears and transactions of less value supersede it. For two decades from the late 1820s the Hudson's Bay Company moved north from the Columbia District headquarters, led with an iron will by Chief Factor John McLoughlin. Forts Langley, Fraser, Rupert, McLoughlin, Naso-Simpson, Victoria, Taku, and Stikine were constructed. In 1839 the Russian agents leased almost the entire mainland of southeastern Alaska to British traders. These hard but generally fair men established a strong and lasting trade. And McLoughlin's efforts were backed up by that truly powerful corporate figure, Sir George Simpson—he who reigned as HBC governor for 40 years from 1821. The old days were over, and it was a constant struggle not only to maintain the fur traffic, but to sustain the Indian population ravaged by new diseases from the Willamette Valley and Columbia River north to Alaska. As an example, in the New Caledonia district (north of McLoughlin's empire) the population appears to be about 2600 in the interior, only half of what it had been in 1829. And of course not all deaths were due to disease. Intertribal and clan warfare had everywhere intensified with the introduction of steel, powder and ball.

But in other ways the natives had changed, as Governor George Simpson noted between his two long journeys in 1824 and 1841. Not only did he observe with much sadness the many semi-deserted villages; he also noted striking changes in native art, for example at Fort Simpson, far up the coast. "They carve steamers, animals, etc., very neatly in stone, wood, and ivory, imitating in short everything that they see, either in reality or in drawings." It was on this journey too that Simpson made an administrative judgment at Fort Stikine, later found intolerable by John McLoughlin at Fort Vancouver. At Sitka he met the chief administrator, a handsome and able Finn named Etolin, and his stylish wife. It was Etolin who, having lost one magnificent ethnographic collection in a fire in Turku, in the Grand Duchy of Finland, gave orders that another of equal interest be gathered, which it was.

Several changes occurred in this period, during the all important 1841 visit of Simpson to the coast and his second visit to Sitka in 1841-42. At this time, with the murder at Fort Stikine of John McLoughlin, Jr., by one of his own men, an unbridgeable gap opens between McLoughlin and Simpson, who appeared at Stikine a few days after the 25 April 1842 shooting. This sad misadventure was in every way mishandled, but the maps used in compiling the evidence of murder are useful to our reconstructions today.

Among other important concerns which the two chief administrators Adolf Etholen and Simpson concerned themselves with was the sale of rum and other spirits to Indians. At the same time the Finnish overseer, who had grown up in the Russian American service, tried to stabilize

These rich ecclesiastical vestments (detail above and opposite) are reminders of the Russian Orthodox Church traditions that were centered at Kodiak, Sitka, and they are a striking reference to the exceptional work of one great priest, Ivan Veniaminov (1797-1879). According to James Gibson the church was "not zealously evangelical." But Veniaminov was untiring and versatile. His work gradually was recognized and his efforts rewarded with the unofficial title of "Apostle of Alaska." Later he returned to Russia and reached the highest church office "Metropolitan of Moscow and Kolomna." (Veniaminov Collections, Cathedral of St. Michael, Sitka)

the annual food supply by increased purchase of wheat, notably in the Cowlitz, Tualatin and Willamette valleys. This system was earlier initiated by McLoughlin and his agents and continued by his successors until the mid 1860s, especially at forts Vancouver and Nisqually. And even though we see McLoughlin passing from the scene, his usually exemplary sense of service was carried on; this despite his explosions of temper somewhat in the Vancouver-Cook tradition but more volcanic.

Some persons with little sense of the past or of the large aspects of history which give a sense of proportion to affairs, regard the wondrously peaceful 49th parallel only to lament and deplore lost opportunities. Some Americans wish that John Calhoun, that masterful Southern foot dragger, had slowed down even more so that the gold strikes of British Columbia in the mid 1850s would have moved the floating population of California to the Fraser River, thereby guaranteeing statehood. Some Canadians believe that the Americans were overly aggressive and greedy at the Treaty of Washington, seeing a most inequitable conclusion squeaking through to a narrow victory against the clock and the elements. They forget that Senator Dayton of New Jersey thought most of the region a barren and irredeemable waste "as the desert of the Sahara." McDuffee of South Carolina in 1846 declared, "I would not give a pinch of snuff for the whole territory" and even in New England the often magisterial Webster said, "What do we want with the vast, worthless area—this region of savage and wild beasts, of deserts of shifting sands and whirlwinds of dusts, of cactus and prairie dogs? . . . a coast of 3000 miles, rock-bound cheerless and uninviting, and not a harbor on it! . . . I will never vote one cent from the public treasury to place the Pacific Coast one inch nearer Boston than it is now." So much for rhetoric. Within 20 years came the American purchase of most of "the great land" including the rich Alaskan panhandle which some Canadians consider part of a heritage that has become part of world history. We have come far from that time in the late eighteenth century when Grigorii Shelikhov, brooding in Irkutsk, hoped that Baranov was trying to find "the best and most loyal American natives to be your spies . . . to obtain information about any foreign ships that appear, including French naval or trading vessels. Then they could sink a foreign ship by cleverly drilling a hole in it, or by setting it afire, or even by luring it into some bay or inlet where it might be wrecked on underwater rocks and reefs." Yes, times had changed considerably since the early years when John Kendrick had emphasized in his instructions to Gray that the natives always be given a square deal. So British Columbia has not been "Americanized" and Canada has her great window on the West. Russia had her view to the east from Kamchatka and the maritime provinces. Who would have dreamed so much would so swiftly come to pass? The "great land" of Russian aspiration and romance fell to the Americans, in part because Russia needed money to pay for her great reform program, and certainly did not want England or France, her European competitors, to have a northern foothold facing Siberia, or anything else in "the quiet ocean."

Today those myriad fisheries remarked upon by Dixon, Gray, Ingraham, Boit and others are waning. The endless forests of "pine" that captured the interest of Cook, King, Vancouver, Malaspina, Bodega and others interested in the wellbeing of their monarchs' ships have been thinned or destroyed. Names have vanished. Hector's Point, named by La Perouse, became Haswell's Rock, but this and Gray's Cove and Roch have long disappeared, along with Virgin's Rocks, Hancock's River, Washington's Islands, Entrada de Juan Perez, Koiyan Straits, Quadra Island and countless Indian names. But so many remain to evoke thoughts of those adventurous, robust men and women. And as with other renewable resources, including the once endangered seal, the sea otter has returned from the edge of extinction. And as is only natural with such a historic and personally enchanting creature, it has again for more engaging reasons captured the livelier part of our interest and imagination.

Because some of those busy sailors of two centuries ago put time aside to keep a journal, we can now relive and understand something of a vigorous, legendary time when men were out searching the broad oceans for the cargoes that we ourselves must continue to win today. Recall John D'Wolf of Rhode Island, trading in Sitka and selling the *Juno.* He sailed off to Okhotsk in his tiny new boat, the open 25 ton *Rostislav,* the kind of voyage that is the stuff of literature, the odyssey, the eternal search. So it was as an honored old sea captain living in

Dorchester overlooking the wharves of Boston harbor. By now a truly ancient mariner "Norwest John" of Bristol reminisced many days with his nephew Herman Melville, a younger Pacific sailor. They voyaged on strange seas of thought together, cruising the shrouded cape, the embayed islands and the deeps of the Pacific in their eras and "as it rolled 5,000 years ago." It was Melville who captured D'Wolf's story of the great whale rising beneath his tiny open boat off Kamchatka. It was he who mingled his own experience with "Norwest John's" spirited enterprises to capture an American saga which has achieved timeless interest, becoming universal literature in *Moby Dick*.

The short lived golden fur trade has vanished, two hundred years have gone by. The great ocean remains almost untapped and untrammeled, offering opportunity to the bold hearted, the persistent and tenacious.

Soft Gold

Objects of Unique Artistry

Northwest Coast Artifacts from the Peabody Museum

Harvard University

Basketry Hats

Wherever whites came to the Northwest Coast they found the people wearing basketry hats. Handsome and practical, these hats protected the wearers from the rain and sun, and furnished a broad surface for decoration or display of prestigious design. These hats were woven in a variety of materials and techniques. In some places certain styles were worn only by privileged individuals. If we can judge by the statements of early mariners and by what we know of the cultural importance of whaling, this may well have been true for the Nootkan conical hats depicting whales and their pursuers made at the very beginning of the historical period.

No. 1 BASKETRY HAT 26x25x26.5cm

32

NO. 1 BASKETRY HAT

A particularly fine example, as well as a most typical one, is this hat, collected at the beginning of the nineteenth century. These hats are extremely rare; there may be no more than fifteen in the world today. All share this unique shape—a small, steep-sided cone with a surmounting cupola-like knob. In material and technique they are unlike the well-known Nootkan basketry of the late nineteenth and early twentieth century (*see* No. 141). The hat is twined on a warp of split spruce root with a weft of black-dyed cedar bark, overlaid in all the light colored areas with the long, narrow and originally bone-white leaves of surf grass, a marine plant. Complex banded geometric patterns cover the knob and its neck and a narrow border at the rim. Between these is *always* a whaling scene, usually with two pairs of very stylized whales and the pursuing hunters in their canoes, with harpoons, harpoon lines and inflated sealskin floats.

As with almost all Nootkan basketry hats, the "whaler's" hats are double, with a rather coarsely woven inner lining of red cedar bark. The inner hat is twined together with the outer one at the rim.

No. 2 BASKETRY HAT

If a knobbed hat with whaling scenes is rare what can be said of one (of only two known examples) with *thunderbirds* and whales? Collected probably at Nootka Sound about 1794 by Captain James Magee, it depicts the mythical struggle between the giant bird and its prey. One thunderbird appears ready to strike the whale with outstretched talons while his counterpart around the hat has already attacked and is carrying the prize to its mountaintop home.

Among the early, and successful, Boston traders seeking sea otter furs on the Northwest Coast was Captain James Magee. On his return from his adventurous voyage of 1791-94 in the *Margaret* he deposited with the Massachusetts Historical Society an excellent collection of artifacts from the Pacific, among which were many fine objects from the Northwest Coast, including this basketry hat. Other Peabody Museum objects in this publication that were originally in the collections of the Massachusetts Historical Society and that were probably from Captain Magee are the comb (No. 131) and the harpoon sheath (No. 39). Some drawings by artists accompanying early voyages show these hats worn by women, but other accounts ascribe them to chiefs only, and probably specifically to whalers, a chiefly prerogative. Recently hats resembling these have been made for sale by skillful Nootkan weavers, but they are made by wrapped twining of cedar bark and grass.

No. 2 BASKETRY HAT 27x27x25cm

No. 3 BASKETRY HAT

Very different in appearance from the knobbed hats, but probably Nootkan nonetheless, is this domed hat of twined spruce root. It is identified in museum records as Kwakiutl, but probably in error. Domed hats with black painted rims and crowns decorated with abstract animal motifs are rare, although not so much as the knobbed whaler's hats. They have the typically Nootkan inner lining of twined cedar bark. A much more common domed hat utilizes no spruce root, but is made entirely of bark, sometimes with wrapped-twined designs of grass. Collection records for black-rimmed hats are meager, so it is not understood just what the relationship between them and the knobbed hats is. This one seems to be the earliest collected black-rimmed hat in existence, supposedly acquired during the first years of the nineteenth century.

There is good reason to believe that this hat was collected by Lewis and Clark at the mouth of the Columbia River, where they saw hats such as this one and described them in their journal. This hat came from Charles Wilson Peale's museum, which received Lewis and Clark material, including a hat from the Columbia River. Hats of this kind must have been traded from the Nootkan tribes to the north.

No. 4 BASKETRY HAT

Most woven hats of the northern part of the coast have a flaring profile and are twined of split spruce root. This very early example is from the southern limit of the flaring hat, northern Vancouver Island. It is made of a combination of twining stitches—diagonal twining over paired warps at the top, skip-stitch twining producing the pattern of diagonal ridges in the center, and plain twining over single warps at the rim. This arrangement is exactly like that on a hat collected at Nootka Sound in 1778, on Cook's third expedition. The crown is painted with a stylized animal representation in a southern variant of the northern formline design system.

Several hats pictured in drawings of the early contact period show tassels such as the ones on this hat, which are of buckskin strung with short sections of dentalium shells. Both Kwakiutl and Nootka fished for these shells on the west coast of Vancouver Island and traded them widely. They achieved even wider distribution when the Hudson's Bay Company bartered for them for use in the fur trade. Enormous quantities of dentalia were traded to Plains Indians in the nineteenth century where they were prized for ear pendants, necklaces and women's dress yokes, often covered with thousands of shells. They were called "Iroquois shells" in fur trade inventories, probably a corruption of the Nootka (and Chinook jargon) name "hyakwa."

No. 3 BASKETRY HAT 38x38x12cm

No. 4 BASKETRY HAT 31x31x17cm

35

No. 5 BASKETRY HAT 27x27x28cm

36

No. 5 BASKETRY HAT
No. 6 BASKETRY HAT COVER

Among the great achievements of the basketmakers' art is the northern crest hat, here represented by an extremely fine example and its protective cover. This Tlingit hat was probably made early in the nineteenth century. It is of spruce root, in three-strand, plain and skip-stitch twining, the latter forming a pattern of concentric diamonds.

The five basketry cylinders surmounting the hat, and hung with an ermine skin, are prestigious emblems, often called "potlatch rings." An over-simplification of their significance is that they represent the number of potlatches given by the hat owner. More likely they originally referred to the number of times the hat itself had been publically displayed and revalidated as a crest object, but in most cases the number of rings was stabilized at some time and remained an integral part of the hat as a family emblem. They were woven as a continuous stack, each cylinder around an enclosed, light wooden ring.

The crown of the hat is painted with an elegant formline design depicting a clan crest animal, but so abstractly that it is difficult (and probably presumptuous) for us to identify it. The rim and the top cylinders are painted pale blue-green, a typical color in northern Northwest Coast art.

All the colors appear to be native pigments, mixed in a medium prepared by chewing salmon eggs. A lump of the pigment material was rubbed on a stone palette in the salmon egg-saliva mixture and the resulting paint was durable and waterproof. This blue color has often been assumed to be from some copper ore, but recent and ongoing investigation of native paint sources suggests that it may be from celadonite, an iron silicate, present on the Northwest Coast.

The importance of this hat is underlined by its utilitarian cover, plain-twined with a simple, zigzig skip-stitch rim design. The crest hat was kept in this cover and only brought out on important state and ceremonial occasions.

No. 6 BASKETRY HAT COVER 28x28x29 cm

37

No. 7 BASKETRY HAT 37x37x20cm

No. 7 BASKETRY HAT

Not all painted hats were true clan emblems, although the designs on them were often crest figures. This hat is a typical northern dress-up hat of twined spruce root. Such hats were worn by both women and men. The design is a whale, with the head taking up most of the available space. It was probably made in the late nineteenth century. Although the painting follows the conventions of the art, the difference in quality between this one and the elaborate Tlingit crest hat (*see* No. 5) is striking.

No. 8 BASKETRY HAT
No. 9 BASKETRY HAT

A pair of jaunty hats, probably Tlingit made, imitate hats worn by white visitors. Most of these must have been made for sale, since they do not appear to have had a native use. These are woven, as most Tlingit baskets, of spruce root, one (No. 9) with spaced bands of grass false embroidery and a hatband indicated by dyed spruce root weft. The other (No. 8) is plain twining, the dyed-weft hat band with alternating vertical stripes and checkerboard pattern. These patterns are achieved by using one dyed and one natural strand in each weft pair, manipulating the sequence on each twining row to achieve two designs. Complex basketry shapes like these require great skill on the weaver's part in adding and subtracting warps to make smooth transitions from one form to another.

No. 8 BASKETRY HAT 27x27x12cm

No. 9 BASKETRY HAT 32x32x12cm

No. 10 BASKETRY HAT

A number of "sailor's caps" and low-crowned, brimmed hats appear in nineteenth century collections, but this may be the only spruce root "top hat" in existence. Elegant bands of dyed-weft patterns elaborate both crown and brim. The dotted pattern is achieved by alternating solid-color weft pairs with two-color weft pairs. As with the low-crowned hats, this one has no real place in coastal culture, and must have been made as an exotic object for trade. The style of decoration in weft-dyed bands suggests Haida work, but the twining direction is more characteristic of Tlingit basketry.

No. 10 BASKETRY HAT 35x35x16cm

39

No. 11 BASKETRY HAT 28x28x14 cm

No. 11 BASKETRY HAT

Tlingit basketworkers were virtuosi who had no trouble in imitating almost any form they chose, even various peculiar hats worn by the newcomers. This one appears to be a copy of a sailor's cap of the nineteenth century. Twined of spruce root and embellished with typical Tlingit basketry designs in grass, using a false embroidery technique, it sports a deep brownish-black band of maidenhair fern stem to represent the ever-present ribbon. Only a few of these hats survive today. The Tlingit adopted a similar sailor's cap style for their social dancing regalia.

40

No. 12   BASKETRY HAT 38.5x38x19cm

No. 12   BASKETRY HAT
This spruce root hat was probably new when James G. Swan collected it in Alaska in 1876. The painting probably represents the mythical sea grizzly, with its large head, toothed mouth and ears covering the crown and front rim of the hat, while the fluked tail and clawed feet appear on the back rim and the two pectoral fins, in red, are displayed on the sides. The clear rich color of the red paint identifies it as vermilion, an important item of trade throughout North America. It was very popular on the Northwest Coast from earliest trade times, but it never fully supplanted the less brilliant native ochre red, probably made from hematite.

Canoe Models

The stereotypical emblem of Northwest Coast culture is the totem pole. But a far more appropriate candidate for the position would be the sea-going cedar canoe, upon which in a large measure the unique character of coastal lifestyle was built.

The Northern two thirds of the coast is characterized by high mountain ranges crowding the shores of the Pacific and the straits, their deep valleys forming winding fjords and a jumble of islands. There was (and is) almost no land travel of any distance possible, so almost all communication and commerce was canoe-born by sea.

Canoes also made possible utilization of the most important food resource of the area, the varied marine life which was hunted, gathered and transported with the aid of canoes. Ritual and warfare involved canoes in both practical and symbolic ways. Those great vessels provided the armature for some of the most spectacular painting and sculpture of the region. They can be seen as marvelous sculptural art in themselves.

Real canoes were not collected in the early days of contact. Ranging in size from one-man craft to impressive vessels 60 or 70 feet long, even the smallest would have made a bulky souvenir for European and American traders. Fortunately we have two forms of records about the canoes seen by eighteenth and nineteenth century explorers and traders. The journals of these visitors were often illustrated with drawings of native canoes, some of them detailed and accurate; additional drawings by John Webber, George Davidson, Sigismund Bacstrom, and the French naval officer Blondel, among other artists, preserved a record of the unusual form of the Northwest Coast canoes. The other form, the native canoe models, is the only other record we have of these early canoes.

No. 13 CANOE MODEL 112x20x25cm

No. 13 CANOE MODEL

This ancient canoe (a "head canoe") is characterized by thin, flat fore
and aft fins extending from the gracefully flared hull. As with most
other Northwest Coast canoes this style of canoe was carved from a
single cedar log, widened and brought to its final form by steaming and
springing outward the gunwales. The model illustrates the very peculiar
and unique form of the early northern type. It is an accurate representation except for the disproportion it shares with most Indian canoe
models, being nearly half as long as it should be in relation to its
height and beam. In spite of appearances, the long slanting end is the
stern and the broad, vertical fin is at the bow (some of these models
are equipped with carved crewmen who are frequently reversed when
the model is assembled for exhibition, since curators have a hard time
believing that the vertical fin is forward).

This model was collected before 1837 and was very likely made for
sale, although models were certainly also made as toys for Indian
children. While this is an early example of "tourist art," the craftsmanship
as well as the artistic quality of the painting is of the highest order.
The design, painted with red primary formlines and black secondary
detail, is too abstract to be confidently interpreted, but it is expertly
done and perfectly illustrates the conventions of an ancient system of
flat design which was closely adhered to by artists of the Northwest
Coast throughout the fur trade period.

No. 14 CANOE MODEL 180x26x29cm

No. 14   CANOE MODEL

A few models, like this one, approach the proportions of actual canoes (the flat extensions are still probably exaggerated). Judging from the perfect similarity of painting styles, it is very likely that this model and the previous one (*see* No. 13) were made by the same artist. It is impossible at this point to identify him, or even his tribal affiliation, since this design system was so closely followed by artists of all the northern tribes—Haida, Tsimshian and Tlingit (records indicate the model was collected around 1849, but no tribal source is given). Whoever the artist may have been, he was a master with a perfect understanding of the principles of the design system.

These archaic canoes share many features of later types, such as the shallow groove along the inner side of the gunwales (*see* No. 17). The function, if any, of this very uniform feature is not known, but it is intriguing to note how much it resembles a very similar feature of certain carved bowls (*see* No. 20).

44

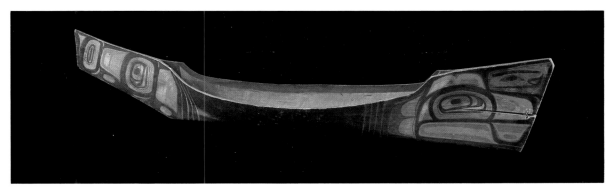

No. 15 CANOE MODEL

In contrast to the two previous canoe models, this one is painted with black primary formlines while the secondary elements are red. In addition, tertiary areas are painted in a soft blue, which is the traditional color when these spaces are painted. As in the other two, the extreme stylization of the painting makes interpretation uncertain, but in all three examples it is clear that the head of the represented animal is at the bow, and its hind quarters are at the stern. Typical in later nineteenth century northern canoes, the center section of the hull is painted black. The black and blue pigments are probably of native origin, while the red is that rich color, vermilion, acquired from the traders almost from the beginning of the period of European contact.

No. 16 CANOE MODEL 100x17x21cm

No. 16 (detail)

No. 16   CANOE MODEL

Carved figures were often fastened to the bows of large canoes for
ceremonies. A number of these full-sized figureheads have been collected,
as well as many models illustrating their use. This one is typical. The
figure appears to represent a familiar Tlingit theme, a sorcerer with his
long hair pulled back and tied to his arms, said to represent a torture
used to extract a confession of witchcraft. Other figureheads were
carved to represent the "Land Otter Man," a fearsome supernatural
being. Perhaps dangerous beings such as these were applied to canoe
bows for war, although it is possible that they would be appropriate to
the figurative antagonism expressed in ceremonial context. Stylistically
the carved figure suggests a Tlingit origin.

This canoe's painting illustrates another northern formline variant;
the red primary formlines are nearly worn away, but once dominated
the design. One might expect that the design painted on each side
would be the same, but this model proves that was not always the case.
The northern artists had propensity to vary designs which we would
expect to be symmetrical.

The catalogue record inaccurately describes this model as a "boat-
shape dish." Some carved bowls were made in the form of a canoe, but
they are always extremely foreshortened.

46

No. 17 CANOE MODEL 81x18x13cm

No. 17 CANOE MODEL

Early in the nineteenth century a new canoe type found favor on the Northwest Coast, superseding the head canoe (not one of that earlier type has survived). The new canoe evolved from several small canoe types. Exaggerated fins were dropped and a gracefully upswept bow and stern adopted. The bow has a vertical cutwater, perhaps a vestige of the head canoe's flat bow fin. The gunwale groove and, on larger canoes, the stylized formline painting are retained. This model's painting is very likely the work of the artist who painted model Nos. 13 and 14 (the former collected before 1837, when head canoes may still have been in use).

Unfortunately the top of the stern has been broken off, at the exact point where, on a real canoe, a separate carved block of wood was fastened. A similar bow block was always grooved for a harpoon vent or for the mast. While most scholars believe that canoes were not sailed before European contact, almost all nineteenth century canoes were fitted with masts and sails. Early mariners stated that the Northwest Coast Indians did not sail until white sailors taught them, but these comments must be taken in the context of the seaman's conceptions and vocabulary. Precontact canoes were sailed before the wind with simple mat or board sails. But in seamen's terms "sailing" meant reaching and beating as well. The sailing rigs of nineteenth century canoes usually imitated the ship's boats of the contact period.

47

Wooden Bowls

From ancient times, bowls carved of hardwood were used the length of the Northwest Coast. Elaborately decorated wooden bowls have been recovered from prehistoric wet sites and are to be found in collections made by the first Europeans to trade with the Northwest Coast people. On the northern coast these carved bowls can be divided into three different types – square bowls, high-end bowls and animal-form bowls. All three categories share certain characteristics of form, chief of which are an undulating rim, higher on the ends, and either bowed or bulging sides. The rim itself is usually rather broad with a lip or flange overhanging the inner surface of the bowl.

Some bowls are free of surface or sculptural decoration, and depend for their artistic effect on intrinsic form and elegant proportion. But most northern Northwest Coast bowls in museum collections show varying amounts of decorative detail.

No. 18   CARVED WOODEN BOWL

This small "square bowl," probably of alder, is a good example of the use of decorative detail. The flaring ends are elaborated with conventionalized formline faces similar to one another in composition but differing in some details. These symmetrical faces are characteristic of the end designs of square bowls, and are usually carved, as in this piece, in shallow relief. The clarity of the colors and absence of wear or accumulation of surface dirt gives the bowl the appearance of newness, but museum records suggest a collection date of before 1819, and the broad, black, somewhat angular formlines and other stylistic features are consistent with work from the early contact period. The colors (black, dark red and blue) may all be native pigments in a salmon egg tempera medium. The bowl was probably new and unused when collected.

Small bowls were used to hold the rendered candlefish or seal oil in which certain foods were dipped before eating. Larger bowls held other foods, but all those that have been much used show characteristic staining, a discoloration this example lacks.

On each side, and adjacent to the corners, is a peculiar design of parallel vertical grooves with their lower ends stopped by a gently slanting line. This detail is unlike the painting on the ends, and in fact seems almost out of place on a Northwest Coast bowl decorated with the familiar formline figures. Yet, of the literally hundreds of square, carved bowls of this type in existence, less than half a dozen are known to lack this detail. It is so uniform in shape and placement that it was clearly considered an indispensable feature of square-bowl design. The best explanation for its presence is that it is a *skeuomorph,* a representation of a once structural or functional detail. Certain birchbark bowls of the interior tribes of northern British Columbia and Alaska almost exactly mirror the proportions and form of the carved bowl. In forming the square bark bowl the maker folds and pleats the material at the corners, resulting in triangular patches of overlapped bark in exactly the same places on the vessel as the grooved design on the carved bowl. The reason for representing this detail of bark construction in carving is unclear, but, perhaps, interior people migrating to coastal areas imitated in carved bowls the familiar features of their traditional utensils.

Many of these bowls are decorated along the broad flange of the rim with an inlay of glossy white shells. These are opercula, or "trap doors" of a marine snail, the red turban shell (*astraea gibberosa*), common to some parts of the coast. Opercula were also used as decorative inlay on the lids of chests and boxes, as well as for teeth in masks and other carvings (see examples throughout this volume). It is still easy to gather enough opercula for inlays if one can find the places where mink, who eat the snails, discard the shells.

No. 18 CARVED WOODEN BOWL 20x18x13cm

No. 19 CARVED WOODEN BOWL

Another small square bowl exemplifies the characteristic features of the type, but is unusual in having the designs painted but uncarved. Such bowls are extremely rare, and most seem to have been made for sale, as few of them show signs of use. Even so, the symmetrical formline faces and the skeuomorphic corner designs are present. Typically the seemingly identical end patterns show variations in detail.

This bowl was collected in the 1860s and illustrates a very different style of painting from that on No. 18, with rounded design units of narrow formlines and open tertiary areas, left unpainted. However, the organization of the designs is basically similar, illustrating the vitality of the formline system over time and the strength of the conventions of bowl decoration.

No. 20 CARVED WOODEN BOWL

Several distinct wooden bowl types were made on the Northwest Coast, one of them the high-ended bowl. It resembles closely in form and detail small northern coastal bowls made of mountain sheep horn. (The high, upswept ends of the horn bowl result in part from the technique of manufacture, which involves cutting a section from the outside curve of the horn, carving the walls to the required thinness and steaming and spreading it to shape much in the manner of forming a canoe. The ends are sharply raised as a result.) Wooden high-end bowls such as this one are not spread, but are carved to form. Bowls of both materials typically are decorated on the inner surface with a raised ridge paralleling the rim, with vertical ribs joining it and the upper corners. These ridges resemble pleats and reinforcing rods on some interior birchbark bowls and are probably skeuomorphic (*see* No. 18). The resulting hollow under the bowl rim echoes the grooves under the gunwales of canoes, illustrating the complex network of relationships of concept, form and structure of canoes and bowls of wood, horn and birchbark.

Formline faces elaborate the ends of the bowls, with other body parts, highly conventionalized, spread around the sides. The design is too abstract to safely interpret. The artist has tricked us again into thinking that the side patterns are symmetrical. Many high-end bowls omit the formline patterns in the centers of the sides and instead show parallel rows of short, carved grooves that closely resemble the natural texture of birch-bark.

Probably most such bowls, including this one, were originally painted, but the oil that they held during feasts penetrates the wood and destroys the adhesion of the paint medium. Sometimes only faint traces of staining will indicate the earlier presence of paint.

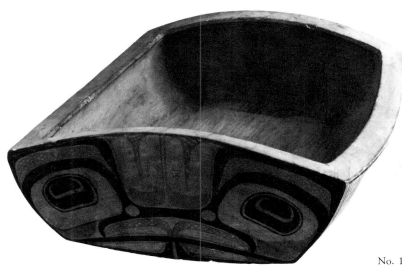

No. 19 CARVED WOODEN BOWL 27x21x9cm

No. 20 CARVED WOODEN BOWL 41x33.5x17cm

51

No. 21 CARVED WOODEN BOWL

Although the documentation for this small grease bowl has been lost, it can safely be dated to the early nineteenth century on the basis of its style. It is an example of a third carved bowl type, the animal-form bowl. The head and tail are sculptured in full, three-dimensional form on the ends, while the limbs, shoulders and pelvis are carved in low relief formlines on the sides. Carved of hardwood, probably alder, it may represent an otter.

The dark staining on the bowl, especially on the ends, is the result of the infused oil oozing to the surface and oxidizing. Sometimes a heavy incrustation of this sticky material obscures the carving on old bowls, which have long rested in museum storage. The stains are darker on the ends of the bowl where the carving cuts across the wood cells along which the oil migrates.

No. 22 CARVED WOODEN BOWL

This very old animal-form grease bowl was collected before 1820, and shows the effects of long use and wear before that. It may well have been made before European seamen reached the Tlingit country. That it is Tlingit is indicated by the features of the two end faces, with the long and heavy-lidded eyes and rounded contours, and the massive formline structure of the legs and claws, all of which resemble those of Tlingit pieces collected in the earliest years of white contact.

This bowl is carved remarkably thin, yet has withstood the vicissitudes of its long life surprisingly well. The long-beaked creature on one end has been called a mosquito, and it might represent that insect, although it could also be one of a number of long-billed birds. The other face resembles the somewhat humanoid bears seen on early Tlingit pieces (however, the absence of ears, which are important features of the bear, makes this identification somewhat questionable). All of which serves to illustrate the difficulties of interpretation without adequate record of the artist's intent.

No. 21 CARVED WOODEN BOWL 16x9x7cm

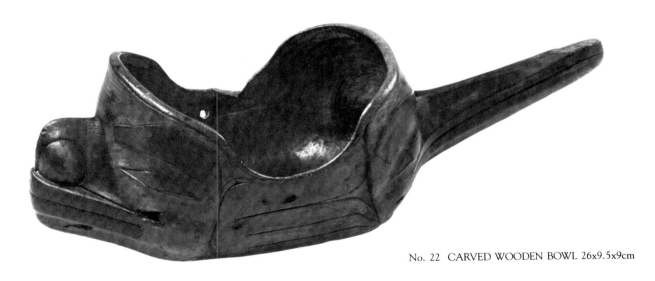

No. 22 CARVED WOODEN BOWL 26x9.5x9cm

53

No. 23 BENT-CORNER BOWL 29x27.5x16cm

No. 23   BENT-CORNER WOODEN BOWL

A feat of technology for which Northwest Coast craftsmen were justly famous was the forming of the four sides of rectangular containers – boxes, chests and bowls – from a single plank. The bending of the corners was accomplished by carving deep and sometimes complex kerfs (or grooves) across the board at three measured points and softening and making flexible the resultant thin wood. The fourth corner, at which the ends of the plank met, was fastened by pegging or sewing through drilled holes. The careful fitting of this joint, to the point of water-tightness, was equaled by the joining of the bottom plank. Bowls made by this method were often hardwood, probably maple in this example, with the bottom board of red cedar.

Bent-corner bowls exhibit the usual bowl characteristics of undulating flanged rim and bulging sides, which are carved into the plank before bending. However, the bent corners are of necessity straight and vertical. The juxtaposition of the vertical corners with the swelling sides results in an interesting play of form.

There is no remaining trace of paint on this bowl. Whether it was painted or not, the principles of design structure seen in northern formline painting are followed. The symmetrical ends represent head and tail of the represented creature, but the extreme abstraction of the parts makes it impossible to interpret. On bowls in which there are identifiable heads and tails the joined corner always falls on the tail end, as in this example. The two side designs, which appear to be mirror images of one another, show different treatment of almost every detail. A geometrically grooved band borders the upper edge. This contrasting band is seen on many bowls of this type and is very likely skeuomorphic.

The bowl was acquired from the Gitksan people of the upper Skeena River by the indefatigable collector, George T. Emmons, in the early years of this century.

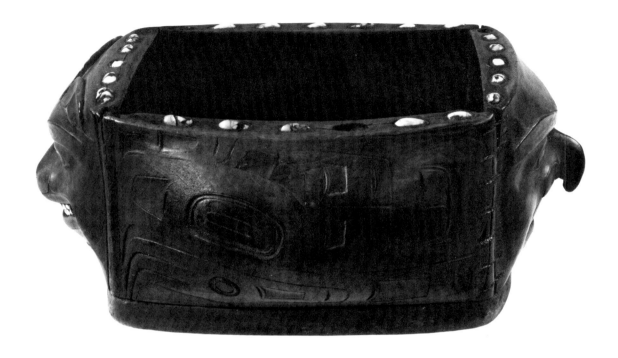

No. 24 BENT-CORNER BOWL 33x36.5x14cm

No. 24   BENT-CORNER BOWL

Scholars tend to be conservative in estimates of the age of artifacts such as this Tlingit bowl, collected in Alaska in 1880, but the style of the sculptured faces and formline detailing of the sides, as well as the deep patination and wear, suggest that it had been in use for generations before that time. There is every likelihood that this piece was in use when the fur trade period began.

The front of the bowl (opposite, lower left) is deeply sculptured in the form of a grizzly bear's head, the eyes inlaid with abalone shell and the wide mouth set with opercula "teeth." On the sides of the bowl the grizzly's shoulders and forelegs with long, sharply bent claws are rendered in broad, compact formlines. The ovoid shoulder joints from the eyes of implicit birds' heads, which may be significant or may be an artist's play on form. The rest of the bear's body is not clearly recognizable, and, in fact, formline U complexes resembling fins attached to the shoulders and elbows suggest the identification of a sea-grizzly, a mythological undersea monster.

The face on the back end (identified by the joined corner) is of the form usually called a hawk (opposite, lower right) characterized by a humanoid face with sharply hooked, beak-like nose. This identification is uncertain. The human mouth of the "hawk" retains a few opercula teeth.

Rich color and black staining are the result of oil infusion. Typical of bent-corner bowls, the dark stains and incrustation appear near the corners, where the carved surface crosses the wood fibers. The characteristic rim inlay of opercula elaborates this masterpiece.

No. 25 COLUMBIA RIVER SHEEP-HORN BOWL 19x16x12cm

No. 25 COLUMBIA RIVER SHEEP-HORN BOWL

Mountain sheep horn as a material for bowls and spoons was common to native people throughout that animal's range. In the northern part of the Northwest Coast sheep-horn bowls and high-end wooden bowls shared characteristics of form and decoration, and were usually carved with animal or bird heads on the ends, with the creatures' body parts represented in formline patterns over the remaining surface. Another tradition of sheep-horn bowl design flourished near the southern coast. Most of the bowls of this type were actually made in the area of the Columbia River Plateau, but intertribal trade between the interior and the coast was brisk along the river, and many of these bowls were collected from the people of western Washington. This Columbia River bowl is catalogued as Skokomish, a tribe living on the west side of Puget Sound.

The technology involved in horn work is simple in concept but complex in practice. The horn is a tough, resilient material that can be carved with woodworking tools. Its most important property for the bowl or spoon maker, however, is its flexibility when subjected to heat by boiling or steaming. When removed from the sheep's skull the horn is a massive spiral shape, narrow in cross section and with a tapered hollow extending part way into the base that fits over a bone core projecting from the sheep's skull. The rough horn was cut to shape, hollowed further, steamed and spread wide to form the bowl.

Columbia River bowls are often wider than long, as is this one, illustrating an extreme spread of nearly four times its original width of the horn at the rim. These bowls were typically trimmed to a flat profile with rectangular upright flanges, which are extensions of a broad band carved from the outer curve of the horn, running under the bowl from end to end. The flanges are usually pierced with rectangular and triangular holes forming a pattern of slats and zigzags (see details). The zigzag motif, derived from rows of interlocking incised triangles, is the principal design unit and is typically arranged in multiple rows around the rim and along the encircling band. Other geometric figures are common; incised concentric circles or rectangles are usual. Many bowls have flat-oval humanoid faces, and sometimes complete figures with geometrically patterned skeletal details are carved on the band.

Most of these bowls show every indication of great age; the normally pale, translucent horn is deep brown or nearly black from age and oil. They often resemble old wood to the point of being misidentified. They are sometimes still seen, highly prized as family heirlooms, among Indians of the Columbia Plateau.

No. 26 COLUMBIA RIVER SHEEP-HORN BOWL
Another version of the sheep-horn bowl, this artifact is inferior in design to the previous one.

No. 26 COLUMBIA RIVER SHEEP-HORN BOWL 20x20x10cm

Weapons

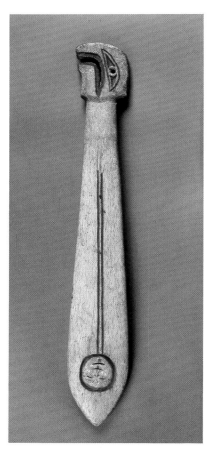

No. 27 WHALEBONE CLUB 51x8x2cm

No. 27 WHALEBONE CLUB

Although it is described in museum records as "a club for killing deer," this whalebone weapon is a typical example of the war clubs that many voyagers, from James Cook on, collected on Vancouver Island. Whalebone clubs of somewhat similar form were used all along the coast wherever the material was available. Cook and his successors considered them so like the bone clubs they had seen on the Pacific islands that they used the Polynesian terms for the Nootkan clubs when describing them in their journals.

Much simpler and less well finished than many early bone clubs, this one still exhibits most of their characteristics. The long, leaf-shaped blade, with elliptical cross section, is engraved with a pair of medial lines terminating in a human head. On many clubs this medial stripe is elaborately detailed with incised triangles and circles. The human head is said to be a reference to the function of the club in war. The pommel is carved with the head of a thunderbird, the usual choice for this decoration on bone clubs. Again, they are frequently more complex than this one, with supplemental bird, animal or human heads incorporated into the design. The sharply hooked beak, however, is the dominant feature of most club pommels. They are always pierced for the wrist thong, which is usually missing in extant clubs. This one is pierced through the eye, which is unusual.

No. 28 WHALEBONE CLUB

An unusual and spectacular variant on the Nootkan whalebone club, this early example keeps the tradition of heavy elliptical blade and thunderbird pommel. The sky monster's head is given a perfectly square silhouette ingeniously made to represent the fiercely hooked and upthrust beak by the placement of a piercing representing the bird's open mouth. The treatment of the eyelids as a crescent paralleling the line of the beak is unusual, but very effective, as are the feather-like forms radiating upward from the eyelid. The greatest deviation from standard bone club design is the substitution for the usual elaborated median line of three starlike patterns incised on the blade. These incisions are filled with a glittering material which appears to be crushed shell set in a matrix, perhaps of pitch.

Most extant clubs of this kind have lost their original grip binding, but it remains here. Various materials were used for this wrapping, the purpose of which was to give the warrior better control of the weapon than would be possible with a polished bone grip. The wrapping on this club is of a fine four-ply cord of what appears to be human hair.

Although this club and the one opposite (*see* No. 27) were thought to have been collected by Captain James Magee in 1792-93, there is no mention of them in the accession report of the Massachusetts Historical Society in its *Proceedings* for 1794, when the Magee material was received. More likely they were among the Northwest Coast weapons received from John Boit, Jr., in 1798. Boit had sailed with Robert Gray on the *Columbia* in 1790-93 and later commanded the *Union* on a voyage to the Northwest Coast. The clubs could have been acquired on either occasion.

No. 28 WHALEBONE CLUB 51x7.5x2cm

No. 29 WHALEBONE CLUB 43x6.5x2cm

No. 29   WHALEBONE CLUB

The Niska town of Gitlakhdamkh on the Nass River was a totempole village in 1914, when George Emmons collected this bone club there. Only a few years later all the poles had disapppeared, cut down, it is said, under the influence of a missionary. The old customs and arts of the Niska and their Gitksan and Tsimshian relatives were rapidly eroding. It was a time when George Emmons, Marius Barbeau and others acquired many treasures, like this elegantly engraved club, for the great museum collections.

A killer whale is represented on the blade, shallowly carved in the conventional formline manner. It is another example of how this sophisticated design system pervaded every facet of northern Northwest Coast art. The part of the club occupied by the whale is thought of as a designed space in which the formlines, while serving their required function of representing the head, ribs, fins and tail of the killer whale, at the same time divide the area into visually interesting and subtly interrelated patterns.

This may be a seal-killing club, rather than a war club. Many northern seal clubs, generally of wood, were carved as killer whales or sea lions, both of which prey on seals. The figures seem to be standardized to such clubs and probably do not have a crest significance. This one was very likely at least a half-century old when Emmons collected it.

62

No. 30 STONE DAGGER

The ancient fighting dagger of the Vancouver Island tribes was a stone weapon with a short wedged point jutting from a spool-like handle almost identical to the stone maul used for driving wedges and stakes. The broad pommel disk was often embellished with the face of a bird or human, like this one with its beak-like nose and mouth open for a wrist thong. Cook and other early voyagers described and collected stone daggers, and others have been found in ancient sites. They are probably all of precontact origin.

The art of sculpting complex forms in stone without the use of hard metal tools was well developed on the Northwest Coast. Daggers and the similar mauls were shaped out of elongate boulders by "pecking," or striking the stone sharply with a hard pebble, to pulverize a bit of the surface. After the shape was achieved, the surface was finished by rubbing with abrasive stone. Although this process was laborious and time consuming, thousands of tools and weapons were made this way. The stone dagger is an example of this simple technique.

It has become popular to call these weapons "slave killers," but there is no evidence that they were made for that purpose. The Kwakiutl did sometimes refer to them as "copper breakers," because the person cutting, or "breaking," a copper may ceremonially strike the copper with such a dagger, as if killing a man, before the actual cutting. (A copper was a somewhat shield-like plaque of great value, and was important in Northwest Coast ceremonial life as a prestige symbol.) Kwakiutl chiefs cut pieces from their coppers and gave them in retaliation to those who harmed or insulted them. This gift required a reciprocation in kind to avoid shame.

No. 30 STONE DAGGER 34x10x10cm

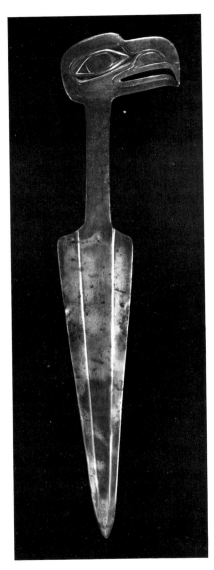

No. 31 COPPER DAGGER 38.5x9x0.5cm

No. 31   COPPER DAGGER

Daggers of metal (usually copper, iron or steel) exhibiting workmanship
of the kind not expected from cultures not known to have a tradition
of smithing, are fairly common in Northwest Coast collections. Since
copper was available to the Indians of the coast before the arrival of
Europeans, and is known to have been used for ornaments and imple-
ments, it is generally supposed that copper daggers were prototypes for
the steel daggers of the historic period. Copper is fairly easily shaped
and finished without special equipment, since it is very soft when annealed by quenching the heated metal in water. It will return to its
hardest state when worked by pounding to bring it to its proposed thick-
ness. Projectile points were made in this way, and it seems certain that
daggers were also produced. Shapes were refined by grinding with abrasive
stones, a technique well developed on the Northwest Coast for the
production of tool blades of nephrite and other suitable stones long
before the historic period. This dagger may be of native copper, but
since trade copper was in good supply by this time it seems more likely
to be of that material.

 The best of these daggers were beautifully designed and finished,
and this one is among the finest early examples. Although old records
are not conclusive, they suggest that it was collected in the first quarter
of the nineteenth century and it can be identified beyond any doubt as
from the northern coast, on the basis of its form and the style of decoration. It has the appearance of having been formed largely by cold
forging, after having been annealed, and finished by grinding and engraving. The last technique was almost certainly introduced early in the
contact period, and requires, at least for work of this character, the use
of steel tools.

 While some scholars have suggested that early metal carving like
this example was done by trained European or even Asian craftsmen for
trade, the subtleties of the traditional forms in the design of the eagle's
head on the pommel are so perfectly followed that it seems highly unlikely
in this case. There are many known examples of non-native copies of
Northwest Coast designs dating from earliest contact to the present
day, and unless the artist, no matter how skilled, understood the princi-

ples of the design tradition, the results were invariably unsatisfactory. The eagle head pommel shows perfect understanding of the formline design system as well as mastery of the techniques involved in its making.

The blade form is typical of early historic daggers, broad and tapered, double-edged, and with a rather abruptly converging point. The pair of ridges stiffening the blade converge near the point and form a wide, shallow flute the length of the blade. Forming these ridges is a challenging task even for an experienced metalsmith with a full complement of tools, and speaks well for the skill of this native craftsman.

The grip was probably wound with a leather thong or braided human hair. The relatively thin copper blade is too soft to be functional, and the dagger was probably intended for display. Such weapons often acquired the status of clan treasures and were passed down chiefly lines, often accompanied by detailed histories of their origins and adventures. Many copper daggers were made in the later years of the nineteenth century, so the material itself cannot be taken as a sign of great age.

No. 31 (detail)

No. 32 STEEL DAGGER

If it were not for the statements of early travelers on the Northwest Coast it would be difficult to believe that the many beautifully forged steel daggers collected there were made by native smiths. The perfection of form and finish they display would tax the skills of a professional blacksmith, and no other evidence of complex metal working of this sort is known from the Northwest Coast. Yet early journals, such as those of the Spaniards Galiano and Valdez in 1792, report that on several parts of the coast natives made fluted daggers, and fine specimens were collected by George Dixon on the northern coast in 1786, very early in the trade period.

Furthermore, native traditions claim indigenous manufacture of iron daggers long before European contact. One such tradition, recorded by Holmberg in 1854 and still held by the Tlingits, tells of a

Chilkat woman who made fluted daggers of meteoric iron on a stone anvil, even before white men came to the Alaskan coast (a spectacular old dagger believed to have been made by this female smith has been found not to be of meteoric iron, but appears nonetheless to be of great age). Other sources of iron in precontact times were through intertribal trade from the east, and in wreckage and drift from across the Pacific. A famous example is the dagger "Ghost of Courageous Adventurer," now at the University Museum, University of Pennsylvania, which was made out of a spike from a driftwood timber. Many steel daggers appear to have been made of files. John Dunn described the Indians in the early 1840s as making from files "beautifully fluted daggers, some eighteen inches long, as highly finished as if they had been turned out of a first rate maker's in London."

Few daggers or swords from the world's armorers can match the elegance of this Tlingit weapon, collected by Edward Fast in Alaska in 1867-68. Fast was on the staff of the military commander at Sitka during the first year of American government in Alaska, and had an unparalleled opportunity to make a large collection of Tlingit material of very high quality. The dagger is one piece of steel, the pommel being an extension of the tang, which is wound with braided skin cord over a wrapping of heavy buckskin. A long skin strap is attached to the grip to be wrapped around the wrist of the warrior to prevent the dagger's loss in battle.

The pommel is forged and carved in the form of a highly stylized bird (see No. 32 detail), perhaps a raven, with the beak forming a pointed blade. This is an elaboration of more utilitarian daggers which have a short version of the primary blade at the pommel. Typically, fluted daggers are flat, or slightly concave on the reverse, although some very early examples are fluted on both sides.

The scabbard of heavy hide with suspension strap is standard. A wooden plug at the point protects the scabbard from the sharp blade.

No. 32 (detail)

No. 33 (detail)

No. 33   STEEL DAGGER

Daggers with carved hilts of wood, bone, horn or ivory were carried by Northwest Coast warriors. Almost any hard, dense wood available might be used; a favorite choice was a scrap of walnut from a musket stock. (Firearms were common articles of trade almost from the first European contact and literally thousands of muskets ended up on the coast, and stocks of worn-out guns were utilized for small, fine carvings, particularly dagger hilts and pipes.) Wooden hilts, like this one, were carved with totemic figures, often inlaid with iridescent blue-green abalone shell in the eyes, teeth and joints. A combined eagle and man form the pommel, and a simple, shallowly carved formline face decorates the guard area, which characteristically covers the heel of the blade with the copper overlays on double-bladed daggers. The securing strap is firmly entwined in the grip wrapping. A slit in the end of the strap was slipped over the warrior's thumb before he wrapped it around his wrist.

Blades of naval swords, bayonets and even butcher knives were utilized for daggers with carved hilts. Some, of course, were forged especially for the purpose, but were never of the fluted types. This blade is double-edged and beveled on both faces.

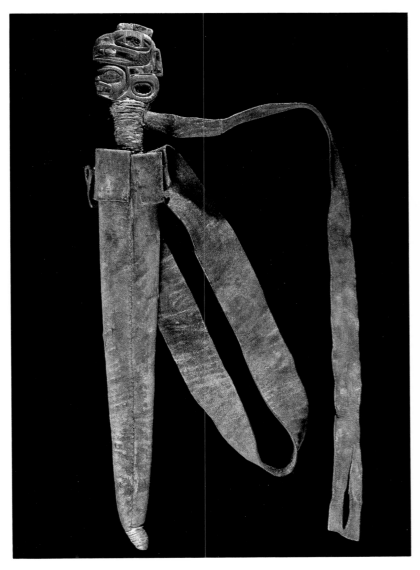

No. 33 STEEL DAGGER 55x3.5x8cm

No. 33 (detail)

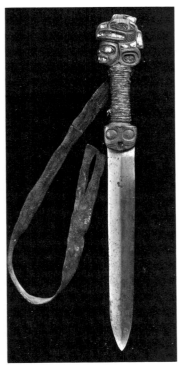

69

No. 34 STEEL DAGGER
A double-bladed dagger and its
sheath from the Edward Fast Collection illustrates the multifluted
blade form. The ridges converge
at two places near the point, and
the effect of the three grooves, or
fullers, is extended to the upper
blade, in the central shark face
and its surrounding groove. Expert
craftsmanship and elegant proportions distinguish this dagger.

No. 34 STEEL DAGGER 50x6x3cm

No. 35   STEEL DAGGER

A greatly simplified face, probably representing the shark or dogfish, decorates the pommel blade of this fine Tlingit dagger. Also from the Fast Collection, it must have been quite old when collected in the 1860s. Simple piercings represent the eyes and mouth of the shark. Copper overlays at the heels of the blade are more elaborately detailed by repoussé, engraving and inlay of abalone shell. The spiral motifs flanking these copper faces are similar to the spirals on the hilts of interior Athapaskan daggers and on Tlingit women's forged iron or copper hair ornaments.

The blade form of old Northwest Coast one-piece daggers, with their rounded heels, ogival shaped silhouette, raised midrib or flutes and clipped point, is startlingly reminiscent of early European Bronze Age daggers. This resemblance must be fortuitous. It would certainly be difficult to establish any link between the two.

No. 35   STEEL DAGGER 52x7x3cm

No. 36 STEEL DAGGER 54x7.5x3cm

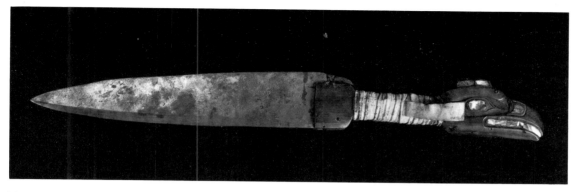

No. 36 STEEL DAGGER

Five flutes on the blade and seven on the pommel distinguish this elaborate dagger. The creature represented may be a wolf, its features defined by grooves and ridges. Thin copper overlays cover the blade heels. It is evident from this piece why Edward Fast described them in his catalogue as swords, rather than daggers. They are fearsome weapons. Young William Sturgis's 1799 account of the formal execution, with daggers, by the Kaigani of two Queen Charlotte Islands' Haida chiefs and the subsequent mutilation of their bodies, is a chilling tribute to their effectiveness.

No. 37 STEEL DAGGER

A single-edged blade with false edge similar to that on early naval cutlasses was another familiar form for carved-hilt daggers. The hilt of this dagger from the Fast Collection is most unusual, being formed of two flat pieces of whale baleen riveted together around the tang of the blade. The baleen is carved to represent a raven, with eye, ear, nostril and mouth inset with abalone shell. Lashed to the grip is a small buckskin loop which secured the dagger to the warrior's thumb – another method of preventing loss of the weapon in the heat of the battle. An old Haida warrior who narrated the battles of his youth to John Swanton described wrapping his dagger to his hand when preparing to fight.

73

No. 38 STEEL DAGGER
The head of a grizzly bear, carved in gun-stock walnut, forms the pommel of a relatively simple dagger. The blade is single-edged and the grip is wrapped with skin. The usual way of attaching the hilt was to fit the blade tang into a recess carved in an extension of the pommel and cover it with a matching piece of wood, binding the two parts firmly together with the tang between. Sometimes the end of the tang was bent to fit into a carved notch, which locked it in place.

No. 38 STEEL DAGGER 55x9x4cm

74

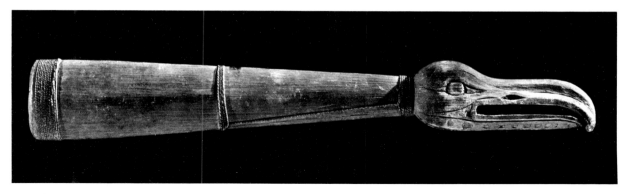

No. 39 WOODEN SHEATH

The true use and place of origin of this fine wooden sheath are unknown, and are hard to deduce from its form. It is one of the pieces transferred from the Massachusetts Historical Society and may be from the collections made on the Northwest Coast by James Magee or John Boit, Jr., at the end of the eighteenth century. It is probably a harpoon sheath and is neatly made of wood bound with fine, two-ply sinew cord.

The style of representing the bird's head is reminiscent of Nootkan carving, with its simple, smoothly curving forms. However, the fine sinew binding, carried between wrapped sections, resembles northern work (for example, the binding on harpoon darts and arrows of the northern Tlingit and their Chugach and Koniag neighbors). The carving itself could be northern coastal work. In any case it is a fine early piece of decorated functional material.

No. 40 THROWING STICK (ATLATL)

One third of all the known Tlingit throwing sticks or *atlatls* in the world are in the collections of the Peabody Museum at Harvard University. These four pieces were, like all the others with known collection histories, acquired in the early years of the fur trade.

The use of throwing sticks to cast darts or harpoons was once almost universal in the Americas, but was largely superseded by the bow everywhere except on the Arctic coasts. There, where hunters stalked their sea mammal prey in narrow skin boats, the atlatl held its own against the bow, which required two hands and more space. Tlingit hunters, in their relatively roomy canoes, could have utilized the somewhat more efficient bow, adapting the ingenious Eskimo harpoon-dart to an arrow form. Nevertheless, Vancouver and a few of his contemporaries found and collected distinctively Tlingit atatls in southeastern Alaska. They are all highly decorated but uncomfortable to hold and use compared to the totally functional, no-frills throwing sticks of the Eskimo. There are so few, and their use is so little remembered by the Tlingit, that they may have been used for only a few years.

This one has the typical configuration: a grip carved in the form of an animal or animal head, an index finger hole with raised rim and a shaft surmounted by another carved figure. In this case the animal whose head forms the grip is unidentifiable (perhaps it is a bird, judging from the feathers and joints represented by delicately engraved formlines extending along the shaft). A little smiling man crouches at the end and stares down at the creature, whose eyes are made of brass-headed tacks.

Although the records are not entirely clear, this atlatl and the two following are believed to have been acquired by Roderic McKenzie and deposited with the American Antiquarian Society in 1819.

No. 40 THROWING STICK (ATLATL) 39x4.5x3.5cm

No. 41 THROWING STICK

The figures carved on the handle of this atlatl closely resemble the complex arrangements on the backs of the oyster catcher rattles used by Tlingit shamans (*see* No. 83). The little reclining man, hands on drawn-up knees, is encircled by the "horns" of the animal at the grip. His feet terminate in a frog's head. This group, so suggestive of carvings on shamans' paraphernalia, leads one to guess that the group is associated with the control of supernatural power. The carved figures are not obviously related to hunting or the prey sought with the atlatl, such as seals and sea otters. The meaning of this enigmatic carving remains to be discovered.

The bird at the opposite end, perching on a bear's head, suggests a raven. The two figures are simply, but skillfully, carved, and the two-dimensional details of wing joints and feathers is a sensitive utilization of the formline design system seen on so many northern coastal carvings and paintings.

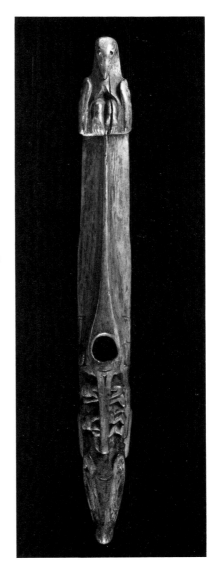

No. 41 THROWING STICK 35x4x3.5cm

No. 42 THROWING STICK

The shamanistic character of the sculpture is continued in this throwing stick. The figures are complex and difficult to identify. The grip is terminated by a long-beaked creature holding a small animal's head in its bill. The animal resembles an otter, often associated with shamans' work. Flanked by the terminal creature's wings is a boldly carved human face with closed eyes, its tongue protruding and bitten by the otter. This extended, or joined, tongue is common in Northwest Coast art, often on shamanistic paraphernalia, but on other objects as well. The extended tongue's meaning is unclear, although many have ventured guesses. Most agree that some kind of power transfer is represented. Another tongue exchange is shown at the end of the long, plain shaft, this time between an eagle and an unidentifiable creature.

No. 43 THROWING STICK

The last of the throwing sticks was acquired by Captain Thomas Robinson before 1813. As with the two preceding examples, the grip of the stick resembles a shaman's rattle or amulet. Here an

No. 42 THROWING STICK 34.5x5x5cm

animal, probably a wolf, carries two tiny men (one in profile and one full face) on his back, firmly held there by the wolf's rigid tail. (There is the possibility that the principal figure is an otter, rather than a wolf.) An eagle with formline wings and a bead eye perches at the opposite end, his beak turned down to his breast. On the opposite side, the eagle's tail forms the platform on which the butt of the harpoon is set, as it lays in the shallow groove running the length of the atlatl, and under the grip, a third little man is crowded inside the wolf.

In use the atlatl is held by the grip with the index finger in the hold. The shaft of the dart or harpoon, with its butt resting on the shelf, is held between the thumb and second finger. As the dart is thrown it is released and the atlatl acts as an extension of the hunter's arm, greatly increasing the dart's velocity. The term *atlatl*, by which the instrument is known to anthropologists, is of Aztec origin.

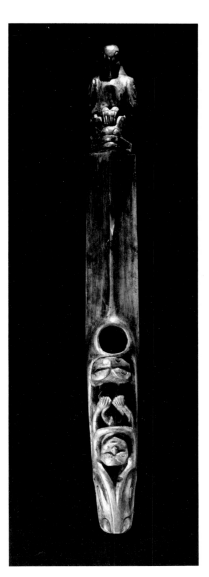

No. 43 THROWING STICK 39x4.5x3.5cm

Armor

At the time of first European contact, Tlingit warriors of noble rank were bound by a code of chivalry and heraldic rules as rigid and complex as those of the knights of Europe in the Middle Ages. Their armor was of wood and hide, rather than of steel, but there were many parallels between the customs and dress of Tlingit warriors and their medieval counterparts. Crest figures of mythical animals painted on the warriors' slat armor or hide tunics were as fanciful and as deeply imbedded in family history as the armorial bearings emblazoned on ancient European knights' tabards. And, as with the knight of old, the Tlingit noble warrior, completely encased in helmet and body armor, presented a fearsome sight to his enemies. Early European observers who saw Tlingits in full armor described their grotesque helmets, and Russian accounts of a battle in 1792 proclaimed (in exaggeration) them impervious to their bullets. Other European accounts tell of musket balls penetrating native armor, to the chagrin of the owners.

No. 44   HELMET
This is a typical example of functional armor combined with fear-inspiring imagery and crest significance. Probably collected in the 1790s, it likely saw use. It is a naturalistic representation of a grizzly (or brown bear), with the sculptured wooden form covered with skin of the animal's head, complete with nostrils and eyelids. Applied over the carved hardwood helmet when fresh, this skin was pegged in place and dried, shrinking it tightly to the wood. Iron domes form the eyes, and the ears once supported small wooden masks of humanoid bears, one of which remains. Opercula set in grooves imitate the bear's ferocious teeth.

War helmets were carved of hardwood, usually maple, often from a twisted or burly piece, and left thick to resist splitting from a club or dagger blow. The helmet came down to the warrior's eyes and was worn in conjunction with a decorated collar or wood visor, bent to encircle the head and cover the face below the eyes. The warrior held the piece in place by biting a loop of spruce root fastened to the mask's surface. The effect was of a fearsome head surmounting a heavy neck, the warrior's face being almost completely concealed.

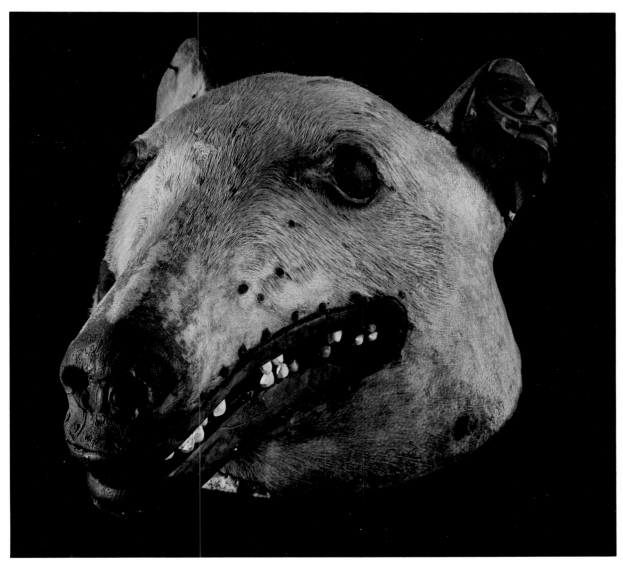

No. 44 HELMET 40x26x20cm

No. 45   HELMET 32.5x29x19.5cm

No. 46   ROD-AND-SLAT ARMOR 65x60x8cm

82

No. 45   HELMET

A functional helmet with restrained decoration, this probably represents a sea monster's head in highly stylized form. Broad red formlines delineate the nostrils, and an attached dorsal fin with a human face carved at the base terminates in an elegantly carved spiral. The hair fringe sweeping back from the fin is common on Tlingit carvings and may represent the creature's breath. Several sources have been mentioned for the hair used on ceremonial objects—the scalps of enemies, the hair of slaves, hair cut in mourning and hair presented in a marriage contract. The traditional histories of the objects often mention the origin of the hair used.

The broad black band at the rim, studded with opercula, is unique among helmets. It is consistent with the abstract character of the entire object. No doubt it was significant, but any meaning assigned it today would be conjectural.

No. 46   ROD-AND-SLAT ARMOR

Body armor of wooden rods, or rods and slats, twined together with cord, was known from the coast of California to the Aleutian Islands. Conceptually it is related to armor from the arctic and eastern Asia. Tlingit rod-and-slat cuirasses (combined breast and backplates) from the early historic period are characterized by the combination of slats at breast and back with rods under the arms, rectangular extensions at the upper edge, and shaped lower edge. The rods at the slanting transition between the sides and the low back are carved with extended flanges to form an even contour, and to retain the twining of tightly braided sinew or human hair. This twining holds the wooden parts tightly together yet allows complete flexibility between them. The slats are also carefully carved, each in slightly elliptical cross section. The upper extensions are joined to the body of the armor with strips of heavy hide laced in place, and shoulder straps of the same material complete the piece.

The cuirass was worn over a tunic of leather, sometimes with sleeves, and was donned from the right side, after which the shoulder strap was fastened with a toggle. The right side of the cuirass was closed with a skin tie. Greaves for the lower legs, made of twined rods, were also worn.

No. 47 ROD-AND-SLAT ARMOR 63x53x8cm

No. 47   ROD-AND-SLAT ARMOR

Twined wooden armor had been out of fashion for many years when Edward Fast collected these two examples in the late 1860s (they were probably 50 years old at the time). Although there is no sign of it here, the rectangular panels left free of twining at front and back were typically painted with crest designs, analogous to the insignia worn by European knights or the *mon* of Japanese samurai. They proclaimed the identity of the warrior who was hidden by his helmet and visor. Rank and identity was primary in the formalized intertribal and interclan warfare of the Tlingit. In this exacting system, peace between warring factions could not be concluded until the "score" had been evened—the dead on each side equal in number and rank, sometimes requiring the ritual sacrifice of a noble warrior who went, voluntarily and alone, dressed in his armor, against the enemy's fighting men to die as in battle.

No. 48 HIDE ARMOR 100x90cm

No. 48 HIDE ARMOR

The fur trade on the Northwest Coast was marked by several instances of direct exchange between white traders and Indians of furs for furs. The most intriguing of these was the trading of ermine skins, highly prized for ceremonial regalia by Northwest Coast chiefs (*see* No. 51), by Captain William Sturgis in 1804. Sturgis, recognizing the demand for ermine, bought all those available at the Leipzig fur fair and brought them to the Northwest Coast to trade to the Indians for sea otter pelts.

A less spectacular exchange than ermines for sea otters, but of more importance to the fur trade, was the supplying of southern coast elk hides to northerners for armor. Thick and tough, elk hides were prized. Traders put in at villages at the mouth of the Columbia and in Juan de Fuca Strait and bought, with European goods, tanned elk skins which were called "clemmons" in the language of the fur trade (the origin of this term is not known, but presumably it is derived from a native word). The northern warriors apparently found this trade advantageous, exchanging relatively easily procured sea otter pelts for hides which were difficult to procure through native trade networks, and getting delivery in the bargain.

This hide armor shirt is typical. It is closed on the left side, with an opening for the arm equipped with a protective flap, or epaulet, for the shoulder, and furnished with ties to close the right side. Decorative flaps elaborate the seam on the left. The chest crest figure is a grizzly, in a straightforward formline rendering. Faces in the ears suggest a supernatural creature. The full face rendering of the bear's head can be seen as two profiles joined at the muzzle, or perhaps as the "unwrapped" surface of the whole head. Secondary red formlines elaborate the body and perhaps represent internal organs. The armor shirt was collected by George Emmons.

No. 49 HIDE ARMOR

Although we commonly conceive of armor as of metal, hide or leather armor anciently had worldwide distribution. In fact, the term for torso armor, cuirass, is derived through French from a Latin word for skin. This spectacularly painted tunic is among the finest specimens of Northwest Coast hide armor. It is of the simplest form, perfectly rectangular, with openings for neck and left arm, pendant tabs on the left seam and ties for the right side. Its importance rests in the painted crest, a bear, or possibly the Sea Bear, rendered in masterful red formlines, with black inner ovoids and secondary detail and pale blue-green tertiary areas.

Without any doubt one of the great masterpieces of Northwest Coast painting, it exemplifies the abilities of the northern artists to represent significant creatures in highly abstract form, sensitively organizing the various elements of the body in an overall and very satisfying design. The creature bites a human head whose arms stretch to the limits of the gaping mouth. Surprisingly, but not beyond the imagination of the northern artist, the little man has another set of arms attached to a complete body, within the torso of the Sea Bear. The figure's hairy legs and clawlike feet suggest part-bear ancestry, perhaps an illusion to the widely known Bear Mother myth in which a woman, kidnapped by a grizzly prince, delivered half-bear children. The Sea Bear interpretation is suggested by the whale fluke-like design at the bear's tail, and reinforced by the ovoid-enclosed human face between his ears, a common convention for a sea creature's blow hole. The elaborated band at the tunic's edge cannot be interpreted with confidence, since similar bands were given widely different meanings, ranging from the prey of the principal creature, to the rock on which it sits. It could be read as an animal, possibly a seal or sea lion, with wide, toothed mouth and flanking flippers.

Edward Fast collected this magnificent example of classic northern art. It closely resembles painted leather pieces collected by Russians in Alaska in the early nineteenth century.

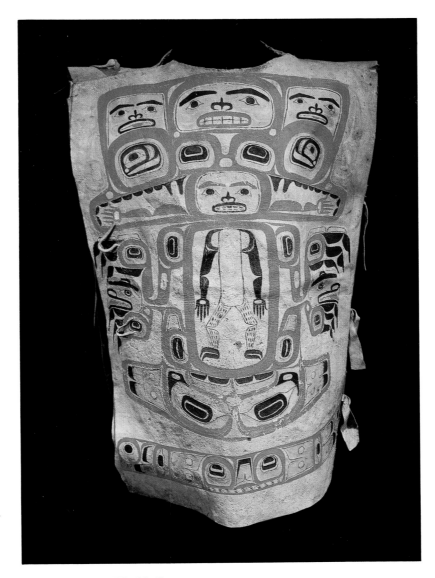

NO. 49 HIDE ARMOR 100x69cm

Headdresses & Masks

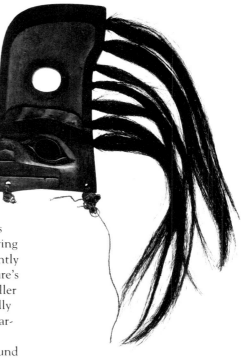

No. 50 CARVED WHALE FIN 25x13x2cm

No. 50 CARVED WHALE FIN

This small, nicely carved whale fin with its trailing shock of hair was once part of a headdress. It was probably fastened to the top of a flaring hat, either of woven spruce root or of wood. Killer whale fins frequently were shown with a face at the base, variously explained as the creature's spirit, a person carried by the whale, or the man who first created killer whales of yellow cedar. Explanations for the hole in the fin are equally ambiguous, the most common one being that it signifies the crest character of the specific killer whale.

The backward sweep of the fin at its tip and the raised flange around it are typically Tlingit, as are the sculptural forms of the basal face. Characteristic vermilion and blue-green paint combine to produce a vibrant effect. The carving is probably from the mid-nineteenth century.

No. 51 DANCING HEADDRESS

The chiefs' dancing headdress with carved and inlaid forehead plaque, sea lion whisker crown and trailing rows of ermine skins is one of the richest productions of Northwest Coast art. Its use spread, according to tradition, from its originators, the northern Wakashan people, to Vancouver Island in the south and beyond Yakutat Bay in the north. Everywhere, it was worn by high-ranking dancers who scattered white bird down from the crown of the headdress as they performed. The down, usually from eagles but sometimes swans, was held by the high fence of bristles and was shaken out and scattered by sharp movements of the dancer's head,

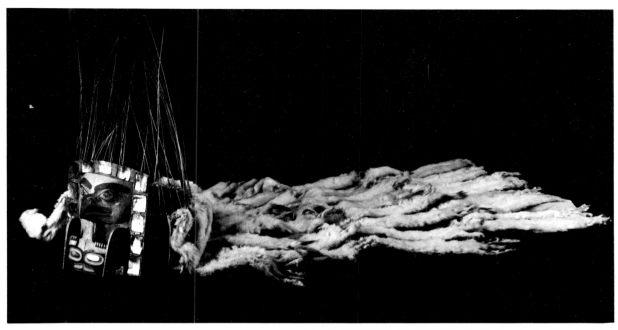

No. 51 DANCING HEADDRESS 30x25x40cm (with 77cm fur train)

then swirled and drifted around him and over the assembled watchers. Following headdress dances, the floor of the house was covered with drifts of white down.

Great care was lavished on the carving of headdress frontlets. Although they probably all were originally representations of clan emblems, they often changed hands through marriage and potlatching, and, especially in the south, lost their specific symbolism. The place of origin of this fine frontlet is not recorded, but it is probably either a northern Haida or Tlingit piece. What is certain is that it was worn by the famous Haida artist and chief, Tom Price, in a photograph taken at the turn of the century.

The principal figure is a raptor, probably an eagle or perhaps an owl. Its formline-detailed wings flank what appears to be an upturned whale's tail, the flukes folded down by the bird's grasping claws. A vertical extension of this figure could be interpreted as a dorsal fin. If it is a whale, the absence of a head is curious. We might be tempted to assign a double meaning of head-tail joint to the ovoid and U complex on the upraised tail, although this would be a very unusual concept.

No. 52 CREST HAT 45x45x62cm

No. 52 CREST HAT

Carved wooden crest hats resembling war helmets, and perhaps derived from them, were worn on important cermonial occasions by Tlingit nobles. They are among the most highly prized of clan treasures. Many of them, and this is an example, are shaped much like basketry hats and they frequently are surmounted by a stack of the prestigious basketry cylinders (*see* No. 5). The carving on the hat, here a grizzly bear, is a representation of a crest animal. The most important hats achieved the status of clan emblems in *themselves,* beyond the significance of the carved image.

The long, amber spires, so prominently displayed rising from the bear's head, are the whiskers of the bull Steller sea lion (*Eumentopias jubata*). These mammoth creatures, renowned for their strength and aggressiveness, were often represented on warriors' helmets, and they furnished, in addition to the springy bristles, thick hide and massive canine teeth, which were carved into shamans' amulets. The long whiskers were most often used as the crown of the dancing headdress (*see* No. 51).

The bear hat is a fine example of Tlingit ceremonial art, at once a visually striking object and treasured emblem, combining the sculptural and two-dimensional art systems in a variety of media: carved and painted wood, woven spruce root, sea lion whiskers, human hair, abalone shell and opercula. Mid-nineteenth century Tlingit sculptural style is well illustrated in the carving of the bear's head with its rounded forms, large open eyes and broad lips. The brightness of the paint colors and absence of wear suggest that the hat was relatively new when collected by Edward Fast.

No. 53   DANCING HEADDRESS FRONTLET
The dogfish, a common shark along the entire coast, is the subject of this Tlingit frontlet collected by Edward Fast. Dogfish is a crest among most of the northern tribes, and among the Tlingit it is an emblem in the Wolf or Eagle moiety. It is easily identified in most examples by a high rounded forehead, downward slanted eyes, often with drooping extensions, and scowling, toothed mouth. Gill slits on the cheeks, an important recognition feature, are absent in this example. Here, the features of the fish are humanoid, the eyes metal-inlaid and the teeth represented by opercula. Sometime since its collection this frontlet has been restored and much of the abalone shell, often missing from old pieces, has been replaced.

The deep blue and green abalone shell, so characteristic of old pieces, was traded from the south, probably even in precontact times. Early explorers found it in great demand and for some time afterward was brought up the coast by traders. Native artists cut it and enhance its brilliance by carving away a layer of brown translucent material that naturally covers part of the inner surface. When seen in action by fire-light, the flashing abalone shell inlays, the whipping and swaying circlet of bristles and the mantle of ermine combine in a dazzling effect, crowning as they do the elaborate dress of the dancer. This dress always includes a blanket, either an appliquéd button blanket (*see* Nos. 77 and 78) or, ideally, a Chilkat blanket (*see* No. 74). Frequently the dancer holds a raven rattle which he shakes rapidly (*see* Nos. 85 and 86).

No. 53   DANCING HEADDRESS FRONTLET
21x17x7.5cm

89

No. 54 SHAMAN'S MASK 20x19.5x12cm

No. 54 SHAMAN'S MASK

On the Northwest Coast, masks are the clearest manifestation of the coexistance of the concrete world and that of supernatural power and myth. They are universally recognized as a feature of Northwest Coast culture. The journals of explorers and traders record the use of masks and many were acquired and brought back to home ports by the seamen who visited the coast, beginning with the earliest voyages. These masks were viewed as curious and grotesque, souvenirs of adventurous visits to a savage land. Occasionally, early observers expressed surprise at the carving skill evidenced in Northwest Coast masks; in 1787, Nathaniel Portlock concluded that some were beyond the abilities of native carvers and must have been left by earlier Spanish visitors!

Although this Tlingit mask was collected by Fast in the late 1860s, it is from a much earlier time. Judging from its condition, it must have been exposed to the elements in a cache or grave for a long time. It is a shaman's mask, representing the spirit of a Tlingit woman. Every Tlingit shaman had a series of masks, each representing a spirit whose power could be assumed by the shaman upon donning the mask and utilized in curing his patient. Many, as with this one, represent women. The asymmetrical painting on the face is indecipherable, and resembles the abstract emblems that Tlingit dancers painted on their own faces at festive occasions. The protruding lower lip, distended by an inserted plug or labret, is a distinctive mark of noble women. White observers were uniformly negative in their impressions of the custom of wearing labrets, and only a few were objective enough to admit that "civilized" nations had their own peculiar ideas about beauty, which were as much distortions of nature as this one.

Although stylized, the carving suggest a close observation of natural form by the artist. Very early Tlingit masks like this often have smaller and more closely (and naturalistically) spaced eyes than later masks (*see* No. 57). Such conventions of carving style, however, may be indicators of the work of different artists or groups of artists, as much as of relative age.

No. 55   SHAMAN'S MASK

Tlingit shamans' masks represented the spirits of many different beings. Some were animals in the ambivalent, quasi-human form so frequently seen in ceremonial art of the Northwest Coast. Wear and damage to this mask complicate the process of identification, since it is impossible to know with certainty its original form. A beak, rather than a muzzle, is suggested by its narrow proportions. The face itself is human; only the upright ears and the beak proclaim its dual nature. Without the beak, the bird cannot be identified.

Typical Tlingit color scheme remains, the red apparently vermilion. If it is, the mask must have been painted very soon after the trade period began, since its style is archaic, and present understanding is that vermilion was not used before that time.

Small perforations of the eyes furnish limited vision for the wearer in this mask, while the example opposite (No. 54) has unpierced eyes. Many Tlingit shamans' masks have no provision for sight, but since the shaman often danced or performed essentially in place, he had no real need for eye holes.

No. 55   SHAMAN'S MASK 25x19x10cm

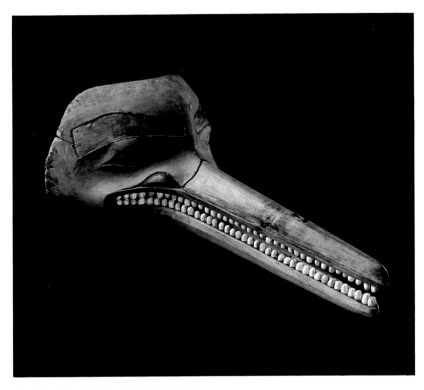

No. 56 SHAMAN'S MASK 37x18x15.5cm

No. 56 SHAMAN'S MASK
The exaggerated length of the narrow beak of this shaman's mask,
and the many opercula teeth, lead
to its identification as a mosquito,
a "man-eater" most familiar to
Northwest Coast people. Another
of those collected by Fast in the
1860s, its style and condition attest
to much greater age. There is no
record to indicate it, but these
three masks (Nos. 54, 55 and 56)
are so similar in condition, and in
stylistic indications of age, that
they may have come from the same
shaman's grave. A shaman's set
usually included masks representing
various human spirits as well as
those of birds, mammals, monstrous beings of different sorts and
even insects, as here. It is possible
that these masks, although very
old when collected, and showing
evidence of having lain in a grave
or cache, could have been in use
when, or shortly before, Edward
Fast collected them. The paraphernalia of a shaman was customarily
retrieved from his grave house by
a successor, for his own use, so
such masks might have an active
life of many generations.

No. 57 SHAMAN'S MASK

A shaman's masks, unlike his amulets and rattles (*see* Nos. 82 and 83), were often complex composites of figures referring to the character of his power sources. A creature closely associated with shamanic power was the land otter. Probably no other animal of the Tlingit world was so closely associated in the minds of the people with dangerous supernatural power. Emerging from the cheeks and between the ears of this mask are three small animals which are probably otters. The large face, although somewhat humanoid in form, has the ears, snout and mouth of an animal like a bear.

The workmanship and design of this mask are superb. Stylistically it is unlike Tlingit pieces collected at the beginning of the nineteenth century and its condition is consistent with its apparent relative newness at the time of collection in 1867-68. The sculptural form of this piece is very much like others collected after the middle of the century. The blue-green paint with details of vermilion and black are typically Tlingit, as are the teeth of opercula.

No. 57 SHAMAN'S MASK 27x20x13cm

No. 58 SHAMAN'S MASKETTE 12.5x9x4cm

No. 58   SHAMAN'S MASKETTE

In the kit of many Tlingit shamans was an elaborate composite headdress to be worn when curing a patient. It was based on a headband covered with the skin of a swan or eagle from which feathers had been pulled, leaving a thick mat of incredibly soft, snow white down. Many other materials were worked into the headdress; clipped tailfeathers of the bald eagle, strands of braided human hair, the tail of a wolverine, or others. But the main ornament was always a carefully carved wooden maskette of a spirit helper of the shaman, tied to the forehead of the headdress. These tiny masks are miniatures of the life-sized spirit masks worn at other times by the shaman. They may display supplementary figures, such as the land otters on the previous mask, or they may be simple faces as in this example, whose characteristics are those of masks known to represent the spirits of dead or dying Tlingit warriors. Slack jaw with swollen, protruding tongue and half-shut eyes are graphic indicators of the ebb of life. A few opercula teeth remain and the shock of hair that once swept upward from the forehead is now gone.

Typical Tlingit blue-green painting is varied by an asymmetrical stripe of vermilion across one eye and cheek. The warrior's moustache and beard are painted in black. Almost all Northwest Coast masks representing humanoid males are shown with whiskers, either painted or inset with human hair or fur. Early European visitors frequently mentioned the sometimes heavy beards of the native men and some Dzawada'enokhw Kwakiutl hunters were said to have smeared the blood of bears they killed on their upper lips to assure luxuriant growth.

No. 59 SHAMAN'S MASK

In this remarkably naturalistic
human mask from the Fast Collection, realistic proportions and
close adherence to anatomical
structure accentuate the expression
of trance or death. A Northwest
Coast convention for these states
is the representation of the eyes
rolled upward, so that the iris is
partly concealed by half-closed
eyelids. A similar effect is achieved
by the Kwakiutl Hamatsa, or man-
eater dancer, whose eyes are rolled
upward when possessed by the
Cannibal Spirit.

Although this mask was collected apparently at Sitka by
Edward Fast, and catalogued as
Tlingit, George Emmons ques-
tioned that attribution, believing
it Haida. It does seem more like
known Haida pieces, but it is
from a time for which very little
stylistic information is available.
It is certainly a northern mask.

The natural color of the wood
suggests sallow skin. A trace of
the fur beard remains; pegs indicate
the former existence of fur moustache and eyebrows. Long hanks
of inset hair fall around the mask.
In use it must have seemed very
real. It was possibly carved as a portrait.

No. 59 SHAMAN'S MASK 18x13.5x12cm

95

No. 60 MASK 20x15x12cm

No. 60 MASK

Many fine early masks collected on the Northwest Coast in the nineteenth century are now believed to have been made for sale to traders rather than for native use. It had become apparent that these foreign visitors were anxious to acquire carvings of various kinds, especially masks, and the local artists obliged them.

Among these early "tourist" carvings were many representing painted female faces wearing very large labrets, which symbolized, for the buyers, the savage Northwest Coast and could be expected to properly amaze friends and family back home. A number of these masks were certainly the work of a single carver, whose sulptural and painting style is recognized by a combination of unique features: round, open eyes with a grooved upper lid; large eye socket; small, narrow nose flattened under the nostrils; rounded, sometimes double chin; wide mouth with very large labret. The face painting is expertly designed of formlines in blue and red. Some of the masks in this group have large, elaborately carved ears, painted red. Several with reasonle collection data were collected in the late 1820s. Their place of origin is unknown, but they were possibly northern Haida.

Although there is no evidence that these masks were made for Indian use they are finely carved, very thin, and expertly painted. They were not turned out hastily for the tourist trade, but are superb examples of the carver's art.

No. 61   MASK

An intriguing inscription on the inner surface of this mask may be a clue to interpretation. It reads "A correct likeness of Jenna Cass, a high chief woman of the North west Coast   J. Goodwin Esq." The most obvious interpretation is that this is a portrait of an actual person, but there is a good possibility that J. Goodwin misunderstood the explanation. Since all the masks and four fully carved figures (*see* Nos. 133 and 134), are strikingly alike in features, and all share a peculiar painting in red to the side of the nose, it seems more likely that the representaiton is of a single mythical woman. The most likely candidate is *Djilakons*, an ancestress of the Haida Eagle moiety, who was usually represented as wearing a very large labret. It may be that Goodwin heard "Jenna Cass" for the name of the fabled Djilakons, who certainly could have been described as a "high chief woman of the North west Coast". The sounds of the letters *l* and *n* are much closer in many Northwest Coast languages than they are in English and there are other examples of similar confusion by early observers.

No. 61   MASK 26.5x21x.5cm

No. 62   MASK

Traditions of almost all Northwest Coast tribes share the belief in man-like beings of great strength, beings who are dangerous to man yet can be a source of wealth or power. This creature has come to be known in English by a number of names, among them "Bigfoot" and "Sasquatch," from a Salish term. The Tsimshian speak of a somewhat analogous being as *ba'wus,* a term borrowed from the Kwakiutl, whose term is *Bukwus* ("Man of the ground"). Although the ba'wus is human like, he is without culture, and acts in ways unacceptable to humans. Of all natural creatures, the one most closely resembling ba'wus is the monkey. Monkeys appeared on the Northwest Coast as seamen's pets in the first half of the nineteenth century, and were represented in a number of carv-

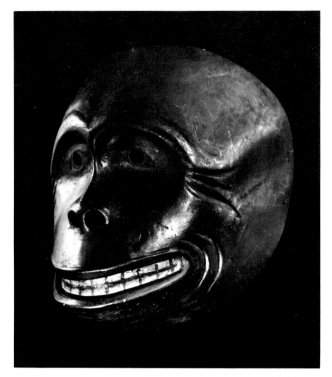

No. 62   MASK 22x19x14cm

ings, notably on argillite pipes. By the time this mask, with its monkey- or ape-like features, was carved, probably at the turn of the century, many Tsimshian had seen monkeys and most were probably familiar with them through pictures and descriptions. So the term ba'wus was translated *Monkey* in English, and this ba'wus mask was carved to resemble, very convincingly, a monkey.

Collected by George T. Emmons from the Tsimshian, it came to the Peabody Museum in 1914. It is painted with graphite black and a dull red. The monkey is represented in a performance dramatizing hereditary spirits called *Nakhnokh,* in which masked dancers portray various humans and animals.

98

No. 63 HEADDRESS 31x31x13cm

No. 63   HEADDRESS

The four carved faces attached to a painted skin headband resemble the maskette on shamans' headdresses. This headdress is recorded as having been worn by Sitka Jack at his potlatch in 1877, along with an elaborately painted skin shirt. Although there is no mention in the record that the shirt and headdress are shamanic, the painting on the shirt resembles those on doctors' garments far more than it does a crest display. It may be that Sitka Jack was a shaman, and wore his regalia on this occasion.

Painting and sculptural form of the maskettes are mid-nineteenth century Tlingit in style. The raised, ribbon-like lip form, so characteristic of this style, is apparent. Asymmetrical painting in the typical color scheme of blue-green and vermilion reinforce the appearance of Tlingit work.

No. 64   COPPER MASK

Copper was available to the Northwest Coast people in ancient times and was highly prized for its decorative qualities as well as for its economic and prestige value. Its desirability was quickly noted by early European visitors who subsequently brought quantities of the metal, in sheet form, to the coast for trading purposes. Although the value was drastically lowered due to the influx, copper continued to be viewed as a prestigious material, based on its importance in mythology and family tradition. Although copper was frequently applied to wooden masks and other ceremonial regalia, very few old masks made of copper are known. Most of those extant are relatively recent, probably dating to the late nineteenth century. This mask is an example.

The creature represented is a humanoid bird. The crownlike decoration over the head probably represents a shaman's headdress of claws. Shamans of the northern tribes wore such headdresses, often made of the foreclaws of grizzly bears attached to a supporting band of hide. Some Tlingit shamans used mountain goat horns in place of bear claws, often elaborately carved with basal faces inlaid with abalone shell. "Claws" made of carved antler, wood, the rims of abalone shells, copper and even beaver teeth were known.

Annealed copper is very mal-
leable and can be shaped and
elaborated using minimal tools.
Many copper articles were made
for sale around the turn of the
century, and it is possible that
this mask is one of them. There is
also the possibility that it was
made for shamanic use.

No. 64 COPPER MASK 22x18x7.5cm

No. 65 DZOONOKWA MASK 33x23x15cm

No. 65 DZOONOKWA MASK

Of all the masking tribes of the Northwest Coast, the Kwakiutl of northern Vancouver Island and adjacent mainland areas probably carried the custom to its greatest elaboration. They, along with their northern relatives the Heiltsuk, have been credited with developing the elaborate and dramatic performances of the Winter Ceremonial, which were acquired and adapted by their northern and southern neighbors. Unfortunately, there are no known documented masks from these people until the middle of the nineteenth century.

A few carvings collected by Cook at Nootka in 1778 may have come from the Nimkish Kwakiutl. The Nootka people had trade and marriage relations with the Nimkish, who lived across Vancouver Island at the mouth of the Nimkish river (George Hewitt, of Vancouver's expedition, identified some of the objects he collected at Nootka as "Namakizat," which is the Nootka name for the Nimkish). In the early nineteenth century sporadic trading with the Kwakiutl occurred around Quatsino Sound and Hope Island, but they were, for practical purposes, off the beaten path until the establishment of Fort Rupert in their country in 1849.

Kwakiutl mythology is crowded with supernatural beings associated with family ancestors, and all were subject to representation in the art and in dramatic reenactment. A few of these creatures are considered by many to be still living in the remote inlets and mountains of British Columbia; the most frequently mentioned is the *Dzoonokwa,* a humanoid giant of great strength, who, although dangerous, is often described as the source of great wealth and power. The Dzoonokwa, along with the Bukwus, is the Kwakiutl equivalent of the Sasquatch.

The Dzoonokwa is described as black and hairy, with bony face, deep-set, often closed eyes, hollow cheeks and lips thrust forward. This mask perfectly illustrates these features. It is not a dance mask, although the Dzoonokwa is represented in dance. This one is called *gikumhl,* or chief's mask, and is worn by a nobleman when he speaks at a potlatch extolling his family's high place and warning potential enemies of his power. He may shout through the mask like the Dzoonokwa, whose cry paralyzed the hearers with fear.

The paint for the chief's mask is traditionally graphite with black, metallic sheen. Long locks of human hair are set in the rim. The mask was collected at the village of Gwa'i on the Kingcome River in 1917, by Dr. C.F. Newcombe. It was probably made around the turn of the century.

102

No. 66 CLAN MASK

Kwakiutl masks often represent ancestors, or the mythical beings associated with them. The dances in which they were worn are essentially dramatic reenactments of those ancient adventures, and as such they are regarded as valuable, inherited privileges. This mask, collected by Dr. Newcombe in 1917, at the village of Dzadzisnokwumi, depicts the ancestor of the *numaym* (or clan), *Dzundzunkaiyo*—who was a *Kolus*, a variety of Thunderbird, before becoming a man and founding that clan. The ancestor is represented in a transitional state, part bird and part man. Dances dramatizing origin stories are usually part of the ritual complex called *Tiasula,* which also includes the dance performed with the ermine headdress (*see* Nos. 51 and 53). However the tufts of red-dyed cedar bark on this mask suggest an association with the Winter Ceremonial, a different ritual.

No. 66 CLAN MASK 33x29x15cm

All the characteristics of late nineteenth and early twentieth century Kwakiutl painted sculpture are present in this clan ancestor mask. The carving is bold and direct with emphatic planes. Generous use of white paint for background and accent is typical of Kwakiutl masks of the period. Broad, contrasting areas of black, red, green and blue, symmetrically arranged and coinciding with the sculptural planes, are characteristic. The green, mask-like painting of eyesockets is a trademark of Kwakiutl painting from the late nineteenth century to the present.

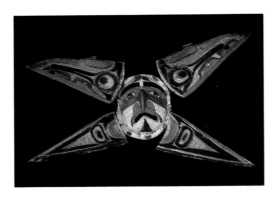

No. 67 TRANSFORMATION MASK (opened)

No. 67 TRANSFORMATION MASK 50x48x33cm

No. 67 TRANSFORMATION MASK

Kwakiutl masters of the dramatic arts spared no efforts to achieve the effects of supernatural powers in their recreations of ancestral adventures. The culmination of these efforts was the transformation mask. Skillfully designed and constructed of multiple parts hinged together and controlled by cords and levers, the mask was made to move and change to illustrate a metamorphosis related in the myth. The classic transformation mask is double, the outer mask depicting one form of the represented being, often an ancestor figure, and the inner mask, suddenly exposed by the splitting of its outer shell, a transformation to another aspect of being (*see* detail). In this example, the outer mask is a raven and the inner mask is the sun. Both of these are crests of the family from whom Dr. Newcombe collected the mask.

The raven, as depicted in the outer mask, is easily recognizable by his heavy beak. The style of carving and painting is distinctly Kwakiutl. Bird skin attached to the top is a remnant of what probably originally covered the frame and secured the mask to the wearer's head. When the control strings, running through wooden fins, were pulled, the raven head split into four triangular rays, their inner surfaces painted to represent the radiating beams of the sun (*see* detail). They flank an anthropomorphic face with a great hooked beak, the usual Kwakiutl convention for the sun.

A performance of such a masked dance in the Tlasula ritual is always preceded by the headdress dance, with eagle down scattered from the elaborate crown of the dancer. Supernatural power emanating from the approaching ancestor spirit overwhelms him and he rushes out of the house. Later an eerie chorus of whistles is heard in the distance, drawing nearer. Attendants investigate and bring the masked dancer into the firelit house. He moves slowly around the floor accompanied by a song belonging to the mask. At the utterance of certain phrases relating to its transformation, the mask suddenly splits, and the inner being is flooded with firelight as the rays of the sun swing outward. The change is almost instantaneous and startlingly complete. The transformation may be demonstrated several times before the dancer leaves the floor.

104

No. 68 HAMATSA CROOKED-BEAK MASK 90x66x29cm

No. 68 HAMATSA CROOKED-BEAK MASK

The most fanciful of the Hamatsa masks is the Crooked Beak. Distinguished by a curved snout rising over a broad mouth and flaring nostrils, it epitomizes the insatiable hunger characteristic of the cannibal spirit and his companions. Hamatsa masks of the nineteenth century were typically restrained in carving and painting details. Fairly early in the twentieth century there began a tendency toward elaboration of form, and later masks became flamboyant and complex. This example is remarkably austere for its time, probably shortly before Newcombe collected it at Gwa'i in 1917. All the forms are beautifully integrated, however, and this, along with its excellent craftsmanship, make it one of the finest examples of Hamatsa masks of the more than 200 in existence.

These great masks are worn on the dancer's forehead, the weight of the beak countered by a strong harness reaching down the dancer's back and tied under his arms. Since much of the dance is done in a squatting position, hopping from side to side while manipulating the massive beak, the dancer must be strong and experienced. A mistake or slip is a serious breach of the Winter Ceremonial and is to be avoided at all cost.

105

No. 69 HAMATSA RAVEN MASK

If any masks can rival the dramatic impact of the transformation mask it must be those of the monster birds who crouch and hop in the firelight in the ritual of taming the Hamatsa. They represent the associates of the man-eating spirit of *Bakhbakwalanooksiwey*, and their presence in the dance house dramatizes the power which has infused the Hamatsa initiate and which must be removed.

The ceremony of taming the Hamatsa is a major part of the important Kwakiutl ritual called *Tseyka*, the Winter Ceremonial. A young man who is heir to the privilege is taken by the man-eating spirit and transformed into a cannibal. He returns, wild, to his village and is captured. In the course of a series of dances and ceremonial observances, the masks representing voracious monster birds appear and dance. One of these is a supernatural raven, represented by a mask with a long, massive beak. The mandibles of the Hamatsa masks are hinged, and at a specific point in the dance, the jaws snap open and shut in a resounding staccato. Masses of shred-

106

ded cedar bark cover the dancer.
The masks are large, heavy and
ungainly, and it takes a strong,
experienced dancer to properly
wear one.

This fine example of early
twentieth century Hamatsa raven
masks was collected by Dr. Newcombe at Memkoomlis village in
1917. It may have been made by
the famous Kwakiutl carver Mungo
Martin, or perhaps his mentor,
Charlie James.

No. 70 MASK
Nootka mask makers exercised
their imagination and skills in
devising many masks with move-
able parts. This one is furnished
with a whirling crown, with scattered eagle down placed in it in a
way reminiscent of the headdresses
of dancers of the northern coast.
Pulling a control cord rotated the
spindle on which it was wrapped;
the momentum of the whirling
crown rewound the cord, then it
could be pulled again, thus spinning the crown first one way,
then the other. These three masks
(Nos. 70, 71 and 72) were collected
around 1900 by B.W. Arnold
along the coast of Vancouver
Island between Alberni Inlet and
Nootka Sound.

No. 70 MASK 32x31x45cm.

107

No. 71   TRANSFORMATION MASK 32x20.5x50cm

No. 71   TRANSFORMATION MASK

This mask utilizes a principle rather uncommon in transformation masks—the inner mask is flanked by vertical iron rods on which the outer mask rises. Both carvings are extremely simple: the smaller, inner face is a half-cylinder with only slight relief for the features; the outer face is boldly carved, with long, narrow nose, eyes flat on the cheek plane, narrow eyebrows and slightly modeled lips. Semi-geometric painting is consistent with Nootkan style. Although much simpler than the Kwakiutl example (see No. 67), the effect of the rising face exposing its inner form is impressive.

Many of the dance traditions of the Nootkan people were lost during the transitional times at the end of the last century, unlike the Kwakiutl ceremonial customs that survived in large measure to the present. Consequently, little is known of the specific uses of many of these masks.

No. 72   MASK

Neighbors of the Kwakiutl along the west coast of Vancouver Island, the Nootkan people share with the Kwakiutl features of Winter Ceremonial and a masking tradition. Although some of the very earliest collecting of masks by Europeans took place among the Nootka in 1778, very few early pieces remain.

Nootka carving is characteristically bold, with simple planes. One ubiquitous feature of sculptured faces is the placement of the large, elliptical eyes on the slanting plane of the cheek, rather than on rounded orbs set in recessed sockets such as is seen in more northerly sculpture. In this mask the separately carved, oval-shaped eyes are pivoted at their ends inside the carved lids. A string control is arranged to roll the eyes, blinking and changing expression. This rolling-eye principle in masks is known throughout most of the coast, but there are probably more examples from the Vancouver Island area than anywhere else.

The hair seems to be of shredded cedar bark, dyed dark. The paint is the commercial variety, applied in typical color arrangement including orange and blue, favorites of the Nootka painters. Fur strips outlining the lids once represented eyelashes. The mask probably depicts an ancestor and would have been used in a way similar to that of the Kwakiutl.

No. 72 MASK 34x26x54cm

109

Textiles & Ceremonial Dress

No. 73 THE "SWIFT BLANKET"

This beautiful twined ceremonial robe of mountain goat wool is one of the world's rarest textiles. There are only three others of the same general type known to have survived, and perhaps another half-dozen of related types, some in fragmentary condition. Of these few, the "Swift blanket" (as it is known, after the collector, Capt. Benjamin Swift) is the finest example, more complex and beautifully made and in more perfect condition than any of the others. When European explorers first met the Tlingit and Haida in what is now southeastern Alaska they were deeply impressed by handsome robes woven in complex designs of the wool of some unknown animal. Descriptions by Spanish, Russian, English, French and American seamen all picture these blankets in the most glowing terms and many were collected, but only this handful is known to exist today. The three most closely resembling this example—one each in the British Museum, the Museum of Anthropology and Ethnography in Leningrad and in the National Museum of Denmark in Copenhagen—may all have been collected on Cook's third expedition, probably at Prince William Sound. The Chugach Eskimo people there wore similar blankets in 1818, judging by a painting by Mikhail Tikhanov, but whether the robes were made there or traded from the Yakutat Tlingit we cannot know. Neither do we know for certain where Captain Swift collected his spectacular robe, but it must have been in southeastern Alaska around 1800.

The Swift blanket differs from later "classic" Chilkat blankets in many ways. The obvious differences are in the rectangular shape, the absence of blue or green color, the tassles of yarn on the surface, and in the entirely geometric design. Less obvious differences are in materials and technique. Chilkat blankets' warp yarns have a core of yellow cedar bark (unlike the plain wool warps of geometric blankets) and the designs are developed by changing weft yarns at the edges of elements. In this and related robes the weft yarns are carried from edge to edge and the color changes are made by using weft yarn pairs of two colors and twisting the yarns to bring

No. 73 THE "SWIFT BLANKET" 165x140cm

the desired color to the front surface. This technique remained in vestigial form in Chilkat blankets only in the corner ties and the teeth designs. The H-shaped figures were formed by inserting extra yarns between the regular wefts and twining both horizontally and vertically, the twining yarn ends hanging down as a tassle. Another unique feature of early geometric robes was the use of skip-stitch twining to produce geometric textures on the plain white surfaces, a technique related to detailing of basketry (*see* No. 5).

We know now that these blankets were woven of the wool of the mountain sheep (*Oreamnos americanus*), in its natural white, yellow dyed with wolf moss, and a deep brown. The wool was expertly spun and plied by hand, and the whole fabric made by twining, without a loom, the warp strands merely hung from a headline attached to a bar.

The blankets were worn, shawl fashion, over the shoulders on ceremonial occasions. They were very highly prized, and at least one visitor, John Hoskins, chief clerk on Gray's *Columbia*, observed in 1791 that the people would not part with them even though they were offered a "very valuable consideration." Of those that were collected only these pitifully few have survived the ravages of time. That the Swift blanket is one is the good fortune of all who have the oportunity to see it.

No. 74 CHILKAT BLANKET 200x125cm

No. 74   CHILKAT BLANKET

The Chilkat dancing blanket, with its long fringe, broad, black and yellow borders and complex totemic design of black, yellow, blue-green and white, represents the epitome of rich display in native North America. It is a foremost emblem of chiefliness on the northern Northwest Coast, yet it is a product of the fur trade era. Although its roots go back far before ships came to the coast from Europe and Euro-America, in twined cedar bark robes from Vancouver Island and the British Columbia mainland tribes and geometric pattern-twined ceremonial blankets of mountain goat wool from Alaska and the Queen Charlottes, no Chilkat blankets of this classic type were recorded or collected before the nineteenth century. The older, firm collection dates for objects of this kind are in the early 1830s, and a single watercolor painting, attributed to an artist with the Lütke expedition of 1826-29, is the earliest known recognizable representation of classic Chilkat weaving. Most were made by weavers of the Chilkat Tlingit village of Klukwan, hence the name.

No. 74   (detail)

A few transitional blankets and fragments remain which combine weaving techniques from the early geometric style with formline designs of the Chilkat technique. Chilkat weaving is an extremely complex form of pattern-twined tapestry work which was developed by weavers endeavoring to reproduce in textile the painted formline designs applied to skin aprons and robes, wooden screens, house fronts, and a myriad of ceremonial objects. They succeeded admirably, and the best examples of Chilkat weaving perfectly reproduce the subtly varied forms on the painted boards used as pattern and guide by the weavers.

All Chilkat blanket designs are representational. They are stylized crest figures, spread-out and distorted to fill the space of the blanket. The central panel of this blanket represents a diving whale, with broad head filling the lower half and spread-out tail-flukes along the upper border. The square, human face in the center occupies the whale's body. Black formlines on a white background delineate the creature, with yellow and blue used in the tertiary areas.

Chilkat blankets have always been valuable and highly prized, both for their crest significance and for their beauty and fine workmanship. The labor in producing one is prodigious, involving the procuring and preparing of the materials, spinning great lengths of goat wool weft and combined bark and wool warp, dying the colored weft and the ultimate complex weaving. Toward the end of the nineteenth century many were made for sale, always at a high price. A very few blankets are being made today.

No. 75   DANCING APRON

When a northern chief greeted his potlatch guests with a "peace dance," shaking eagle down from his headdress, he usually wore under his dancing blanket an elaborate fringed apron hung with rattling deer hooves or the beaks of tufted puffins (*Lunda cirrhata*). A shaman impersonating a healing spirit over his patient wore the same kind of apron, often as his only garment. Long enough to encircle the waist and with fringes hanging below the wearer's knees, these aprons were made of painted deerskin, trade cloth decorated with contrasting appliqué or embroidery of porcupine quillwork or dentalium shells, or—most splendid of all—wool yarn woven in the "Chilkat" technique. This apron is a very fine, early example of painted skin. It probably represents the prototypical form from which those of other materials and decoration were derived.

No. 75   DANCING APRON 100x57cm

At one time each fringe was tipped with a deer hoof or puffin beak, and every movement of the dancer swayed the fringe, clattering the hard, resonant pendants together. Deer hooves' sound is a forceful clammer, puffin beaks produce a softer rustling or tinkling effect. The fringe is always of leather, regardless of the material of the apron itself. The shape seen in this skin apron, with its central or frontal flap, is typical.

The apron was collected by George Emmons, presumably from the Tlingit around the turn of the century, but the painting is of a very old style, and the apron probably was many generations old at that time. An abstracted creature, rendered in red primary formlines, holds a human figure in the mouth, its head occupying the area between the creature's eyes. This design is reminiscent of the similar figures on the armor shirt (*see* No. 49).

114

No. 76 LEGGINGS

Leggings to match the apron were part of a chief's dancing regalia. The same materials, or combinations of materials, were used. Worn wrapped around the lower legs, the designs take on a three-dimensional character which is enhanced by the use of fringes and shaping of the edges.

The clear, unworn painting in rather unusual dark brown and green belies the age of this beautiful pair of skin leggings. They are probably from the early part of the nineteenth century. The animals represented are unidentified, but their heads appear, nose down and flanked by forelegs and paws, in the centers of the designs. Although we might expect each legging to be the same as its mate, the artist has chosen to vary the design so that the two are unlike in most details.

No. 76 LEGGINGS 42x42x1cm (each)

A subtle detail of design which might go unnoticed marks the high quality of workmanship. The upper fringes were once wrapped at the base with porcupine quills, some of which remain. Quill-wrapped fringe was a feature of fine old Northwest Coast skin work, and was part of a continent-wide tradition. Another elegant touch was an edging of fur, but only narrow strips of skin, sewn to the upper edges of the leggings, remain.

No. 77 BUTTON BLANKET 175x145cm

116

No. 77   BUTTON BLANKET

With the advent of trade and the influx of new materials it brought to the Northwest Coast, native artists and craftsmen demonstrated their creativity in the adaptation of those materials to traditional forms. The button blanket is one of the best examples of this meld. Woolen cloth was one of the first materials traded to the Northwest Coast people, and buttons held an attraction for bartering natives. But it was not until the second half of the nineteenth century that the mantle we call a button blanket was standardized as the customary ceremonial robe.

This example, probably Tlingit, is characteristic of late nineteenth century northern button blankets. The foundation is a heavy Hudson's Bay Company blanket, dark blue with a black band at each end. The red flannel border, traditionally on only three sides, is broken in the center of the top and the space filled with an insert of striped cloth. When worn, this part of the edge encircles the wearer's neck and is the first part of the blanket to become soiled and worn, and is easily removed and replaced. The name of the robe comes from the hundreds of pearl buttons which are stitched. The figure here is an eagle, shown with two heads. This may be an example of the principle of "splitting," that is, rendering the two sides of an animal in profile, in order to show the whole creature on a flat field, and in order to keep the design symmetrical. Although the design and use of the button blanket are traditional, all the materials used in it were obtained in trade.

No. 78   CEDAR-BARK NECKRING 97x13.5x10cm

No. 78   CEDAR-BARK NECKRING

Ropelike rings were worn by dancers all along the coast and became insignia of certain dances. Shamans also wore them at their work. Edward Fast collected this ring. Unusually, it is embellished with an ivory cylinder, with figures like those on shamans' amulets and rattles. The style and subjects are Tlingit. A humanoid face with bear's ears and claws forms one side, on the other a figure grasps the horns or spines of a monster. Birds' and frogs' (or perhaps otters') heads fill the spaces, and tiny frogs peer out of the man-bear's ears.

No. 79 BUTTON BLANKET
Button blankets were made in all
sizes. This is a child's robe, made
of a piece of Hudson's Bay blanket,
with the traditional red woolen
borders. It is undocumented, but
its stylistic features are clearly
Kwakiutl. These features are the
elaborate button designs on the
borders, the rendering of the
Thunderbird and his curved ears,
the small coppers in the corners
and the use of unusual handmade
Chinese buttons. These buttons,
called *Tsundzus* ("Chinese") by
the Kwakiutl, were apparently
available in Victoria around the
turn of the century and are seen
almost exclusively in Kwakiutl
blankets of that period and later.
Very recently, since the revival of
ceremonial activities on the northern coast, and influenced by
Kwakiutl blankets, some Haida,

No. 79 BUTTON BLANKET 120x84cm

Tlingit and Tsimshian button blankets have been made with elaborated borders, but on earlier blankets the
buttons were used there only to line the inner edge of the border stripe.

The *Tsundzus* and other saltwater mother-of-pearl buttons are very irridescent. In the firelight they gleam
like silver. No museum exhibit can match the sight of a long line of women dancing to honor and pacify the
Hamatsa, with red blanket borders swirling and button outlines flashing the colors of the fire.

118

No. 80   CHILKAT-WOVEN BAG

Chilkat blankets were sometimes cut in strips and distributed at potlatches memorializing deceased chiefs. The pieces were converted, by sewing them together or adding materials, into aprons, blanket borders, hats, leggings and other ceremonial articles. Almost all Chilkat woven dance leggings are made of pieces cut from blankets.

No. 80   CHILKAT-WOVEN BAG 22x22x21cm

This piece is an exception, a bag almost certainly made for sale from a Chilkat blanket fragment. It may have a prototype in Tlingit culture, a utilitarian waterproof bag made of halibut skins. However, the cloth lid with roughly beaded "ALASKA" establishes it as intended for non-native use. The woven strip was cut from a "diving whale" blanket with a conspicuous, configurative dorsal fin and long, narrow tail-flukes, a blanket design of which there are several examples in collections.

No. 81   TWINED CAPE

Conical capes twined of yellow cedar bark warp and usually nettle fiber weft were standard women's wear the length of Vancouver Island before European dress was adopted. The drawings of John Webber and others illustrate the style as seen in the eighteenth century at Nootka, as do Edward Curtis's photographs of Nootka and Kwakiutl of the early twentieth century. Curtis's models were quite familiar with the conical cape although it was no longer in

No. 81   TWINED CAPE 80x43cm

fashion in their times. In fact, one of them, Mrs. George Hunt, made capes of this kind for use in Curtis's motion picture *In the Land of the Head Hunters*.

A few of these garments were made of mountain goat wool yarn, rather than cedar bark, so it is no surprise that, after woolen trade blankets became available, they would be unraveled and the colored yarns be rewoven.

Rattles

Carved wooden rattles shaped like birds were used by dancers and shamans on many parts of the coast. One of the most distinctive rattle types, and one which was exclusively the property of shamans, is the oyster catcher rattle, so called for the bird that the carving represents. The black oyster catcher (*Haematopus bachmani*) is a bird well suited to be associated with shamans. Its appearance alone—black body, fire-red beak and eye with its yellow rim—is unworldly and mysterious. Add the piercing, whistling call and furtive habits to make it manifestly a shaman's bird. The courting display of the black oyster catcher, an agitated, bobbing dance with neck outstretched, accompanied by clattering cries, is imitated in the form of the rattle.

Oyster catcher rattles are usually elaborated with clusters of carved figures on the bird's back. Almost invariably there is a strange, monster head, usually next to the rattle handle; here it is raised against the bird's neck. It has often been called a bear, or, because many have long, curved horns (*see* No. 83), a goat. However, its round eyes and snout and curled lip, sometimes upward-extended tongue, suggest some unknown supernatural monster. Other figures of otters, sea lions, octopus tentacles and shamans are common.

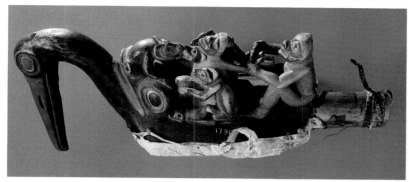

No. 82   OYSTER CATCHER RATTLE

This rattle illustrates a common theme—the torture of a witch to extract a confession of sorcery. A shaman, kneeling behind, has tied the witch's long hair to his hands (which have been secured behind his back). The accused was kept in this position for 8 to 10 days or until he confessed.

A small animal's head, protruding from the witch's chest below his pain-distorted face, bites the tongue of an animal emerging from the round-eyed monster's snout. Other creatures flank the witch. The oyster catcher's curved neck, round eye and long red bill, are naturalistic representations. Ermine skins tied along his wings have long ago lost their fur to insects.

Tlingit shamans shook the oyster catcher rattles when singing over their patients. The rattles are carved of two pieces joined along the sides. The hard wood, usually maple, is hollowed to a very thin shell so that the small pebbles, beads or lead shot contained in the rattle make a resonant sound as it is shaken.

No. 83   OYSTER CATCHER RATTLE

Another shaman's rattle representing an oyster catcher with very long, arched neck has a simple arrangement on the back, of a single reclining shaman singing and grasping the horns of a monster. That creature holds a salmon in his claws, against the handle of the rattle. As is usual with oyster catcher rattles, the bird's feet are carved raised against its

breast. Fragments of ermine skin are tied along the juncture of the rattle.

Because of its vulnerable shape, the beak of the oyster catcher rattle is always of a separate piece of wood (sometimes bone or ivory), morticed into the bird's head (if it were carved in one piece with the rattle, the wood grain would run across the thin beak and it would be easily broken). Rattles of this kind have been referred to as "crane" rattles, but it is clear that they represent the black oyster catcher.

No. 84   RATTLE

Round or oval rattles, everywhere on the coast, are generally thought to be shamans' rattles. Some of them are carved to leave a round hole right through the center. The meaning of this configuration is unknown. In this finely made rattle, collected by Fast in the 1860s, shallow relief-carved ravens' heads flank the hole, two on each side of the rattle.

The forms are painted in ochre red, black and much worn blue-green. For some reason, perhaps a chemical incompatability between the pigment and the salmon egg medium, blue paint on old Northwest Coast pieces seems less durable than the red or black, and frequently is worn away before the other colors.

No. 84   RATTLE 24x10.5x5cm

122

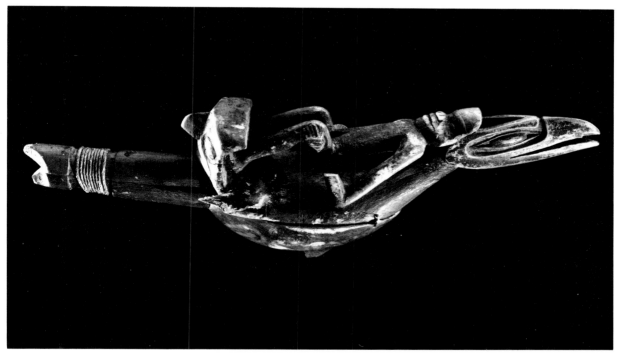

No. 85   RAVEN RATTLE

Another very early rattle, also collected in 1880 by Lt. Woodworth, has no sign of a frog or tongue. The tail-bird, with short, blunt beak, faces the handle of the rattle. The reclining man is carefully carved, with fingers and ankle joints represented. As usual, his head is flattened and hollowed on the back, resembling a mask. Whether this and the vertical piercing of the raven's head are for lightness and resonance, or have some symbolic purpose, is not known.

The features of the face on the breast have been indicated by rather rough painting. Since relief carving traditionally was done after the painting was finished, it is possible that this rattle was never completed. In any case it saw long use before it left native hands.

No. 86 RAVEN RATTLE 28x8.5x7.5cm

No. 86 RAVEN RATTLE

The best known rattle of the Northwest Coast is the "raven rattle." It is carved in the shape of that bird, with upraised tail forming another bird's head and with a reclining man on the back. Usually the man's tongue is protruding and held by the beak of the "tail-bird," or by a frog, which either sits on the man's chest or is itself bitten by the tail-bird. In this very old raven rattle the tail-bird was broken off long ago and the break roughly reshaped, so that there is no way to know how it related to the man's tongue. The meaning of this peculiar arrangement has been debated over the years, and we are no closer now to understanding it. Recorded Indian traditions of the origin of the rattles do not shed light on it. Most scholars agree that the tongue held by frog or bird probably signifies a communication or transfer of power. This leads to the assumption that the raven rattle originated as a shaman's implement. In historic times, however, it has been a dancing rattle, used by a noble person performing with the frontlet headdress (see Nos. 51 and 53).

Although collected in 1880 by Lt. S.E. Woodworth, U.S.N., this rattle is from the early years of European contact, if not before. The carving of the man's face and the two-dimensional details of the raven's head and wings, and the beaked face on the raven's breast, are in early Tlingit style. Early rattles also tend to represent the man as flat on the raven's back, while later examples are raised and touch only at the feet, elbows and head.

124

No. 87 COPPER RATTLE (32x24x9cm)

No. 87 COPPER RATTLE (reverse side)

No. 87 COPPER RATTLE

A few rattles formed of copper are known from the northern coast. Most of them are relatively recent, probably dating from the last part of the nineteenth century. Some of them must have been made for use, but others were made to sell to collectors. It is not possible to know for certain to which category this piece belongs. In any case it is a striking example of the use of the material in conjunction with abalone shell and human hair.

The copper rattle has the form of a shaman's instrument. Unfortunately the record of its significance and use which accompanied it seems to be fanciful. The style of sculpture, and the two-dimensional detailing of the face and forehead, resemble Tlingit work of the late nineteenth century.

125

Pipes

No. 89 WOODEN PIPE 3.5x6.5x7cm

No. 88 STONE PIPE 6x5x8cm

No. 88 STONE PIPE

Tobacco was known and used on the northern coast long before Europeans came. It was the only plant truly cultivated there in pre-contact time. Colnett, Malaspina and Whidbey all saw and described tobacco gardens of the Tlingit in the eighteenth century. However, the Tlingit and their neighbors did not smoke their tobacco, but mixed the dried and pulverized leaves with ash and sometimes lime and sucked the combination. They were introduced to the custom of smoking by white seamen and very quickly forsook both their native tobacco and method of using it for the introduced material and technique.

Tobacco chewing or sucking had been an important feature of certain ceremonies, especially the feasts in honor of the dead. But here, too, smoking took over the ceremonial position of chewing as it did the recreational use. Pipes for ritual use were elaborately carved, perhaps with crest figures. Most were of wood, but a few were of other materials, primarily stone and horn.

This is one of a very few stone pipes extant. It, like almost all the many Tlingit pipes in the Peabody Museum collection, was collected by Edward Fast.

Unfortunately, Fast apparently recorded nothing about the meaning of these pipes, so any interpretation depends entirely on resemblance to other known pieces. The stone pipe represents a bird, probably a raven, with a much compressed body. The legs are tucked under the bill, the

126

wings sweep around under the cheeks, and the tail, with a face in the joint, runs up the back of the bird's head. The material is fairly soft, and was probably carved with steel tools.

No. 89 WOODEN PIPE
Wood was the usual material for Tlingit pipes. A favorite subject for the carved figure was a young bird with the bowl of the pipe in the gaping mouth. The large round eye and stubby tail of this pipe contribute to the image of a baby bird. Conventions of Tlingit design are expertly followed in rendering the wings and back. A simple stem of a shoot with the pith pushed out was inserted in the hole between the wings. Very few of these stems survive.

A short section of a gun barrel forms the pipe bowl itself. Most of those measured prove to be about 58 caliber, the standard bore of the so-called "Northwest gun," a musket type traded all over North America and common on the Northwest Coast. Muskets worn or damaged beyond repair furnished materials for pipe bowls, tools, hair ornaments and small carvings (*see* Nos. 33 and 38).

No. 90 WOODEN PIPE
Another baby bird, fat and very hungry, has a sheet copper lining for his pipe bowl mouth. It is more elaborately, if not so cleanly, carved than No. 89. A large, bulging human head with small hands takes the place of the bird's tail. Massive formlines elaborate the wings and breast, and tiny claws grasp a perch. The rather rough execution is compensated by the monumentality of the carving.

No. 91 WOODEN PIPE
A lining of sheet brass, probably from the buttplate of the same trade musket that furnished the barrel section for the pipe bowl, decorates the open mouth of another bird pipe. This one is of coarse, open-grain wood. The carving is bold and rather rough. Profile stylized faces fill the wing joints, and a small sculptured human face forms the joint of the tail.

No. 90 WOODEN PIPE 7x6x9.5cm

No. 91 WOODEN PIPE 14x5x9cm

127

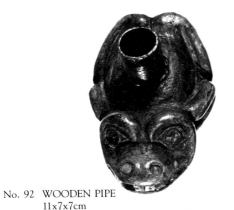

No. 92 WOODEN PIPE
11x7x7cm

No. 92 WOODEN PIPE
The compact form of a crouching frog makes an ideal pipe and was frequently used. This one is probably made of walnut from a musket stock, inlaid with abalone shell. The gun barrel bowl bore is larger than most, approximately 70 caliber. This is within the range of sizes of military musket bores of the early nineteenth century, rather than the somewhat smaller size of the standard trade musket. In the early days of the fur trade on the Northwest Coast, most guns traded were probably surplus military arms.

No. 93 WOODEN PIPE
14x4.5x9.5cm

No. 93 WOODEN PIPE
The joined tongue motif seen on rattles and shamans' charms is illustrated again on this pipe, carved of an open-grain wood. The bird biting the tongue of the man is probably a raven. A very compact killer whale makes up the rest of the pipe. A gun barrel section is set in the whale's blowhole; smoke rising from it represents the whale's spout. The barrel is ringed with two filed grooves, so that it has the appearance and the meaning of the basketry rings on a crest hat. It is of military caliber. The handling of formline detail throughout this pipe is excellent.

No. 94 WOODEN PIPE
16x6x15cm

No. 94 WOODEN PIPE
Pipe carvings often have a narrative quality, with multiple figures combined in portrayal of incidents in myths. It is unfortunate that Edward Fast failed to record such information. This pipe clearly refers to a specific story. A search of recorded Tlingit myths might help to identify the squatting winged figure biting his nose, and the cluster of miniature nose-biters and other figures surrounding the pipe bowl. It is cut from a trade gun barrel, and the wood is from the butt of a walnut stock.

No. 95 WOODEN PIPE
Another gunstock pipe with large caliber barrel bowl illustrates an unknown myth. A bear-like creature squats at the end of a trough, which may be a river; salmon swim toward a spiral figure which may represent a whirlpool. The banks of the "river" are nicely designed with abstract formlines, and a human figure with upraised hands merges with the bear's back.

No. 95 WOODEN PIPE 16x5x11.5cm

No. 96 WOODEN PIPE
Gunstock and barrel furnish material for this pipe. The meaning is obscure. A crouching, scowling man merges with the block of the pipe, surrounded by abstract ovoid and U forms. No doubt it illustrates a mythical being or incident. The crouching position of the figure, the snarling expression and his small, round ears suggest the "land otter man" *Kushdaka*, a fearsome supernatural who takes the spirits of drowned people.

No. 96 WOODEN PIPE 10x5x11cm

No. 97 WOODEN PIPE
Many pipes are carved with simple, single figures, such as this raven with segmented neck. The bowl is raised and faced with sheet metal. The large capacity of such pipes was utilized in smoking feasts when the pipes were passed and everyone smoked heavily. The tobacco smoked was considered to go to the dead for their pleasure.

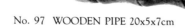

No. 97 WOODEN PIPE 20x5x7cm

No. 98   WOODEN PIPE
In this pipe, a wolf, judging by the tail and tapered ears, stands over an emaciated bear with lolling tongue. The bear's ribs show prominently and he is submissive to the wolf. Gunstock wood and a tall section of the barrel of a "Northwest gun" are the materials used.

No. 98   WOODEN PIPE 13x5x12cm

No. 99   WOODEN PIPE
An embossed tubular bowl of brass, salvaged from some unknown object of European manufacture, distinguishes this pipe. A bear, intent on devouring a salmon, stands over a crouching frog. The carving is simple and direct. With one clawed foot the bear pins the salmon's tail, with the other the head, while he rips the flesh from the exposed bones. The suggestion of sexual activity in the relationship of the bear and frog may be more apparent than real.

No. 99   WOODEN PIPE 11x4.5x11cm

No. 100   WOODEN PIPE
Some Tlingit pipes, and those of their Athapascan neighbors, were fashioned after European pipes, with bulbous bowls and cylindrical stems. A wolf sits on the stem of a pipe of this type, his tail curled up over his back, and ribs showing. Traces of red, black and blue paint remain. The bowl of this pipe is cut from an octagonal gun barrel, set in a copper base.

No. 100   WOODEN PIPE 13x5.5x9cm

130

No. 101 WOODEN PIPE

Imagination and superb workmanship combine to make the bear's foot pipe one of the most interesting. The sturdy, barrel-shaped leg is expertly elaborated with formline designs carved in shallow relief, as is the rectangular socket for the stem. Even the sole of the clawed foot is finely carved.

No. 101 WOODEN PIPE 9x14x7cm

No. 102 WOODEN PIPE

What appears to be a lathe-turned finial of oak is the basis for this pipe. The symmetrical form is unaltered, the surface only being covered with relief-carved formlines. They appear to delineate a raven's head and compressed body and wings, but the arrangement is so abstract that several interpretations are possible. The bowl is faced with thin sheet brass, crimped over the edge of the wood.

No. 102 WOODEN PIPE 6.5x6.5x10.5cm

131

No. 103 WOODEN AND IVORY PIPE 32x8x9.5cm

No. 103   WOODEN AND IVORY PIPE

Although this pipe is made of wood and ivory, it is really a part of the argillite carving tradition (*see* following pages). At least one other similar pipe is known, in the collection of the Cranbrook Institute of Science. The two pipes are certainly by the same unknown carver.

The master sculptor who fashioned this exquisite figure from gunstock walnut and walrus ivory was inspired both by the appearance of a nineteenth century ship's officer and the figurehead of the ship itself. The cape, whose folds swirl into a pipe bowl, and the decorative fillet crowning the boldly sculptured locks must be derived from the neoclassic drapery and details of figurehead sculpture. Even the arched pose reflects that source. It is corroborated by the crisply carved billet head and trailboard detail along the figure's legs.

Just as in many other Euro-Americans represented in argillite ship pipes and as free-standing figures, the pale complexion of the subject has been indicated by the use of ivory for face and hands. The carving is portrait-like. Perhaps a specific captain was intended—more likely he was a generic "Boston Man" as envisioned by the anonymous pipe carver. It is quite possible that this pipe, and its near twin, were specially commissioned from some highly regarded artist for presentation to a patron or friend back in New England.

132

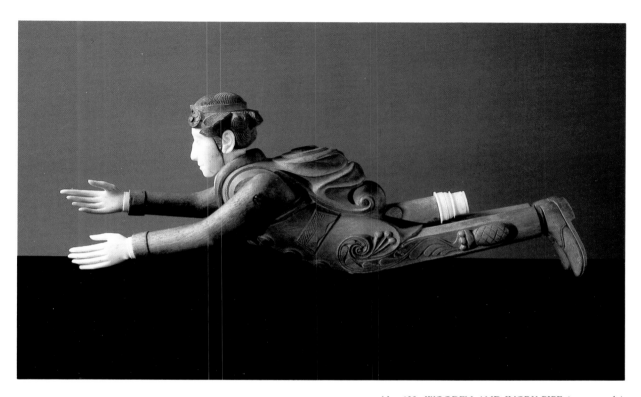

No. 103 WOODEN AND IVORY PIPE (reverse side)

Argillite Carvings

On a steep, heavily timbered mountainside overlooking Skidegate Inlet in the Queen Charlotte Islands, a vein of fine-grained, dark gray shale, soft enough to cut and carve to a lustrous black finish, has been quarried by Haida carvers for at least one-and-a-half centuries. The material is called argillite, and from it were fashioned some of the masterpieces of Haida art.

Although it now seems certain that argillite was used long before the advent of white men in the Haida country for small carvings such as amulets and labrets, there is no real evidence, either archaeological or traditional, for anything like the volume of production of art objects which began early in the nineteenth century for sale to the foreign visitors.

The usual estimate for the date of the beginning of this trade in argillite "curios" is about 1820. Recent research seems to bear this estimate out, although some of the earliest dates assigned to the collection of argillite pieces now in museums have proven to be erroneous. Careful scholars, such as Robin Wright and Peter Macnair, have been working to sort out myth from reality.

By sometime in the first quarter of the century, a thriving commerce in these objects began. They were eagerly sought as souvenirs of visits to the Northwest Coast and a great many found their way to collections in Europe and the eastern American seaboard. Pipes were by far the most common of these souvenirs until the latter part of the century. The earliest examples, like this one, can be smoked.

No. 104 ARGILLITE PIPE 11.5x2.5x9cm

No. 104 ARGILLITE PIPE

Although the McKenzie pipe may be the earliest example known, it was carved by an artist who must have had considerable experience with the medium. Argillite is easy to carve, but it is extremely brittle. The structure of this complex pipe suggests that the maker was well aware of the fragility of the material and compensated consciously for it. Since the style of carving is essentially like that practiced in wood, mountain sheep and goat horn, bone and ivory, the forms and details of the design were merely transferred to the new medium.

The same figures represented in art for Haida use were incorporated in the early argillite pipes. A whale juts out to one side, biting the body of a man whose head is twisted back under the whale's jaw, hands gripping the creature's mouth, and legs drawn up under his chin. The whale's tail curls under his body and his pectoral fins thrust backward, flanking the tall pipe bowl. From the whale's back rises a humanoid face with hooked beak, perhaps a representation of the Thunderbird. Opposite the whale a bird, probably a raven, surmounts a crouching man. What seem to be the raven's wings rise over his head. These wings, and the whale's flippers, tail and head, are detailed with beautifully organized and perfectly shaped formlines, crisply incised in the soft stone. Although it shows abrasion and wear, the pipe is essentially undamaged, despite its fragile nature and the 163 years of its existence, much of this time without special care. It is quite amazing that so much argillite sculpture has survived.

No. 105 ARGILLITE PIPE 8.5x4.5x8cm

No. 105 ARGILLITE PIPE

The second of two pipes believed to have been collected by McKenzie before 1819 also depicts a whale as its main figure. Formline-designed flippers elaborate the sides, and the whale's tail, curved forward, is held by a frog suspended head-down from the whale's mouth. Back-to-back with the whale is a crouching man with extended tongue.

The earliest argillite pipes are of this kind—traditional Haida motifs in compact, full sculptural form. They resemble some of the narrative style wooden pipes. Their bowls are large and functional, although they almost never show signs of having been smoked.

No. 106   ARGILLITE PIPE

No. 106   ARGILLITE PIPE

As the argillite tradition developed the carvings became larger and more flamboyant. Figures multiplied—this pipe has ten distinct creatures represented—and their relationships to one another became intricate and convoluted. During the first decade or so of the development of the art, pipes were usually rather thick in cross section, the figures in full three-dimensional form, and as the pipes grew longer in the 1830s the artists began to open the compositions and pierce the argillite between the figures.

In this pipe, the bowl is still large, and is in the back of a whale in place of a dorsal fin, or perhaps a blow hole. The figures are all creatures seen in Haida sculpture produced for themselves, on spoon handles for example, but the less restrictive shapes available in argillite pipes and the fact that they were made for export, allowed the artists much greater freedom in designing and choosing the figures.

No. 107   ARGILLITE PIPE

As the trade in argillite pipes increased, some makers began to produce very thin, flat carvings, which have come to be called "panel pipes." Since these fragile panel pipes are often a mere centimeter thick, the figures are treated as relief carved flat designs, with considerable attention given to the formline elaboration of wings, ears and fins. Although panel pipes are too thin to allow for a functional bowl, they are almost always drilled in its place with a vertical hole, which meets a long horizontal hole. Their purpose seems solely to justify the carvings as nominal pipes.

This panel pipe seems unfinished, since the eyes of the central "eagle" figure are uncarved, and since none of the traditionally beveled or hollowed tertiary spaces, except most of the eye and joint sockets, are completed. The figures are straightforward: an eagle, at the narrow end, a raven facing the unfinished eagle, a being with coiled proboscis usually identified as a butterfly, another raven and a goose. The pipe is probably from the period just prior to the mid-nineteenth century.

136

No. 107 ARGILLITE PIPE 26x7.5x1.5cm

No. 108 ARGILLITE "PIPE" 33x10x2cm

No. 108 ARGILLITE "PIPE"

Foreign seamen and vessels were every bit as exotic in the eyes of the early nineteenth century Haida as were the Northwest Coast people to the sailors. Argillite pipes imitating in varying degrees of realism and fantasy trading ships and their strange crews began to be carved before 1830. In the next decade they became very popular.

Although this carving is not drilled, it matches every other characteristic of the typical Haida "ship pipe." The carvings are pierced and sometimes inlaid or elaborated with bone or ivory.

The designation "ship pipe" is an appropriate one. The spiral detail at the "bow" is derived from a ship's billet head, and many of the geometric details are straight from cabins, stern and quarter galleries, railings, rigging and other structural ships' details. Large, elaborate rosettes must be representations of paddle wheels.

137

No. 109 ARGILLITE "PIPE" 27x12x2cm

No. 109 ARGILLITE "PIPE"

The hand of the same artist as the maker of No. 108 is evident in this undrilled argillite panel. Ship pipe features are evident, with the billet head scroll reduced to a small spiral under a spray of foliate forms. The paddle wheel is suggested by a quarter segment of a spoked rosette. The actors on this argillite stage are, like those on the first example, compact little fellows, unlike those on many ship pipes, who are often lanky and angular. Haida carvers were facinated by the clothing, and especially the shoes of the foreigners, and they depicted them in great detail. Here the shoes, with their thick, stiff soles and prominent heels, show in little cutouts in the full cloak of a man who is seated before a structure of unknown significance. Just what these people are up to is hard to say. Part of the fun of ship pipes is in trying to figure out what the people are doing and with what they are doing it!

138

No. 110 ARGILLITE PIPE 28x8.5x1.5cm

No. 110   ARGILLITE PIPE

There is no record of the identity of any of the early argillite carvers, but the distinctive styles of individual artists allow us to group their work and recognize that there were many carvers supplying the demands of their white customers. The three ship pipes in this group are all from the hands of a single artist. His penchant for complex window framing, the distinctive foliate scrollwork and, most of all, the stubby white men with large heads and sensitively sculptured faces, all act in lieu of his signature.

Although it has been suggested that this panel was inspired by a railroad car, that source is highly unlikely. Railroads were in use in the eastern United States in the 1840s, when the pipe was probably carved, but the chance that a Haida carver might have seen one, or even a picture, is very slight. On the other hand, the ship characteristics are well illustrated, most emphatically by a majestic figurehead in the form of an eagle proudly displayed over the billet head scroll. Floral panels along the base closely resemble the details of trail boards, carved panels running along ships' bows aft of the figurehead.

No. 111   ARGILLITE FIGURE

Standing figures of white men (probably ships' officers judging by their dress) were popular with purchasers of argillite carvings in the mid-nineteenth century. Usually posed solidly erect with legs spread and hands in pockets, the sculptured seamen gave Haida carvers the chance to express their perception of the dress and character of the visitors. Every seam, button and decoration was shown in detail, and hair and sideburns or whatever fashion of beard or moustache was appropriate framed faces as un-Indian as Haida artists could make them.

Probably the largest of these sculptured men, and distinguished by a head and shirt collar of contrasting red argillite, is this proud, young gentleman. From his boots to his carefully groomed hair he is a picture of Yankee self-confidence. Hands in pockets, as usual, draw back the tails of his coat, so that the drop-front and fly of his trousers, with their fancy buttons, and his striped waistcoat, show. Haida carvers' conventions for white features—angular face with long, pointed nose, small, tight-lipped mouth and parted hair with sideburns—are well shown in this figure.

No. 111   ARGILLITE FIGURE 18x12x61.5cm

140

No. 112 ARGILLITE FIGURE

A very few argillite carvings of white men represent them seated. For one thing it takes a much thicker slab of the material than is needed for a standing figure. Argillite splits into irregular layers, generally about four or five centimeters thick, when quarried, and it takes special care to remove thicker slabs. In this example the man's face and cravat are of ivory. The seams of his shoes and clothing are carefully rendered, the latter by fine, dentate lines recalling stitching. Striped waistcoat and fancy buttons complete the impression of fine dress.

Open books, sometimes with writing or printing on the open pages, appear occasionally in argillite sculpture. One such book, read by a tiny man in the cabin of a ship pipe, has a fragment of some publication in Hawaiian glued to the open book.

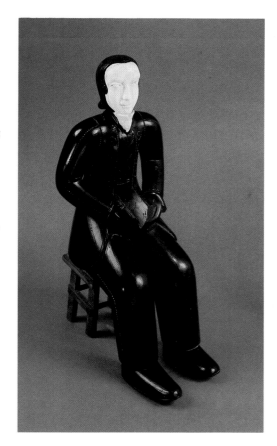

No. 112 ARGILLITE FIGURE 17x11x28.5cm

141

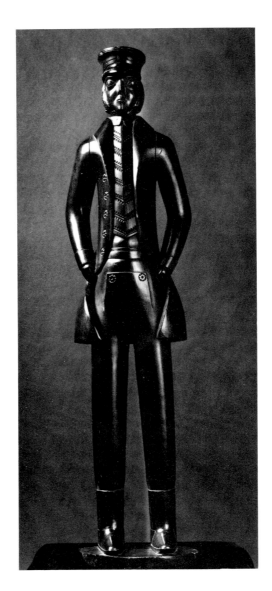

No. 113   ARGILLITE FIGURE
Another very large standing seaman, by the carver of No. 111,
wears a carefully detailed, peaked
cap and sports heavy sideburns of
black argillite, setting off his red
face. He too takes the hands-in-
pockets, legs-apart stance. His
trousers are tucked in his boot
tops.

At about the same time as
these argillite statues were being
carved, or perhaps a bit earlier,
naturalistic figures of Haida couples
were being made in painted wood,
and were for sale. Some of these
are very detailed, with sensitively
sculptured faces and well-rendered
clothing. But is was not until the
late years of the nineteenth century, years after Euro-American
figures had gone out of style, that
the argillite carvers began to produce single figures or figural groups
of native subjects, usualy shamans,
dancing chiefs or characters inter-
acting in mythical incidents.

No. 113   ARGILLITE FIGURE 15x9x60cm

142

No. 114 ARGILLITE FIGURE
Alongside the large, red-faced
seamen figures, this little man is
less than imposing. But what he
lacks in stature and fancy clothes
is more than made up by the power
and expression of his face. Of all
argillite figures, this one is most
surely a portrait. The features are
so individualistic that it seems
inconceivable that a carver would
render them this way without a
specific face in mind. Perhaps one
day we will recognize him from
some picture of a mid-century fur
trader with a high, prominent
forehead, large, sad eyes, a long
nose and muttonchop whiskers.

No. 114 ARGILLITE FIGURE 7.5x6x26cm

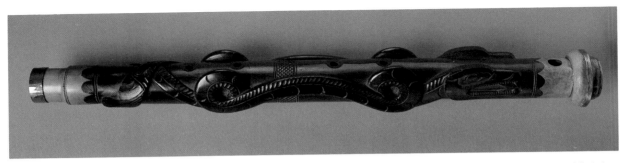

No. 115   ARGILLITE FLUTE

Whistles constructed on the principle of the fipple flute or recorder had an important place in the ceremonies of many Northwest Coast tribes. They were blown in secret to represent the presence of supernatural power. The whistle mechanism may have been in existence on the Northwest Coast before the arrival of Europeans, but there are no examples from early collections or from pre-contact archaeological sites. Some ceremonial whistles were multi-toned, constructed to produce dissonant chords, adding to their eerie effect. However, they were not made with holes which could be stopped to vary the pitch and produce melodies.

End-blown flutes with holes were imitations of European recorders. Quite a number of these instruments were made of argillite, beginning prior to 1850 until about the turn of the century. Early flutes were usually decorated with floral patterns, rosettes and sculptured figures similar to those on argillite pipes of the period. Often, as in this flute, the ends including the mouthpiece were cast of lead. The holes are usually of even size and spacing, resulting in a scale of notes that corresponds neither to that used by the Indians nor the white men. Like argillite pipes, they could be used, but probably were not really expected to be.

The writhing serpent carved in relief on each side of this flute ties it directly to the fur trade. The design is an adaptation of the coiling brass serpent or "dragon" used as the sideplate of the "Northwest guns" (see example shown in the Introduction) which were traded to Indians all across America from colonial times to the beginning of the twentieth century. An indispensable feature of these muskets, the dragon sideplate, although varying slightly in detail from one maker or period to another, always kept a fixed basic form. Argillite carvers seized on the brass dragon as a theme, and copied the sinuous beast on argillite pipes and on at least one chest lid. The sideplate creature has a single, circular loop among his undulations, and his head is usually turned sharply back. The tongue always has a barbed, harpoonlike tip, and fins and tail are rendered as foliate plumes.

Trading companies ordering muskets always specified that the makers adhere to the time-tested eighteenth century design, including the dragon sideplate, since the conservative Indian customers judged the quality of the trade gun by those features. It was not until early in the twentieth century that the Northwest gun was discontinued.

144

No. 116   ARGILLITE TOTEM POLE

Model totem poles are the best known products of the argillite carvers' art. The earliest dated examples are from the 1860s, perhaps the heyday of the monumental poles fronting Haida villages. During the following century, model totem poles dominated production. The earliest examples were true models, echoing the half-cylindrical format and strongly formline oriented design of the massive wooden prototypes. As the old villages were abandoned and as model totem poles became the staple of the carvers' repertoire, they became more freely sculptural. The limitation of form imposed by the tree trunk on the carver of large poles was gone. The figures on argillite poles were freed from that half-cylindrical limit.

Some of the finest argillite models were made around the turn of the century. A few of the best carvers had made the last of the large poles for traditional purposes. One of those was John Robson, the probable carver of this fine model. Robson also made wooden models for the American Museum of Natural History, illustrating various types of monuments and the different figures represented on them. Robson's models were traditional in form, differing from the old, full-sized poles mainly in the greater three-dimensionality of the figures.

The lowest figure on this pole is a beaver, with a stick in his mouth. The human face at the base of his flat tail is probably an elaboration of a traditional formline joint design. The next figure is a raven holding a frog in his beak. The uppermost creature is a bear, who grasps the cylinders of the raven's hat.

There is no documentation as to the maker of this model. The Robson attribution is on the basis of similarity to documented carvings by him. Both the sculptural characteristics and of those of the flat decoration on wings and ears match known Robson work.

No. 117   ARGILLITE TOTEM POLE

The best known of all Haida, and possibly of all Northwest Coast, artists was the master carver, painter and engraver Charles Edensaw. His reputation is so great and his work of such high quality that any piece that can be shown to be by his hand immediately attracts the attention of collectors and curators. Edensaw reached his peak of skill and artistry in the last quarter of the nineteenth century, and he produced many outstanding works after the turn of the century. He was one of a group of Haida artists who were working at a time when their culture was undergoing profound changes; who produced ceremonial and crest art for their own people

145

but at the same time devoted much of their artistic effort to the curio market as well as to filling commissions from museums and anthropologists.

By the 1870s Charles Edensaw's style, both sculptural and two-dimensional, had developed to a point where it was very distinctive, although he always worked well within the restrictions of tribal art tradition. He was a prolific carver of argillite, producing examples of almost every sort—model poles and houses, platters and bowls, chests and figures, although there are no known pipes or flutes attributed to him. His work is characteristically uncluttered, with great attention given to the integration of the various figures in the composition. Forms are markedly rounded, which gives his work a kind of benign quality.

Edensaw worked in the period when narrative Haida art was at its peak, and he was a foremost practitioner of it. His model poles invariably cluster figures related by mythical event. The specific stories from which these figures come are not known, but they seem to be from the adventures of Raven. The lower figure is probably Raven in part human form, holding a killer whale. The central large figure is Raven in the guise of a woman, with a large labret in his human mouth and his raven's beak hanging below. He holds a frog. The upper figure is a boy holding Raven's hat. He wears the skin of a monster whose legs flank the boy's face and whose fins wrap around him.

No. 118 ARGILLITE FIGURE GROUP 19x14x19cm

No. 118 ARGILLITE FIGURE GROUP

Haida artists turned more and more to illustrative figural groups in their sculpture around 1900. Many of these represented shamans at their practice and others were illustrations of specific incidents in the myths from which traditional prerogatives came. A favorite of many carvers was the widely known tale of the Bear Mother (*see* No. 49). A young woman who had insulted the bears was induced to marry a strange, handsome nobleman who, it turns out, was a grizzly bear chief in human form. The union produced sons who were part bear and part human. Eventually the woman's brothers rescued her and killed her husband, who had predicted his own death and instructed his wife in the proper way to treat his body. This sculptural group, from the late nineteenth century, is probably an illustration of that story.

Although the bears' heads are carved within traditional sculptural style limits, their bodies are naturalistic. The natural position of a large bear's grasping forelegs and claws and the contorted position of the human are characteristics of argillite sculpture of the time.

146

No. 119   ARGILLITE PLATTER
Late in the nineteenth and early
in the twentieth centuries Haida
carvers turned to platters again.
This time they almost always
chose traditional Haida motifs,
and many plates were made depicting, in narrative style, events
in the mythology. Argillite platters
were never functional—the material is too brittle and easily
scratched to survive actual use
without damage—so the carvers
began to incorporate sculptural
detail. Although retaining the
trappings of actual plates—rim,
foot and hollowed surface—they
became in fact framed vignettes of
Haida myths.

No. 119   ARGILLITE PLATTER 52x27.5x4cm

    Three hapless canoemen (one
shows only his hand) battle a
giant octopus. The decorated bow
and tip of the stern of their canoe
can be seen between the monster's
tentacles. The trauma of the mo-
ment is reflected in the anguished expressions and frantic clubbing of the victims. This kind of action was
altogether new in Haida art. In earlier times the representations of the most violent mythical incidents were
restrained and without overt expression of emotion.

    Traditional Haida tenets of art minimized spacial depth. Creatures interacting with one another were
very seldom drawn with one overlapping another, as is so dramatically done here, with the octopus dominating
the composition, covering nearly all of the canoe and its crew. Even less traditional is the deliberate overlapping
of the abstract arrangement of ovoids and Us forming the background. This background pattern makes no
structural or symbolic sense. The platter is a product of a time when Haida culture, society and art were
undergoing dramatic transformation.

No. 120   ARGILLITE PLATTER

Round and oval platters of argillite, whose form derived from tableware brought to the Northwest Coast from Europe or the American ports, were part of the early production. The first were decorated with complex combinations of elaborate, compass-designed rosettes and floral motifs. Many of these, with sprays of crescentic leaves and small round berries, are thought to represent the native-grown tobacco plant. Others must be derived from floral and geometric motifs on imported dinnerware, perhaps even from pressed glassware, which was just becoming popular at the time.

This oval platter illustrates, in addition to rosettes, tobacco motifs and geometric and stylized floral patterns, two other adaptations of foreign design. In an elliptical cartouche in the center, an eagle, wings spread, grasps a cluster of arrows. Although lacking a starred and striped shield (seen on a number of similar argillite platters), the eagle cannot be anything but the American emblem, with his sheaf of arrows and olive branch,

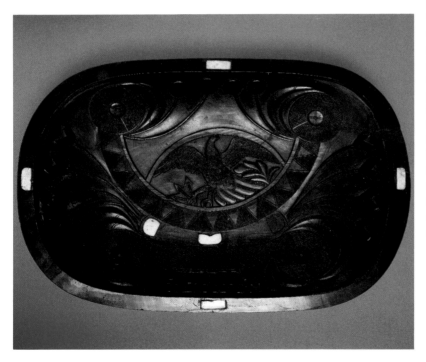

represented by the leaf spray under the bird's wing. These American eagles were seen on ships' carvings and coins, from which most argillite examples are derived. The other foreign motif is a line of pseudo letters, carved in relief near the rim. On some examples the lettering and date on a coin are fairly accurately copied, but here the artist has used the characters decoratively and without understanding, in the same way that copyists not familiar with the conventions of Northwest Coast design have distorted them.

No. 120   ARGILLITE PLATTER 37x24x55cm

148

No. 121 ARGILLITE BIRD

Since most argillite carving was
done expressly for sale to what
were the tourists of the time,
fanciful figures and creatures new
and little understood by the carvers, but perceived to be of interest
to the buyers, were incorporated
into the repertoire. If this carving
is a representation of a particular
bird, we can only guess what it
might have been. Fashioned of
several pieces of argillite combined
with whalebone, it has little resemblance to any bird, natural or
supernatural, known to the Haidas.
The long legs and comb suggest a
domestic rooster, but Northwest
Coast rattles and pipes intended
to portray that bird feature the
long, arching tail feathers. Perhaps
if the beak were not missing it
might give us a clue.

Surface detail on the argillite
bird combines semi-naturalistic
feathers, fanciful, geometric pat-
terning and conventional northern
formlines. Mixed designs like this
and the combination of argillite
and whalebone were characteristics
of mid-century carvings made for
sale to white men.

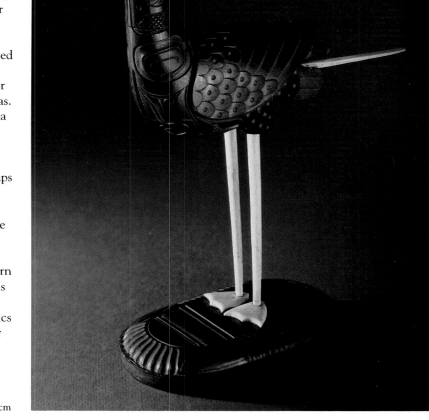

No. 121 ARGILLITE BIRD 23x7x27.5cm

Tools

No. 122 HAND ADZE 21x6.5x11cm

No. 123 HAND ADZE 22.5x6x13cm

When the first European explorers met Northwest Coast Indians they found them using a few iron tools among those of stone, shell and bone. These rare tools were highly prized by their owners and rightly so, for the advantage of iron and steel blades over those of other materials available was enormous. Indians discovered that the newcomers were fantastically rich in iron and the first of those visitors had a hard time protecting their ships from being dismantled surreptitiously by covetous tribesmen. Iron and steel and ready-made blades soon became a major part of the stock of traders, and before long the coast was saturated. The material, however, never lost its importance. Once generally available, all other blade material was discarded. Almost all Northwest Coast carved objects in museums were made with steel tools.

No. 122 HAND ADZE

Although steel replaced stone and shell for tool blades, the forms of those tools and the methods of using them remained little altered. The adze was the principal carving tool. On the southern and central coast it had a very short handle, sometimes joined at both ends to the blade, leading to a D-shaped configuration. D-shaped adzes were versatile tools, enabling the carver to remove wood quickly with deep cuts, or to lightly plane the surface. By allowing the adze to rock slightly with every stroke, each chip could be cleanly removed, leaving a regular texture that was admired and widely used as a decorative finish on canoes, houseposts and other carvings.

The handle of this D-shaped adze is carved from hardwood, perhaps maple, and decorated with an incised eye form similar to those on Nootka warclubs (*see* No. 28). The flaring projection at the blade end of the grip, curved to fit the heel of the carver's hand, is a characteristic of adze handles from the southern part of Vancouver Island and from Washington state.

No. 123   HAND ADZE

Whalebone, the tough, heavy material used by coastal warriors for clubs, was ideal for adze handles. Although rather porous, the carved surface takes a fine polish, and adzes made from whalebone are often decorated with carved figures. This example is recorded as having been collected at Quinault, on the Washington coast.

The blade is probably cut down from a small axe head, although there is some evidence that blades of this form were sometimes blacksmith made for the purpose. The lashing may be of twisted whale or sea lion sinew. It is protected from wear by being lashed through the eye of the blade, the great advantage of this form.

No. 124   HAND ADZE

Most adzes on the coast were utilitarian tools, with a minimum of decorative detail. This example, from the village of Gwa'i in the Kwakiutl country, was collected by D. F. Newcombe in 1917, and is a good example of the functional adze used at that time. The Kwakiutl, living at the geographic point of overlap of the two forms, used both the southern D-shaped adze and the northern long-handled, or "elbow" adze. Each tool has its advantages and disadvantages.

Native carvers still use the tool in this same form, and find it ideal for carving. They are not slow to pick up new tools when they see any advantage to doing so. Nevertheless the native-style adzes are still in use, having withstood the test of efficiency in competition with modern tools.

No. 124   HAND ADZE 20x4x8cm

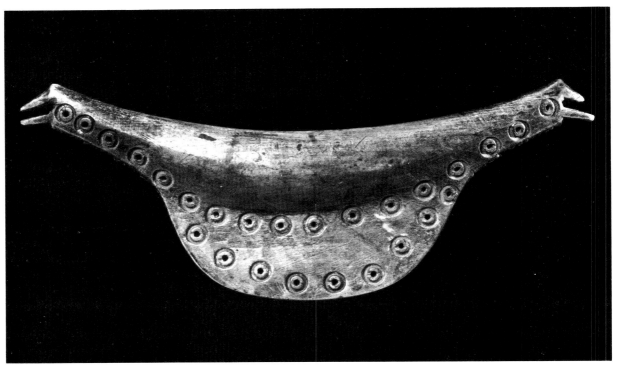

No. 125   MAT CREASER

Mats of various materials were important to the comfort and well-being of the people of the coast. Cedar bark was the material used most widely for these textiles, which were put to service as covering for cargo in canoes, insulation and partitions in houses, raincoats, "tablecloths," seats and even canoe sails. On the southern coast mats were commonly made of leaves of the cattail (*Typha latifolia*). Certain thick leaves were collected and dried in enormous quantities. The mats were made, not by weaving, but by sewing the leaves edge-to-edge with a very long hardwood needle. As many leaves as could be strung on the needle were pierced and while it was still in place the mat creaser was run firmly over the leaves. A groove along the bottom edge of the creaser matched in form the triangular cross section of the needle, and parallel creases were scored on the leaves on each side of it. This prevented the leaves from splitting when the twisted sewing cord was drawn through. The mat was sewn across in this way at intervals. Cattail mats were used as mattresses, partitions,

152

insulation, coverings of temporary shelters and many other useful objects.

Salish mat creasers were often finely made, frequently with the ends carved as animal or bird heads. This one has a smoothly swelling form, ideal for a comfortable grip. Decorative lines of circle-dot designs terminated as the birds' eyes. Collected at the Hoh River on Washington's outer coast, before 1905, it was probably in use at that time. Mat creasers are unchanged in form from those found in archaeological sites to creasers in use in the twentieth century. This one is among the most elegant, and is a fine example of the little-known art of the Coast Salish.

No. 126 TRAP STICK

Trap sticks, usually of whalebone (as in this example), are fairly common in collections of northern coastal material, but the particulars of their use are not understood at all. George Emmons, who collected many of them among the Tlingit, gave several contradictory descriptions in his notes, and the other references to them in ethnographic literature are confusing, unclear or fanciful. Perhaps the answer lies buried in someone's field notes or in the memory of an old Tlingit or Athapascan trapper.

This trap stick is not complete, the narrow end missing some five centimeters. They always have this swelling, curved shape, and the carved section at the end always projects on the convex side of the shaft. The trap stick must be part of a deadfall, or perhaps snare, trigger. The other parts accompany some specimens, but even they give few clues to their function.

Here the carving represents two animals neatly juxtaposed, their legs joined to form zigzag patterns. Carvings on trap sticks are thought to be amulets to aid the trapper in his work. Or they may be ownership marks. Every kind of creature is represented on them, even helmeted and visored warriors' heads.

No. 126 TRAP STICK 19x5.5x1cm

No. 127 ANTLER TOOL

Another problematical tool of unique form is carved of antler in the shape of an otter. If it were not for the curious holes piercing it, it would probably be identified as an amulet. Edward Fast, who collected it, referred to it as a gauge for gambling sticks and horn spoons. Lacking other information, we must consider this identification in trying to reconstruct its function.

The row of four graduated holes in the otter's tail may have had the purpose of grading, or perhaps smoothing, the finely finished, perfectly regular cylindrical gambling sticks used by the northern people. The larger, tapered oval hole in the animal's back could have been used as a wrench in reversing the curve in the handles of mountain goat horn spoons. After the spoon bowl was cut to shape and spread to its final form the handle was heated and bent backwards. An antler wrench such as this one could give the leverage necessary to shape the handle.

The otter carving is a nice example of the northern artist's propensity to decorate utilitarian objects, fitting the sculpture comfortably to the available shape.

No. 127 ANTLER TOOL 20x3x2.5cm

154

No. 128   CAP HORN

Muzzle-loading muskets require a set of complementary equipment for loading and priming. At minimum, a horn or flask of gunpowder, a pouch containing balls or shot, a charger or powder measure, a short loading rod or "short starter" and, for a percussion gun, a container for caps are needed. All of these could be and were made by Northwest Coast natives. Frequently they were decorated by carving.

A handy container for percussion caps was often made of the base of a mountain goat horn, closed at the large end with a fixed wooden plug, and at the small end, drilled to pass a single cap, with a stopper. The cap horn could be carried loose in a shooting bag, or attached by a cord to the powderhorn strap. This beautifully carved cap horn may have had a tethering cord tied around the neck of the Thunderbird or strung through his recurved beak. The little bird, with folded formline wings, perches on the flukes of a whale's tail. The head of the whale and his flippers fill the large end of the horn. Abalone shell inlay in the eyes and shoulder joints of the Thunderbird contrast with the lustrous black of the goat horn.

No. 128   CAP HORN 4x3x8.5cm

155

Miscellaneous Carvings

No. 129   MOUNTAIN GOAT HORN
BRACELET 8x5x2.5cm

No. 130   MOUNTAIN GOAT HORN
BRACELET 8x6x2.5cm

No. 129   MOUNTAIN GOAT HORN BRACELET
Examples of Salish art from the early contact period are extremely rare.
Only a handful of elaborately carved bracelets of mountain goat horn
survive—of the sixteen known, only three are in the United States. All
with documentation were collected in the eighteenth or early nineteenth
centuries. This bracelet is part of the collection believed to have been
made before 1819 by Roderic McKenzie.

  The bracelets were ingeniously made of a strip cut from the outer
curve of the black, tapered horn. After soaking, the horn was heated,
probably by boiling, and bent to shape. A simple, but very effective,
clasp was made in which the small tip of the horn was inserted in a
hole cut in the broad end and locked in place by a clever system of
offsets.

No. 130   MOUNTAIN GOAT HORN BRACELET
An undulating design of carved concentric circles flanked by clustered
crescents differentiates this bracelet from the more open character of
the other design. Both arrangements are characteristic of early Salish
horn bracelets. It is only recently that these objects have been recognized
as distinctly Salish and are being given serious attention by scholars.
Their extreme rarity and the absence of concrete data are among the
difficulties faced by researchers in dealing with them and other southern
coastal material from the early contact period.

No. 131 WOODEN COMB

The small, pre-1819, collection identified with Roderic McKenzie includes some of the most important early Northwest Coast material in existence. This double-ended comb is one of the finest examples of the unique Salish two-dimensional design system known. Both sides are carved, utilizing the same basic elements as the abstract horn bracelet designs, but arranging them to form animal shapes. On one side a configurative representation of a quadruped, perhaps a wolf, is seen; on the other a complex overall pattern of two interlocking animal profiles. A sophisticated form of symmetry is employed in this design, in which the repeated elements mirror one another rotationally. Opposed crescent and triangles combine to form the eyes, lips, claws and other parts of the creatures.

No. 132 BONE COMB

James Magee collected this delicately engraved comb during his voyage of 1791-94. The animal head, possibly a whale, utilizes the formline concept, with narrow relieving slits outlining broad formline ovoids and U shapes. T-shaped reliefs at the rear corners and the curved relief slit defining the edges of lip and cheek are graphic examples of the conceptual relationship between this Haida or Tlingit piece and the Georgia Strait Salish comb.

The teeth of this northern comb show worn grooves usually associated with weaving. Although the technique of twining used in the geometric blankets of Magee's time allowed the weaver to pack stitches tightly without any implement, it is possible that a comb of this kind was used.

No. 131 WOODEN COMB 21.5x5x2cm

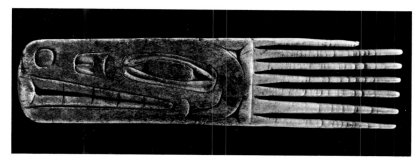

No. 132 BONE COMB 13x3x1cm

157

No. 133   WOODEN STAFF

A great variety of carved staffs were used by the Tlingits. Some, with carved, inlaid and hair-fringed killer whale fins, were referred to as dance paddles and were wielded by leaders of group dances with motions to indicate changes in time and movement. Others, carved with individual or stacked crest figures resembling totem poles, were carried as lineage emblems by noble persons when dancing or speaking. Shamans also had carved staffs that represented supernatural beings from which power emanated. Fast identified this staff, with its bird head finial, as a medicine man's.

The shaft is quite plain except for encircling grooves and red paint. The grooves divide the shaft into cylinders that resemble hat rings, but also could represent vertabrae. This skeletal allusion reinforces the shamanic association. The bird's head is two-dimensionally organized, with minimal sculpture, and shallowly recessed and painted formlines. A human hair fringe is set into the upper edge of the head.

No. 134   CRADLE MODEL

The Chinook people, near the mouth of the Columbia River, shared culture features with their coastal neighbors and with the upriver people with whom they had trade relations. The style of decoration on this model cradle is part of the same tradition seen on sheep horn bowls and ladles all along the Columbia into the interior Plateau (*see* No. 25). The cradle form, a boxlike receptacle carved from a block of wood, is typical of the southern coast, but related to Nootkan and Kwakiutl cradles of steam-bent boards and coiled basketry cradles of the Fraser River Salish. Cedar bark bedding is typical over much of the coast.

This model is probably one of the oldest and most complete of its type. It was received in the museum in 1918, but must have been made no later than the mid-nineteenth century. Almost all Columbia River objects with this style of ornamentation show evidence of great age. The child represented by the carved figure shows the flattened head form artificially achieved by the Chinook and their neighbors.

158

No. 133 WOODEN STAFF 112x3.4x9cm

No. 134 CRADLE MODEL 33.5x12x9cm

159

No. 135 WOODEN FIGURE 13x9x46cm

No. 135 WOODEN FIGURE
No. 136 WOODEN FIGURE
The maker of the "Jenna Cass" mask and others of its type (*see* Nos. 60 and 61) in the 1820s, also produced at least four female figures, all of which are now in museums in New England. The formal characteristics of the features and painting correspond exactly to those of the masks.

Like the masks, they are carefully and expertly carved. There is no doubt that they were carved for sale to white visitors—there is no real precedent for them in traditional native art. Later the carving for sale of naturalistic figures of native people became a relatively common activity. Some of them were carved as nude and dressed with miniature clothing. Whether these figures were clothed when collected is not known. The other two extant figures wear plain cotton smocks, but these may have been added in the nineteenth century, as was the custom when displaying figures such as these in museums.

It is unfortunate that none of the masks or figures by this artist has any solid documentation as to its place of origin.

No. 136 WOODEN FIGURE 8x5.5x20cm

No. 137 WOODEN FIGURE
This tiny and exquisitely carved
Tlingit figure is of unknown use.
Edward Fast referred to it as an
idol. It is very possibly a figure
such as shamans used in much the
same manner as other spirit carvings. It may also have been attached to part of a shaman's regalia.

Whatever its use, it is a fine
example of mid-century Tlingit
miniature sculpture. Although
Northwest Coast carvers had fine
abrasives—shark skin and horsetail
rush—with which to smooth and
polish carvings, they more often
finished their work with very fine
cuts of a knife. These tiny slices,
overlapping all over the carved
surface, leave subtle facets, which
can be seen on this figure.

Facial features follow Tlingit
stylization. The flattened kneecaps
are a carving convention seen
almost everywhere along the coast,
for instance on the figures with
knees drawn up on raven and
oyster catcher rattles (*see* Nos. 85
and 83).

No. 137 WOODEN FIGURE 14.5x5x5cm

No. 138 BONE SOUL CATCHER 18.5x3x3cm

No. 138 BONE SOUL CATCHER

Much of a Northwest Coast shaman's work in curing illness was in restoring a soul which had been separated from its corporeal body. Tsimshian, and perhaps Haida, shamans used a remarkable carved object in their efforts to capture and return such an errant soul. This instrument was a tube of a bear's leg bone, carved in the form of a double-headed monster, in which the soul could be confined, restrained by stoppers of shredded cedar bark.

The bone from which the tube is cut flares at the ends, heightening the effect of gaping mouths. The features of the represented being are carved in low relief, utilizing the formline principles. Although the original shape of the bone is hardly altered, the whole implement acquires a sculptural quality from the relief carving. Often there is a human face in the center. This has led some to refer to the whole figure as a *sisiutl*, which is a specific serpent-like creature of Kwakiutl mythology, but that term is inappropriate for the soul catcher. The derivation of this design is unclear, but the heads have been described as wolves.

Basketry

Tlingit basketry twined of split spruce root has been renowned since the beginning of the historic period. The trailing roots of the Sitka spruce were dug, peeled and split into fine strands to be used as warp and weft of baskets. Baskets ranged in size from tiny cylindrical eagle down containers with telescoping lids to large storage and berry picking baskets. Tlingit basket makers utilized several decorative techniques. Skipstitch twining, as used on the brims of basketry hats (*see* No. 5) produced raised textures on the surface. Dyeing the root itself resulted in colored bands circling the basket. These dyed bands were utilized as background color for designs in dyed and split grass stems and the dark brown stems of the maidenhair fern, applied in a technique called "false embroidery." The design elements were apparently of great age and were combined, within a somewhat fixed format, in almost limitless arrangements.

No. 139 SPRUCE ROOT BASKET 27x23x22cm

No. 139   SPRUCE ROOT BASKET
This fine basket is from around the turn of the century, made for sale to whites. Basketry had become, late in the nineteenth century, one of the few sources of cash for Northwest Coast native women. Tlingit women excelled in the art and produced thousands of baskets that today make up a large part of museum and private collections of Northwest Coast basketry.

The designs on this basket were called "shaman's hat" (at the top and bottom) and "winding around" (in the center).

No. 140   SPRUCE ROOT BASKET
A specialty of Tlingit basket makers was a cylindrical, lidded basket, nearly completely covered with designs in false embroidery, with a hollow knob on the lid containing bird shot or tiny pebbles, which rattle when shaken. Rattle-top baskets were favorites of the customers, and they remain highly prized today. Although the vast majority of those in collections were made for sale, Tlingit women did produce and use them for storage of special treasures.

The designs on this basket were named "fireweed" (at top and bottom) and "cross" (in the center).

No. 140 SPRUCE ROOT BASKET 22x22x12cm

165

No. 141   BASKETRY-COVERED BOTTLE

Northwest Coast basket makers
were extremely skilled at controlling the shape of their work, and
many bottles, as well as other
objects including shells and even
deer antlers, were tightly covered
with basketry for the collectors'
market. Especially active in this
aspect of basketry were the women
of the west coasts of Vancouver
Island and Washington state's
Olympic Peninsula.

The materials used here were
split red cedar bark as warp and
inner weft, and split grass for the
outer, wrapping weft. The technique was wrapped twining, and
designs were made by changing
the color of the outer weft at
appropriate times. The technique
is not of great age in the area,
first appearing in the last half of
the nineteenth century.

166

No. 142   BASKETRY-COVERED
BOTTLE

Collected about 1875, this
wrapped-twined basketry-covered
bottle is an early example of the
technique. Nootkan wrapped
twining has a characteristic spiral
texture, the result of the constant
pitch of the wrapping weft without
an opposing pitch of the inner
weft. This and a usually plaited
cedar bark start in the center of
the bottom are the identifying
features of Nootkan wrapped
twined basketry.

Many small to medium lidded
baskets were also made by the
Nootkan weavers, as well as other
specialized types. Nootkan wrapped
twining probably developed from
openwork burden baskets made of
split root by a similar technique.

Soft Gold

The Brilliant Visual Record of the Fur Trade

From the Oregon Historical Society, North American & International Collections

The geographic distances mentioned in this volume are impressive. James Cook on the Second Voyage alone sailed 55,000 miles. The Dane, Bering, in his two voyages, counting land and sea journeys between St. Petersburg and Kamchatka, and the Saint Elias shore, traveled over 20,000 miles. La Perouse traveled almost 20,000 sea miles from Paris to his death on the Santa Cruz Island reefs—or on the nearby shore. Vancouver, who returned home from his three-year voyage (mooring at Shannon in Ireland) traveled approximately 65,000 miles on this, his last of the three Pacific voyages (the first two were with the Great Navigator—Cook). Vancouver in his disciplined and meticulous way may have been the second greatest. The American Wilkes conducted a remarkable scientific voyage for the United States 20 years before the Civil War, including his Antarctic tour. His journeys affected the Oregon boundary negotiations and the subsequent purchase of the Great Land—Alaska.

The following illustrations are laid out to generally suggest the New England sea route down to the Falkland Islands (Malvinas), then to Cape Horn and around, up to the Hawaiian Islands (a predictable route). Some moved over to the Oregon coast and the Columbia River, progressing up the west coast of Vancouver Island, particularly to Nootka and its Friendly Cove; others eventually moved through the Strait of Juan de Fuca, through the Strait of Georgia and the Inside Passage. Other routes moved toward Baranof Island and Sitka, Prince of Wales Island and up to Cook Inlet, to Kodiak Island and the Aleutian chain and the Pribilov Islands, to Petropavlovsk in Āvacha Bay on Kamchatka Peninsula, or to Macao and to Canton in the Pearl River delta in South China. No one of them was a pleasure cruise.

Perhaps the greatest of America's merchant explorer exemplars was Robert Gray of Tiverton, who first sailed from Boston Harbor in 1787. On his first big voyage after sea service in the American Revolution, Gray rounded the Horn, reached the Northwest Coast, and his small ship (the size most favored for the hazardous and narrow waters of the Northwest Coast) entered Tillamook Bay and the Strait of Juan de Fuca. When he arrived home in 1790 he had completed the first American circumnavigation. His senior associate John Kendrick dropped out; he never did go home, ending his career in Hawaii. It is interesting that when Gray returned safely home to the India wharf in Boston harbor he was received rather quietly, almost routinely. He had sailed about 27,000 miles. He hired a horse and rode an hour and a half home to Mrs. Gray. Within a short time Gray returned to sea in the *Columbia Rediviva* in which ship the following year he entered and named the Columbia River on 11 May 1792. Again he followed the rough triangular pattern sailing to Canton and then back to Boston.

New England ships bound for the Horn and the Pacific invariably stopped at the Falkland (Malvinas) Islands to water and replenish. As we see water casks are being refilled. John Boit, Jr., says that Robert Gray remained at anchor here 11 days at New Island harbor. "A tent was erected on shore for the Tradesmen . . . The weather generally was very cool. During our stay at these Island[s] we shot upwards of 1,000 Ducks and Geese and 6 *Hogs* . . . There were no trees and the grass was 3 feet high. The face of the Country does not present a very delightful prospect, extensive heaths, mountains and ponds of water are to be seen all over the Island." (G. Davidson, OHS Library)

Cape Hoorn bearing West
distance 5 miles

Terra del fuego — This Land bore N.W.By.N. distance 3 miles

This evocative drawing (above) of Tierra del Fuego and Cape Horn is especially pleasing for its undoubted accuracy and the mood conveyed in "the pale white cold sky with dark clouds—The Sea much darker than the Land deep Indigo Soiled with East India Ink, the Snow remarquably bright." While the view is not dated, it would seem that with luck the ship "would round Cape Hoarn [sic]" the next day to Staten Island, the seal station, on 29 December 1791.

Of special interest is a companion piece, Capt. John Boit's Staten Island view "at the distance of 7 or 8 leagues from the land," drawn while aboard the *Union* in 1795. (S. Bacstrom, Private collection)

Sigismund Bacstrom was remarkable. As Lord Nelson would have said, he had "interest." We do not know his birthdate, but he was serving in the Dutch fleet in 1763 having *perhaps* been trained at the University of Strasburg "as a Physician, Surgeon and Chymist." By 1793 he was surely 50 years old. Douglas Cole, who knows him best, states that he would have gone with Cook on the Second Voyage as a naturalist, but Banks who had employed him pulled out at the last moment and his staff went with him. Our loss.

Bacstrom reached the seal fisheries of Isla de los Estados (Staten Island) one day short of Cape Horn, about 29 December 1792. This

highly detailed drawing is interesting for the topography and the techniques revealed. The *Jack Hall* [*Jackal*] is anchored at this sealery earlier built by Captain Etches. Some men are left at this station by the London-based expedition which then pushes on from Tierra del Fuego via the Marquesas to the Northwest Coast.

Captain W. Brown of the *Butterworth* was the squadron leader and an unsavory character. His vessels played havoc along the Northwest Coast, killing not a few natives in a greedy quest for furs. Luckily Bacstrom was able to leave Brown at Nootka. (S. Bacstrom, Private collection)

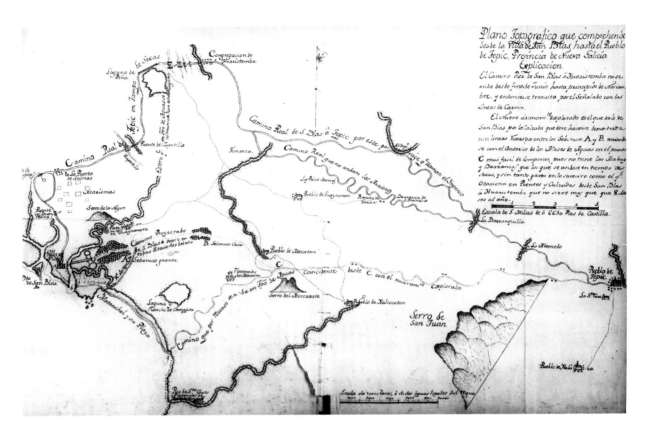

The topographical plan scarcely conveys the rugged aspect of the Mexican countryside between the important crossroads town of Tepic and the Camino Real, which wound down through harsh mountains to the jungle floor and swamps surrounding the fortified seaport of San Blas (1767). Sailors who reported in from Galicia in Spain, the salubrious area of La Coruna and El Ferrol, must have been appalled at this malaria-infested port, which was so critical to the supply of the California settlements and the northern expeditions.

Jacobo Murphy, responsible for this 1809 description, informs us that the road between San Blas and Huanistemba "is not passable from the end of June to the beginning of November." (J. Murphy, Archivo General de La Nacion, Mexico City.)

174

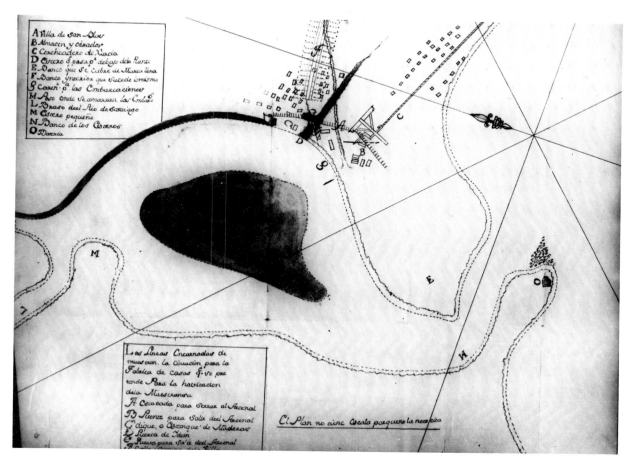

This plan of the colonial military seaport of San Blas cannot suggest the tensions of this critically important site on the Santiago River. Because of the weather and fevers abounding, the shipbuilding center was essentially a seasonal operation. In May, preparations were begun to remove the government personnel up to Tepic, several days away. Each November the government returned to the enshoaled harbor. Despite all these hazards, an extraordinary production schedule was maintained in the colonial shipyards producing many craft, including the *Santiago,* the *Sutil* and *Mexicana.* (F. Segurola, Archivo General de la Nacion, Mexico City)

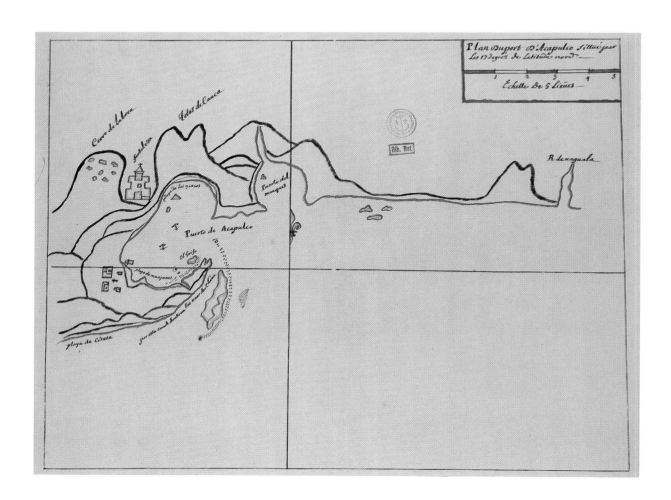

"Chinese goods" came by Manila galleon into Acapulco (1650). An *almojarfizgo* (import tax) was levied on the so-called annual shipment, which tax gradually increased over the years from 10 to around 33 percent. The severe strictures of Seville's powerful merchants restricted trade, limiting all Pacific traffic to the port of Acapulco. The port was closest of the Spanish Pacific ports to Mexico City, but this was scarcely a convenience to other ports north and south, including those in Peru and Chile. (Bibliotheque Nationale, Paris; Museo Naval, Madrid)

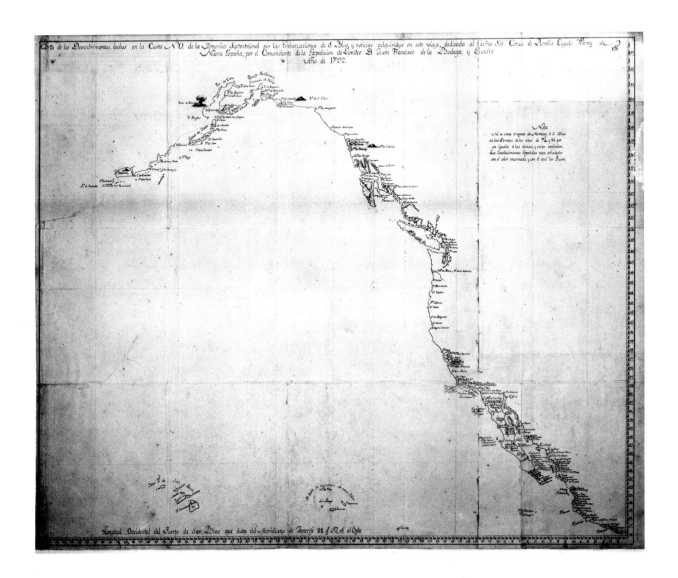

This striking manuscript map shown opposite (83x72 cm) bears out Henry R. Wagner's contention that the Northwest Coast is "all that which extends from Cabo San Lucas [the tip of Lower California] indefinitely to the north." This map of 1792-93 is based on Bodega y Quadra's earlier map of 1791. Dedicated to the Viceroy, Conde Revillagigedo, this overview includes (perhaps for the first time) all the discoveries made by Spanish, British, some Russians and the Boston merchant-trader Robert Gray.

Some Russian establishments are faintly noted in pale blue—at Unalaska Island, Cabo Bonilla, and two on the Kenai shore of what will soon be changed from Cook's River to Cook Inlet. Note the active volcano (Illiamna) across the broad inlet. Far south over two score Spanish missions and other settlements in red array march up California toward San Francisco Bay.

The map surpasses the Bodega y Quadra map used by Wagner, for Puget Sound is shown in great detail as is the Columbia River (this page), here marked "Entrada de Heceta, y Rio de la Columbia." The port of Acapulco, sacked by Francis Drake, is shown and the scope includes the Hawaiian Islands and the Aleutians in the far north. Don Juan Francisco de la Bodega y Quadra has left us a magnificent record of the late eighteenth century Pacific shore. (OHS Library)

179

View at Oahoo on 7–27 Dec: 1792.

Sigismund Bacstrom sailed in the waters of the Sandwich Islands in the British brig *Three Brothers* with Captain W. Alder, on an unlicensed trading venture. The "3 Bs" was probably in the Islands from December 1792 to February 1793, avoiding the storms of the Northwest Coast, a season when many Indians removed from the shore to more protected winter quarters. We have no description of Bacstrom's stay in Hawaii, but this exceptional scene shows Diamond Head and its present-day Maunalua Park beaches to advantage. (S. Bacstrom, Private collection)

Wittity-Bay in the Island Oahoo.

"Whittity-Bay in the Island Oahoo" drawn 29 December, 1792 aboard the "3 Bs" is of course the celebrated beach at Waikiki running along toward Diamond Head on the right. Especially interesting is the rainbow resting on a bank of fog which partially obscures the verdant landscape. This is the site Bacstrom identifies with the recent waterside murder of Hergest, the commander of Vancouver's supply ship *Daedalus*, Gooch, the expedition's astronomer, and a Portuguese seaman in British service. Their bodies disappeared.

When Vancouver returned, a comprehensive review was undertaken in a most scrupulous manner. Three Hawaiians were identified as ring leaders in the affray. Tomohomoho carried the investigation for the islanders, and upon reaching a verdict took the men off in a large canoe where their chief, Tennaveu, eventually executed them by shooting them in the head with a pistol. (S. Bacstrom, Private collection)

181

"The double canoe from the Sandwich Island," is a masterful understatement. Bacstrom's drawings appear to be accurate depictions of things observed; and here we see what most sailors dreamed about, rather explicitly presented, in a most congenial manner. All those pleasures kept many a sailor going on the long cold voyages either side of Hawaii. But the taking became less easy and predictable as Cook's sailors would attest, not to mention Captain Hergest of the *Daedelus*, Gooch and others who were ambushed and killed through the years. But the pleasurable dream, including all that pork, quite naturally lingered on. We have to believe it all because the canoe and the textiles are so faithfully drawn. (S. Bacstrom, Private collection)

Felipe Bauza or Tomas de Suria made a fine sketch (Yndio de Nutka 1791) which is in the Museo de America, Madrid. The subject wears a bearskin and carries a herring rake probably 20 feet in length. Aside from his cape he wears nothing but his chieftain's hat. So it is here 14 years earlier. John Webber has drawn a much more finished picture of "A Man at Nootka Sound" (shown opposite).

He too wears his split cedar bark hat with that characteristic bulb. His hair is dark and lank and he is strongly built. He is very likely carrying a bow of yew, as Gunther suggests, or of some other dark wood. Narrow at the grip, nocked at each end, the weapon is probably strung with sinew. The case for the laterally barbed softwood arrow may be of sea otter skin, or perhaps land otter. The anklets of fur are a novelty, but not the nose ring.

This raiment is typical, whether for hunting in the forest or at sea in a whaling canoe. This chief is unnamed, but he could conceivably be Maquinnah, who by tradition first greeted Cook from his canoe. Cook gave the Moaquat leader a large axe. For the most part the subsequent relationship between Cook's party and the natives was good. There were no fatalities, although the British were often much exasperated by thievery. In leaving, the great navigator said of a chief, "before he went I made him up a small present and in return he present[ed] me with a Beaver [sea otter] skin of greater value. This occasioned me to make some addition to my present, on which he gave me the Beaver Skin cloak he had on, that I knew he set great value upon. . . . He as also many others importuned us much to return to them again and by way of incouragement promised to lay in a good stock of skins for us." The official publication of the Third Voyage was delayed until 1784 in order to include Webber's 78 plates; several of the original drawings are featured here. (J. Webber, Peabody Museum, Harvard University)

"A View of the Habitations in Nootka Sound" (above), April 1778, is duplicated in the British Library Manuscript Collections and engraved in the official publication of Cook's Third Voyage. The village site was visited April 22, "at the west point of the Sound . . . During the time I was at this village Mr. Webber who was with me made drawings of every thing that was curious both within and without doors; I had also an opportunity to inspect more narrowly into their houses, household affairs." This is a wonderful drawing indeed. Clerke is looking for grass for the ship's goats and sheep.

It is not too much to believe that the prow of the dugout in the foreground is pointing directly at Cook completely engrossed in his meeting in company with Capt. Clerke, who said, "we were receiv'd and treated with every kind of civility and attention by the Principals of this habitation; they really made most hospitable offers, but our difference in taste and idea of what is good and palatable, wou'd not permit us to avail ourselves of this part of their kindness." There were two boats. Cook's is a yawl, perfectly drawn, with perhaps four oarsmen—some midshipmen. Of overriding interest is one of the Indians actually holding out what must be a sea otter skin. Cook had been in the Sound for three weeks so this is not the first sea otter skin observed, but as they prepare to leave there is much symbolism in the drawing. (J. Webber, Dixson Library, Sydney, NSW, Australia)

184

Within the village Webber has moved indoors (this page), and he describes the interiors, "appartments" filled with interest. "I sought for an inside which would furnish me with sufficient matter to convey a perfect Idea of the mode these people live in." This rich and attentive drawing is of priceless value to ethnographers. Cook commented on the "two large images, or statues placed abreast of each other and 3 or 4 feet assunder, they bore some resemblance to the human figure but monstrous large; the best idea of them will be had of them in a drawing which Mr. Webber made of the inside of one of their appartments . . . with a small matter of iron or brass, I could have purchased all the gods in the place, for I did not see one that was not offered me, and two or three of the very smalest I got." Above the *parterre* effect are wonderful bentwood storage boxes of cedar. In order to record the scene Webber had to give up most of his brass buttons. (J. Webber, Peabody Museum, Harvard University)

Webber's exceptional interior views (perhaps both are of Yuquot village) together reveal just about everything that is going on in "appartment" life. First the planks are built up and of huge size. We know that finished planks were sometimes of great dimension and value, handed down through generations and moved by water from one village location to another. While the house dimensions were large, the entire space was not always covered. The support beams were heavy.

The larger number of persons are wearing yellow cedar single cloaks, perhaps with dog or goat hair entwined as the loom would suggest. Fish, probably herring, are being roasted, and other kinds are suspended for drying and smoking throughout the dwelling. Splendid woven collecting baskets are everywhere, as are mats and bags. Everyone is barefoot and somehow engrossed. There are few children to be seen, possibly indicating a low birthrate or heavy infant mortality. There are no chimneys, insulation or signs of privacy. (J. Webber, Peabody Museum, Harvard University)

This is a useful drawing of a Nootka woman of quality associated perhaps with Maquinnah. She is wearing her fur-trimmed rain cape of woven yellow cedar (made circular by weaving from the head hole downward, and gradually increasing the diameter with more warp material). She also wears the bulb-top ceremonial rain hat worn by both women and men of the upper class.

Men of the several tribes would very often go naked on pleasant days, wearing only their ornaments, or at sea their hats. Footgear was almost never worn—because of rain. Women usually wore some kind of woven garment but the journals abound with notes concerning how ineffective this cover could and was often meant to be. The only headgear limited to females were the special basketry hats women on the Lower Columbia River wove for themselves. (J. Webber, Peabody Museum, Harvard University)

Unfortunately Webber made only one pencil sketch of the exploring ships; his other views show them at some distance. This is a particular reason why the Ellis drawing (opposite) at King George's Sound, Nootka is so interesting and important. The "Astronomer's Rock" also shows to great advantage, and we are able to see the solitary fir next to the tents which Ellis featured alone in another "Rock" drawing (this page) during the stay at Nootka. The *Resolution,* never a great sailer, is now showing signs of distress and acute wear due to inadequate and hurried shipyard repairs in England.

Her consort *Discovery* in the background is the better ship by far. She does not show the heavy alteration *Resolution* was given, with the "round house" on the stern to provide more commodious quarters for Cook's associates than a regular Whitby-built collier boasted. The *Discovery* was 462-ton burden and carried 12 carriage guns and 12 swivels; she was first entered in the navy lists as HMS *Drake* (certainly an appropriate name for a Pacific voyager). (W. Ellis, National Library of Australia, Canberra)

Cook originally gave the name Sandwich Sound to this great northern water but with some wisdom changed it to Prince William Sound. This watercolor, "A View of Snug Corner Cove in Prince William's Sound," is brilliant, which is more than one can say for Prince William Henry, eventually to become William IV, the Sailor King.

As Murray-Oliver suggests, the ships become insignificant beneath "the grandeur of the great peaks soaring up and up, the whole instinct with the icy stillness of the snowswept landscape."

The ships remained four days and a leak in *Resolution* was examined: "we gave the ship a good heel to port, in order to come at and stop the leak, on riping off the sheathing, it was found to be in the Seams which both in and under the wale, were very open and not a bit of Oakum in them." Snug Corner is today almost at the entrance of Port Fidalgo on the east side of Porcupine Point. (J. Webber, Dixson Library, Sydney, NSW, Australia)

190

Cook studied the inhabitants of Prince William Sound with his usual care. The Russian hunters had encountered much opposition among the tribes whom Cook found unlike those on Vancouver Island. They were small of stature, thickset and good looking. Clerke said: "The Natives here are fine jolly full fac'd Fellows, abounding to all appearance in good living and content: they have very chearfull countenances, and in their conversation with each other, there appears a good deal of repartee and laugh[ter]." (J. Webber, Peabody Museum, Harvard University)

191

The young American, John Ledyard, a British Navy marine corporal, led Cook's landing party ashore 2 October 1778 at Unalaska Island in the Aleutians. Russian traders had established a trading post there years earlier. When their leader Gerasim Izmailov returned Cook's visit, the trader was accompanied by 20 canoes of Russians and natives such as surgeon's mate Ellis has drawn here.

Of special interest were the maps he produced for use by the celebrated navigator. Cook placed much value in them as did Vancouver upon his return. In fact, the Russian government issued orders to cease being so helpful. (W. Ellis, National Library of Australia, Canberra)

Since the villages were often occupied on a seasonal basis Cook could not determine the true population in King George's [Nootka] Sound. He noted their small stature, broad, flat faces and high cheek bones and plump cheeks. "Their mouth is little and round, the nose neither flat nor prominent; their eyes are black little and devoid of sparkling Fire . . . they paint with a liberal hand." In his usual observant manner he found them a docile, courteous, good-natured people, but quick to take offense.

Aside from the black, red and white paint mixed with fish oil or crushed roe he reported, "In this plaster they made various scrawls on the face and particularly on the forehead. Besides this daubing they have another ornament to the Face, which is a small circular plate, or flat ring in the shape of a horse shoe but not more in circumference than a shilling; the upper part is cut asunder. . . . These ornaments were made of either iron or copper and the rims of some of our buttons were appropriated to this use." (J. Webber, Peabody Museum, Harvard University)

The Russians came to Chugach
(Prince William) Sound with the
Irkutsk Company under the leadership of Nikolai Mylnikov and his
partners in the 1770s. St. Constantine's Redoubt was established
on Hinchinbrook Island in 1793,
as was Voskresensk nearby, where
shipyards were built. The high
mountains discouraged agriculture.

This rather fierce-looking
native won the admiration of
Cook. In May 1778 he observed a
group while the *Resolution* was
under repair. He had Crantz's
History of Greenland aboard, and
from it Cook decided the Chugach
group were very similar to the
Greenland natives and unlike the
Indians to the south. Their clothing, hunting gear, body armor and
tradition of tatooing were the
same. Some of his other ideas are
questionable now because we
know that many of the natives
here encountered were Athapascan, not Eskimo. (J. Webber,
Peabody Museum, Harvard University)

194

In this Webber drawing can be seen Captain Cook's ship *Resolution* and *Discovery* on the edge of disaster. The expedition has reached its highest latitude, 70°44′, and the lee shore lies three or four miles off through the haze, with the wind from the west. A massive ice field pushes them toward land also "much incumbered with ice." Just in time a lead opened up to the southwest. For weeks Cook skirted danger on both the American and Russian shores. Lieutenant James King named Cape North (*Mys Schmidta*) and later described the Chukotski Peninsula and tied in with Bering's voyage in 1728 near St. Lawrence Bay.

The *Discovery* was built in 1774 at Whitby and was purchased by the Admiralty in 1776. (J. Webber, Peabody Museum, Salem, Mass.)

Webber's drawings sometimes reflect a curious serenity. Behind the lowering bluffs are great mountains reaching above the usual clouds. Here one might be contemplating a southern lagoon, yet all the important information is here for these people whose single domesticated animal is the dog. They are barefooted it would appear, in and out of their semi-earthen quarters.

The famous baidarka is seen carefully laid up away from the rocks and tides. Russian observers said in the early days the 37-pound boat took over a year to build, but the hide boat could be handled by a seven-year-old boy. There was always a severe shortage of wood for framing, though more driftwood became available as more Europeans entered the north Pacific and more ships were wrecked to cast planks and "float iron" onto the meandering currents. (J. Webber, Peabody Museum, Harvard University)

196

Cook remained three weeks in English Bay (Samgunuda) Unalaska repairing a starboard leak in the *Resolution*. The men caught halibut and salmon and the officers and artists made many important notes concerning the genial but conquered Aleut people and their captors. Short of stature, plump and round-faced, both Aleut men and women wore sealskin garments and intricately sewn bird skins. Theirs was an economy dependent upon the sea and the birds and berries the scattered islands supported. Life in the sub-surface dwellings was comparatively comfortable and relaxed, a fact the British sailors soon unearthed.

The use of the lip ornaments (labrets) was decreasing in deference to Russian taste, but tattooed chins were a tradition with Aleut females. They made "very neat baskets," caps of weasel skin and had much else to trade. (J. Webber, Peabody Museum, Harvard University)

The daughters and wives of the neolithic "marine cossacks" had their special skills. They were superb sewers, and of course they did their best to provide the food and warmth their families needed. But they had no broad experience in food production except for seasonal birds, berries, ground squirrels and products of the sea. They were of a friendly temperament, but the Russian overseers brutalized them and their men were often away. The usual diseases cut the population drastically: typhoid, whooping cough, German measles and of course syphilis. Smallpox was a scourge.

Gibson states that the epidemic of 1835-38 reduced the native population by a quarter. In 1840 the Aleut population was roughly 4,000. This rather engaging young woman, much taken with her tattoos, nose and chin ornaments and a beautifully cut parka trimmed with teeth, cannot see into a future where the otters and Aleuts faced near extinction together. (J. Webber, Peabody Museum, Harvard University)

198

The Russian American Company and the hunters who preceded the Company's formation were dependent on the Aleuts. The Russian administrators said that the Aleuts had become irreplaceable and Governor von Wrangell stated they were "the sole miners of the Company's wealth." Bishop Veniaminov said they would voyage 14 to 20 hours a day during the early summer season. But weather determined success. Many drowned, sometimes whole fleets. In 1834 a party of 80 baidarkas from Kodiak were away hunting for four months of which only a half day was suitable for hunting.

The highly decorated visor is embellished with charms, feathers and seal and walrus whiskers and colorfully painted designs. These glare visors are a wonderful example of form, function and art combined. Sometimes the hunters wore waterproof garments of bear as well as seal gut. The sea lion whiskers standing out from the magical amulets and designs signify the number of walrus killed. Each group of four indicates one animal taken. (J. Webber, Peabody Museum, Harvard University)

The harbor of Awatcha (Avacha), Petropavlovsk (St. Peter and St. Paul) on Kamchatka Peninsula. The first outsiders to see this "well fortified place" were King and Webber, clambering over the late winter ice to the beleaguered village seasonally weakened by fevers, smallpox and scurvy. The sergeant in charge of the Russian detachment sent off for help across the mountains to Bolsheretsk where the district commander Major Magnus von Behm was stationed.

It was to this intelligent and personally too helpful officer that Captain Clerke entrusted the journal of the now dead Cook, plus some of his own and King's journals and charts. Through this trans-Siberian journey England learned of Cook's death from Catherine the Great, who sent his reports on to George III.

The harbor has been transformed today as a Soviet naval fleet anchorage. (W. Ellis, National Library of Australia, Canberra)

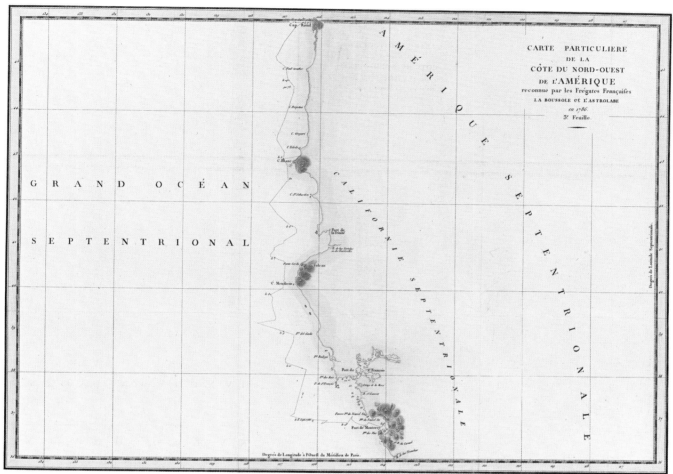

La Perouse map of the west coast of America, 1786 (OHS Library)

In the mid-1780s Jean Francois de Galoup Comte La Perouse harried British settlements in Canada and Hudson Bay with substantial success. Returning to France, La Perouse was sent by Louis XVI (in response to Cook's triumph), from Brest into the Pacific with two vessels.

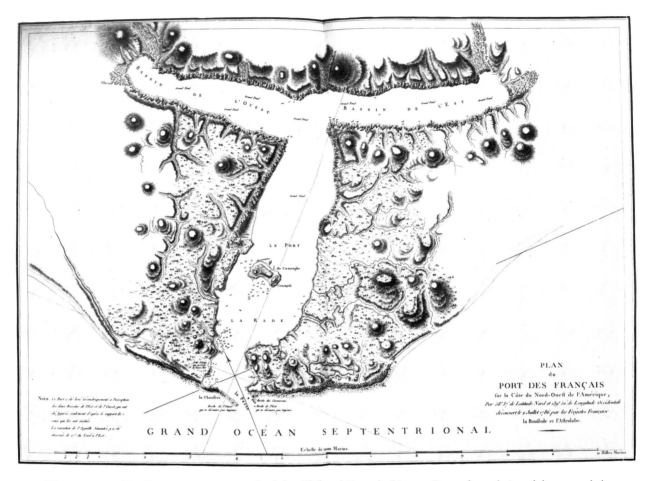

The voyage of La Perouse in command of the ill-fated French frigates *Boussole* and *Astrolabe* moved due north from Hawaii to Port Mulgrave (Yakutat). They experienced a disaster while moving down the Alaskan coast from their first landfall near Mount St. Elias. The expedition was warned of the very hazardous mouth of Port des Francais (now Lituya Bay). La Perouse had observed during soundings that the mouth of his discovery posed special problems; in fact it became a tidal raceway. *Voyage autour de Monde* states that on 13 July 1787 La Perouse sent the yawls from the *Astrolabe* and *Boussole* plus the latter's jolly boat to take soundings.

202

First Lt. d'Escures (a Knight of St. Louis) received very specific orders from the count on safety. "After such instructions . . . what danger could I fear? They were given to a 33-year-old man who commanded ships of war—what greater security could I have?" The boats set out at 6:00 a.m. on an expedition that was part pleasure and part discovery. The yawls were caught stern to in the ebb tide and all hands were lost. The natives were offered presents to rescue anyone, living or dead. Two rescue boats were sent out, and officers searched the beach. La Perouse remained on board to guard against native attack. The natives (Tlingits) then reported they had taken up and buried one body. However they would not point out this grave to the officers who responded to their message. It was never found, if it existed at all, but boat wreckage was produced. "All had disappeared, all were swallowed up!"

On 30 July the expedition sailed south toward Monterey, Hawaii, Australia and the Philippine Islands (some items were sent north to Petropavlovsk). Happily dispatches were sent from there across Siberia to

Port des Francais

Paris. The two frigates then moved southeast and eventually into history. They smashed up on the reefs of Vanikoro, an island in the Santa Cruz Island group. Eventually all succumbed. Obviously some of the best officers and men had drowned earlier in Alaska and in a later massacre in which the captain of the *Boussole* was also killed. The single survivor from the entire expedition was young de Lesseps, who spoke Russian and had been detached at Petropavlovsk with dispatches, charts and other materials gathered up until that date, excepting those separated at Port Jackson, Australia. Unlike Cook who lost his own life but few others, the French emerged with but one survivor; fortunately he was the records courier, and in later years the toast of the town in the diplomatic circles of St. Petersburg.

When La Perouse was somewhere off the Washington shore the crew observed signs of volcanic activity in the mountains. This was more likely Mount Baker than Mount St. Helens. In Macao the Port Francais furs were sold for 9000 Spanish dollars. (OHS Library)

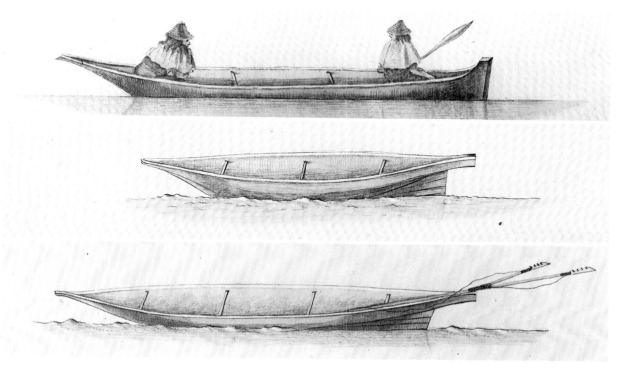

These canoes in their several forms deserve closer study, whether the one-man baidarka of the north, the whaling and sealing canoes, or the awesome vessels of about 70 feet. These craft provided transportation along the Northwest Coast, a land of such broken topography that overland travel is virtually impossible today. The shapes and design of their craft is of lasting interest and we are indebted to all the illustrators, from Bacstrom, Ingraham, Webber, Davidson through Warre and Kane, who recorded them.

Essentially, the canoes were souvenirs too large in size to be placed into a hold or even carried home as deck cargo (*see* canoe models, pp. 42-47). While waiting in the Columbia River for Broughton's return, Manby records that "the first favorable moment I anchored the Vessel [*Chatham*] close to the shore, and purchased a large Canoe from the Indians which fully answered my purpose." But we never hear of it again. The fine example from OHS Museum collections was secured by Hudson's Bay Company Company factor James Birnie, from Grays Harbor. (S. Bacstrom, Private collection)

a View of two Indian Villages round Cape Scott in Lat nearly 51. Dy N at the Entrance of Fitz Hugh Sound

When Spanish explorer Perez reached this general area, this first recorded white leader noted that one of the inhabitants was carrying an iron pointed harpoon.

Of particular interest in this drawing are the special structures comprising the two villages. They are large Waukeshan-style houses which Drucker describes as being roughly 40 x 100 feet in dimension, probably of Haida design. This would be a too accurate view of how many villages appeared after the smallpox epidemics swept north Vancouver Island and the Queen Charlottes.

The Spanish priests who were with Perez kept good watch over matters. Friar Crespi wrote: "They were well formed Indians, with good faces rather fair." His associate, Friar Pena, said of the women: "They are as fair and rosy as any Spanish woman," the lip discs aside. *Santiago* was then compelled by currents and listless winds to move south and on 8 August 1775 Perez paused briefly outside the harbor at Nootka. The ship was much weakened by scurvy and other problems and Perez having once identified the great river of the West could only observe it from offshore. (S. Bacstrom, Private collection)

This drawing (top left, p. 208) was finished in England, but it suggests the Indians of Point Rose area (Queen Charlottes) at the time that Bacstrom visited there in the *Three Brothers* in 1793; it suggests how they looked at home, rather than in ceremonial clothes. The "3 Bs" was an unlicensed brig trading out of Newcastle without authority from the British East India Company.

Point Rose was a hazardous stretch of water and it was there that the HBC ship *Vancouver* later went aground and was ransacked by villagers when the crew precipitately abandoned the steamer. (S. Bacstrom, Private collection)

Cunnyha (top right, p. 208), a Haida chief whom John Boit met 8 June 1795 as drawn by S. Bacstrom in 1793. He came out to Boit's *Union* through an afternoon squall, and stayed overnight while his canoe returned to shore. The next afternoon Cunnyha's wife came out with a gift of two otter skins. Then Boit "detained" another chief "for fear they wou'd not come of[f] again." He discovers that iron and cloth are in demand, "but furs are at least 100 P cent dearer than when the *Columbia* was to the coast."

The next day *Union* was put in close to the village and a large canoe came out carrying Cunnyha's wife. "So I took her on board & let ye Cheif go, & sent the Canoe to inform them of it at ye Village. At 8 Two Canoes came along side from Cunniha Out of which I purchased a Capitall lot of prime furs, & paid well for them." Boit then let "ye Old woman" go with a present, plus presents to all her people. He left carrying away the skins which the village had been saving for Vianna, a Portuguese whom had left the village taking with him to Macao two of the Haida women.

This wonderful drawing suggests that 70-year-old Cunnyha is wearing sailor's trousers with brass buttons and a red wool shirt under his robe, which is bearskin perhaps, or woven cedar bark; his naturally wary eyes are drawn as bright blue (S. Bacstrom, Private collection)

When Bacstrom returned to Haines (Tattesko) Cove on 18 March 1793, it would appear that Cunnyha's eldest daughter (bottom left, p. 208) came out to the ship; although we associate Cunnyha with the Haida village on the north coast of Queen Charlotte Island. Koota-Hilslinga is young and agreeable as the Spanish sailor Camaño has earlier noted. Now she is wearing a wire insert in preparation for her labrets. She has crossed the strait as part of Cunnyha's relocation scheme. At this time Bacstrom was still aboard the "3 Bs." (S. Bacstrom, Private collection)

Decorative and highly finished drawing (bottom center, p. 208) that was finished after Bacstrom returned to England in July 1795. This Chief Tchua may be associated with the village in Norfolk Sound built on a rock. In particular, a special dash has been added to the physical presence indicating some desire at a distance in space and time to enhance the appearance of the subject. In their ceremonial raiment, the Indian leaders presented an altogether striking appearance. (S Bacstrom, Private collection)

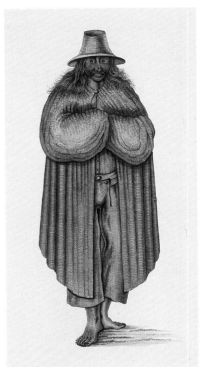

208

209

Hangi, the daughter of a chief, is wearing copper bracelets and anklets and probably a trade dress (top left, p. 209). As we know, natives did not like to give up their jewelry in trade, but these might not be native manufacture. The fork hanging on her blue and white beads is grand, in fact oversize. The display in general is revealing, particularly the blue buttons on her dress and the artfully draped blue cloak clasped about her neck.

She appears full of confidence and every inch a chief's daughter. (S. Bacstrom, Private collection)

It is just possible that this is another study of Clopa Namulth seated on the ground, feet bared (top center, p. 209). He looks about the right age and personality. During his visits to Friendly Cove he made a point of his near equality with Maquinna, but Malaspina, among others, was unimpressed. Yet he made no overt moves against the explorers.

Bostonian William Sturgis, who knew the Northwest Coast so well, later said, "I believe I am the only man living who has a personal knowledge of those early transactions and I can show *that in each and every case* where a vessel was attacked by them [the Indians of the region] it was in direct retaliation for some life taken or some gross outrage committed against *that tribe*." Sturgis is one who early introduced rum into the Northwest Coast trade, a practice which only years of negotiation eliminated. (S. Bacstrom, Private collection)

A drawing (top right, p. 209) of Chief Tzachey completed by Bacstrom after his return to England in 1795. The drawing shows a trade hat, European in design, and the indications of brass buttons. (S. Bacstrom, Private collection)

When the great Malaspina archive one day is published we may be able to determine if "The Portrait of a Nootka Chief and his wife" in the Museo de America Collection (Bauza No. 96) might not be Clopa Namulth the Nootka chief, perched on the rush seat of a chair of English or American design (bottom center, p. 209). The chair looks oversize, but then the chief may have been small. The picture was sketched in 1793 and finished in 1796.

In this period, sophisticated, slave-holding Wickananish was regarded as a great whale hunter, Maquinna the younger as the smartest chief and aged Clopah Namulth as the most cantankerous. He wanted to trade only for iron, powder, shot and firearms, not baubles. And he seems to project this in an admonitory attitude. (S. Bacstrom, Private collection)

These original eighteenth century papers of John Box Hoskins are of considerable importance, including his "Log of the Voyage of the Columbia Around the World."

Professor Samuel Eliot Morison tells so much when he reminds us of a Hoskins letter, "Sir, you'l please to let my mama know that I am well Mr Boit (the fifth mate, aged seventeen) also requests you'l let his parent know he is in health." This from Northwest Coast, latitude 55°0′ N, 15 August 1791, and sent home by the brig *Hancock*, Captain Crowell of Boston. This news was a natural concern since three days earlier Second Mate Joshua Caswell and two seamen were killed by Indians while fishing from the *Columbia's* jolly boat just out of cannon range.

Hoskins became rather critical of Captain Gray in his letters home to Mr. Crowell, too critical perhaps, but his youth might be a factor. The Captain had unfortunately come to regard him as a company spy. (Ms., OHS Library)

View of an Indian Village in Norfolk Sound.
8–29 March 1792.
This drawing was taken when Mount Edgcumbe bore W½ N.

This view may be off Admiralty Island behind present Baranof Island. The village must be a Tlingit settlement. The "curious structures" are of course very impressive sculptures and very much as Malaspina's artists and Ingraham recorded in the same short period. Indians are leaving the shore perhaps to trade. The bearing from this spot toward Mount Edgcumbe is WSW.

Later, P. N. Golovin, the special observer sent by Grand Duke Constantine in 1861, observed: "The Kolosh [Tlingits] are intelligent, warlike and savage; they have a deep aversion to civilization . . . they are always armed with knives and often have pistols and guns which they obtain from the English and Americans. They are all very good shots." (S. Bacstrom, Private collection)

WINTER QUARTERS.

In this sprightly George Davidson original watercolor we see Gray safely anchored in Adventure Cove, a site on the eastern shore of Lemman Inlet on Meares Island. In 1937, Mr. and Mrs. Edmund Hayes and Samuel Eliot Morison sailed the three-man ketch *Seaway* from the Columbia River to the approximate location of this anchorage. The exact location of the sheltered inlet and beach where Fort Defiance was built is latitude 49°9.1′ N; longitude 125°52.3′ West (Boit had made it 49°15′ N ands 125°30′ W). Through the records of Boit, Hoskins, Howay and others at their disposal, the trio established the 1792 location beyond doubt. (G. Davidson, Sanborn Coll., OHS Museum)

"At 4:00 [a.m.] saw a strange sail in the N.W. our anxiety at meeting a sight so new created much satisfaction: by 8 we spoke her and found her to be the *Columbia* of Boston—Grey [Captain Robert Gray] master trading on this coast for peltries of the Sea Otter.

"Scarce any event could be more gratifying than meeting with this man, as a well-known character, who has lately given a voluminous work to the world." This Meares report proved to be a red herring.

Unfortunately in this meeting Vancouver's officers confirmed that John Meares was a falsifier and Robert Gray, who was soon to discover the Columbia River, was a very shrewd Yankee, indeed, having duped Meares on his first voyage. (T. Manby, Ms., OHS Library; G. Davidson, OHS Library)

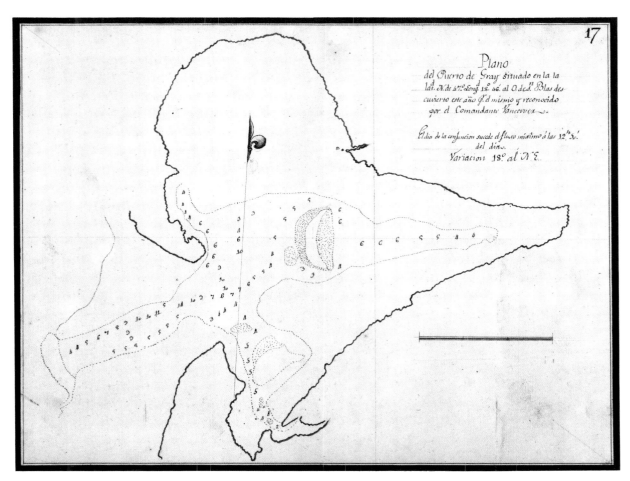

Plano del Puerto de Gray is of course the commodious but shallow harbor on the Washington coast, Grays Harbor. The Boston captain made this discovery 7 May 1792 just prior to entering the Columbia. This manuscript is assuredly the Spanish copy made by Bodega y Quadra that summer from the copy Vancouver made when discussing Gray's new discoveries; it was drawn in either Nootka or Monterey. M. Kraus notes that Vancouver later used this as a small inset, but Wagner did not make note of any separate map. Gray evidently entered the unknown water with a jolly boat, rowing ahead of his ship. (OHS Library)

SURPRISED by the NATIVES of CHICKLESET.

On 8 May 1792, Gray did a brisk business with Indians in his newly found Gray's Harbor, trading blankets and iron. Later that night a large number of canoes packed with natives began to swarm around the *Columbia*, so Gray decided to fire on one that had come within half-a-pistol shot. A nine-pounder loaded with buckshot destroyed the canoe and probably everyone in it. The next day brisk trading continued. Two days later he entered the Columbia River. (G. Davidson, Sanborn Coll., OHS Museum)

ATACKTED at JUAN. DE. FUCA. STRAIT'S.

Gray entered the Columbia River on 11 May 1792. While Captain Gray had enjoyed a peaceful and profitable 10-day stay in the Columbia River his luck again changed when he returned north to Columbia's Cove.

A large war canoe approached the ship in a moonlit night carrying about 25 Indians. According to John Boit there were other canoes following. "We hailed them, but they still persisted . . . Captain Gray ordered us to fire, which we did so effectually as to kill or wound every one in the canoes." (G. Davidson, Sanborn Coll., OHS Museum)

217

From Nootka Thomas Manby wrote: "April 25, 1792. At 1 P.M. it fell little Wind, we found the influence of a current setting the Ship fast towards the Rocks: the Anchor was dropped in 37 fathoms, and soon after the *Chatham* followed our example: the Calm lasted all the afternoon which permitted two canoes with six Indians in each to visit us without hesitation: they came along side, and came on board with little Invitation: being the first Inhabitants of the Continent we had seen. . . . Without any kind of clothing except the skin of some Wild Beast that hung loosely from the Shoulders, not reaching to the middle of some of them. Each man had his quiver hung around him well filled with arrows, the points of them were either of Bones or Stone placed in with great inge- nuity and neatness: the Bow was of yew about three feet in length with a string of twisted sinews. The yellow buttons on our cloaths fixt their attention for these they bartered every thing they possessed.

"We procured from them some curious flint knives about four inches in the blade, and some skins of Bears, Deer, Foxes, Racoons and other small Animals. The Arrows were nicely ornamented with a kind of paint chiefly with red, green and black. We found red ochre in their possession: after mixing it with grease or train oil they smear the face, hair and body over with it, and to make themselves more beautiful in their own opinion, a shining mineral not much unlike writing sand is laid plentifully on the Eyebrows, Nose & chin. It was difficult to read their countenances, so much were they disfigured by their odious fashions: the Septum of the Nose was perforated and a piece of bone four inches long pierced through it lying athwart on the face. By constantly living in the smoak their eyes have acquired a loathsome redness which makes them appear the most furious of the furies."

Of course Manby was 22 and fastidious, so as we can see the young Briton was not much impressed. How vexed he would be to learn that on their voyage up the coast the expedition underestimated the appear- ance of the Columbia River mouth, soon penetrated by Robert Gray. (Manby Journal, OHS Library)

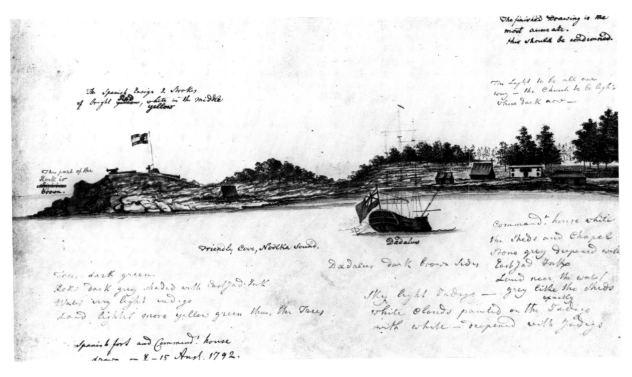

The finished Drawing is the most accurate.
this should be condemned.

The Spanish Ensign 2 Strokes of bright _____, white in the middle, yellow

The light to be all one tone — the Church to be light'd thus dark now —

This part of the Rock is _____ brown.

Friendly Cove, Nootka Sound.

Dædalus

Command'. house white the Sheds and Chapel Stone grey deepened with East Ind Ink Land near the water grey like the Sheds exactly

Trees, dark green.
Rocks dark grey shaded with East Ind. Ink
Water very light indigo
Land light'd more yellow green than the Trees

Dædalus dark brown Sides

Sky light Indigo — white Clouds painted on the Indigo with white — deepened with Indigo

Spanish fort and Command'. house drawn on 8 – 15 Aug'. 1792.

Bacstrom's precise mind is at work here. He wishes to eliminate this drawing because it is not accurate, but for us it is a most useful visual record of how the anchorage and San Miguel fortifications appeared at that time, 15 August 1792. HMS *Daedalus* under Lt. James Hanson sailed in the fall for Tahiti, New Zealand and Botany Bay, returning to Nootka with supplies for Vancouver on 13 October 1793. Missing his commander by one day, he followed him south to Monterey. (S. Bacstrom, Private collection)

View of the Spanish Fort and Cove, at Nootka Sound.

Bacstrom has been away but Governor Salvador Fidalgo, whose white painted residence (some called it "a palace") dominates the far shore, has been busy. Surmounting many problems, he has moved to strengthen the Spanish San Miguel position at Nootka by stripping the *Princesa*, now returned from the unsuccessful Neah Bay colonization. After much effort, her cannons now command the entrance to Friendly Cove. On 9 May 1793 the new governor Ramon Saavedra arrived from San Blas in the *San Carlos*. (S. Bacstrom, Private collection)

A.C.F. David believes this astonishing and wonderful picture to be the only known Vancouver Expedition drawings made by Zachariah Mudge. After three months of dangerous, intricate navigation threading their way through a tide-ripped labyrinth they proved the insularity of the land mass, to be temporarily called Quadra's and then Vancouver's Island. This conclusion coincided with the sudden and dangerous afternoon grounding of HMS *Discovery*. As she struck submerged rocks the tide took her on the starboard and she heeled over "her situation, for a few seconds, was alarming in the highest degree."

Vancouver states that the starboard main chains were within three inches of the surface of the sea. She was floated off the next morning. (Z. Mudge, Dixson Library, Sydney, NSW, Australia)

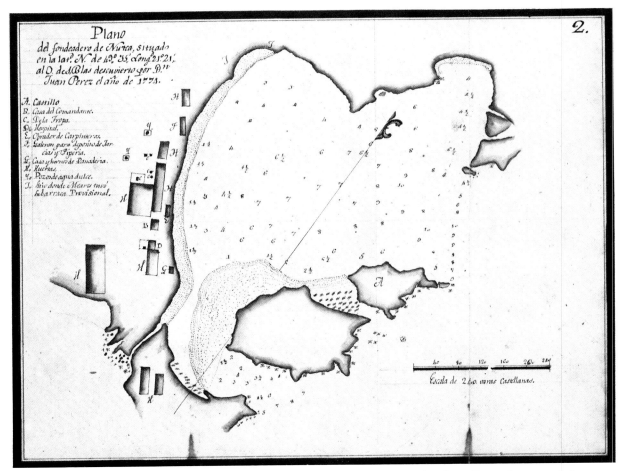

This fine plan (33x25.5 cm) leaves no doubt (in Spanish minds at least) that Juan Perez discovered the port of Nootka in 1775. It minimizes any British claim, suggesting only a small area (J) where Captain Meares "had a provisional sub-lease" on the shore. This original map drawn in response to the Nootka Controversy provided a heavy barrier to Vancouver's position that Spain had no legal territorial claims north of San Francisco. Meares' "British fort" does not appear. The small island (A) will soon be heavily fortified by Governor Fidalgo. (OHS Library)

This very strong drawing has been attributed to Henry Humphrys of Vancouver's expedition. The "residencia" under construction in Jose Cardero's drawing is now complete (see illustration No. 29 in OHS publication *Voyages of Enlightenment*) and Alberni's gardens are flourishing. In the first Alejandro Malaspina voyage of 1791, and then with the *Sutil* and *Mexicana* in 1792, Cardero recorded pictures that Malaspina had evaluated as "those of a simple amateur not devoid of taste or feeling." Felipe Bauza too, sketched the scene. Our interest of course is Humphrys' accuracy rather than his finished style.

The view reflects how the shore must have looked during Vancouver's visit with Quadra in September, 1792. The barracks for Spanish troops are seen and the narrow beach at the right where it is believed Meare's structure stood. It was Meare's claim that sparked the alarms of the world-renowned Nootka Controversy. Perhaps Vancouver is going ashore to confer with the commandant on these points.

National honors were involved, a dangerous thicket indeed, as was that of the increasingly powerful and ambitious British fleet. Secretary to the Admiralty Philip Stephen scrawled his comment with reference to the site: "All that we are really anxious about in this particular part of the Business is the safety for our National honour which renders a Restitution necessary." Stephen further stated: "The true state of the fact appears to be that Meares never was in possession of more than the Hut where the tent now stands in the drawing made by Mr. Humphrys, and therefore in a narrow and literal sense Restitution is compiled with by restoring that spot. . . . I dare say Lord St. Helens will find no great difficulty in persuading the Spanish Minister [in Madrid] to make the Concession absolute which the Spanish Commandant at Nootka [Bodega] did not think himself at liberty to do. The Use of the Harbor must of course remain common to both Parties." (Peabody Museum, Salem, Mass.)

Thomas Manby came from Norfolk. Upon being paid off from the *Illustrious* he received an offer in December 1790 to join George Vancouver as one of his mates. In a 10 December letter to friend John Lees, of Dublin he stated: "Every appearance of war is at an end, the Fleet are fast dismantling, and a long peace is likely to ensue. . . . The Service we are to perform will be exploring the northern regions of the Pacific Ocean, in an unknown and unbeaten track; and if luck attends us in three or four years we shall certainly come back." Through his action-packed career he saw much heroic action and had much bad luck. (T. Manby, Ms., OHS Library)

and the Ship bore up for Attoi a neighbouring Island with Tahooa and the young Indian on board. Tahooa again became very dejected and in the evening he watched an opportunity and jumped overboard swimming toward the shore with all his strength; the Ship was hove to it blowing very fresh. We lost sight of him, and proceeded on our course the land being at this time six leagues distant, we fear he could never reach it.

The Discovery and Chatham in Nootka Sound.

August 30. 1792 The two first days were passed with the Spaniards in visits of form and ceremony. Don Quadra kept a sumptuous table served on plate and gave a general invitation to all the Officers of the British Squadron. He expressed the greatest satisfaction at our arrival, as he wished to restore the place to the English as soon as possible. One of the Houses was cleared for our Sick; and another fitted up for receiving part of the Stores from the Daedalus; every thing went smoothly on for a week. We were busily employed clearing the Store ship the Spaniards were preparing for their departure, and the day was fixt for striking the Spanish Colors and hoisting the British Flag. The arrival of an American Brig stopped the intended plans; the Master of her having sufficient influence with the Spaniards persuaded them that the treaty between the two nations only gave the English the spot which they were dispossessed of by Senr. Martinez. This Brig was in the Sound when Martinez seised the Vessels and Factory belonging to Mr. Mears; in the publication of the latter gentleman, we are informed, these very Americans assisted in forging the Irons to secure the Prisoners. Don Quadra on this information sent an official Letter to Capt. Vancouver acquainting him that altho' he quitted Nootka Sound he should not withdraw the Claim his Catholic Majesty had to the Territory; but at the same time willingly relinquish all Title to the Spot where the English Factory had been erected. Some days passed by Letters going to and from

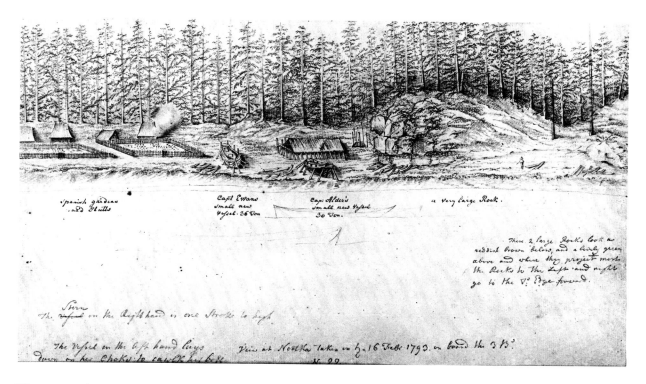

Spanish gardens and Hutts

Capt Ewans Small new Vessel 36 Ton

Cap: Alder's Small new Vessel 30 Ton.

a Very large Rock.

These 2 large Rocks look a reddish brown below, and a lively green above and where they project most the Rocks to the Left and right go to the V. Edge forward.

The Vessel on the Right hand is one Stroke to high

The Vessel in the left hand lays down on her Choks to caulk her bott

View at Nootka taken on Sat 16 Feby 1793 on board the 3 B's.
N. 22.

This very informative view taken 16 February 1793 on board the "*3 Bs*" must have been that ship's return from Hawaii. The drawing instructions and color notes are here, but even more useful is the almost exact description of activities on shore. First is the eternal forest standing in green and endless sentinel. The gardens of course suggest by their stockades that deer are a problem. The two new vessels under construction are in part prefabricated sloops being finished up for the two roving merchant captains, Ewans (Ewing) and Alder. The lively green rocks had a much better use when employed for Cook's astronomical readings. Beyond them, in September 1788, John Meares and his Chinese laborers launched the first ship, the *Northwest America,* which (upon capture) the Spanish renamed *Santa Gertrudis.* (S. Bacstrom, Private collection)

View in <u>Bocarelli Sound</u> in Lat. 55. 14 N.
were we laid at anchor on Tuesday 11 Sept: 1792.

Water very pale Indego
Sky very clear quite pale Azure and white
small delicate white clouds or none
Distant Mountains pale blue green
nearer views lively yellow green
Rocks green and oker

In this view of Bocarelli (*sic*) Sound the 400-ton *Butterworth* under notorious William Brown is seen, possibly with the *Jackal* and *Prince Lee Boo.* It would appear that the squadron is making its way north from Nootka and will shortly anchor in Haines Cove (Tattesko) and return to Nootka 10 October 1792. Soon after, Brown sailed for Hawaii, leaving Bacstrom to join the "3 Bs." Only the *Prince Lee Boo* remained behind. Brown's ship accidentally killed John Kendrick in Hawaii by a shotted signal cannon discharge into his sea cabin in the fall of 1794. Someone was heard to say, "Too much English on the ball."

Shortly afterward Brown, who had used so many natives so wantonly, was killed by Hawaiians, who had come on board the *Jackal* to trade. He was stabbed with iron daggers. (S. Bacstrom, Private collection)

226

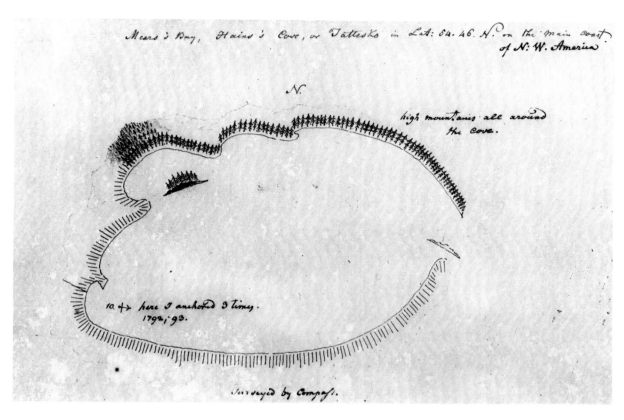

Tattesko (Meares Bay or Haines Cove) was a favored new Haida site on the mainland. Cole identifies it as present Datzkoo Harbor, about six miles from Cunnyha's village of Kiusta. Bacstrom obviously visited the bay at least three times. It is because of this movement back and forth between Parry Sound and Tattesko that Bacstrom encountered Koota Hilslinga. (S. Bacstrom, Private collection)

The handwritten notes on the drawing read:

clear Serene Sky — sun Shine.

all this was in a Strong Light

the dist: mount: a pale very light purple, nearer blue, and nearer green

all this part was in [strong?] with a deep Reflex on the water.

38.

The water here pale Indigo with plenty of Light reflecting from the clear Serene Sky

The water here reflects green somewhat Lighter than the Trees — the green is yellow green Deepened with bluish green

a View out of the Harbour, taken from the Ships Bow — on a beautiful forenoon 9–14 Sept: 1792.

Haines's Harbour in Lat: 54. 42. called by the Indians Vallesko

The Shore from the Trees to the Rocks were all covered with shed yellow Leaves Deepened with red and Brown.

N. 24

The harbor is beautiful as the *Butterworth* leaves on a fine summer morning, 14 September 1792. The maple leaves have started to fall, and the sun is shining, Bacstrom notes, in a clear serene sky. His trees are faithfully recorded in their silent rows and everything except for the presence of the *Butterworth*'s Captain Brown seems pretty right with the world. He will eventually anchor there three times. (S. Bacstrom, Private collection)

Stephan Hill, "2nd Officer with Captain Maggie [Magee]" is without doubt from the *Margaret*. The islands are not referred to by Gray's name, Washington Islands, but they are certainly well described. The several villages noted in the two charts copied lead to the suggestion that this is where the 1,000 otter skins were secured.

Skittigits Sound which Ingraham described is seen, as well as the many dangerous irregularities between Point Rose and the great expanse of shoal water rounding the point to Hancock's River (Masset Sound) proceeding toward the north shore village of the famous chief Cunnyha.

To get even a small inkling of the dangers, let Vancouver speak of anxieties held for boat parties. He spoke of the "violence of the sea, which, from the uninterrupted ocean broke with great fury on the southern shores." But wherever the boat crews were he spoke of "my anxious concern on these perilous occasions." Among other concerns were the large canoes that would suddenly appear from coves and around capes, filled with natives bent on plunder. (S. Bacstrom, Private collection)

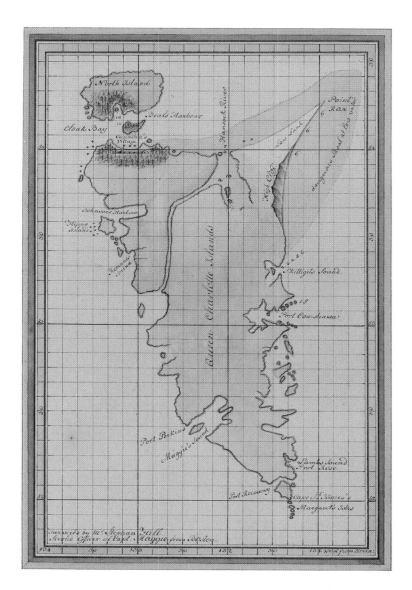

229

James Magee was captain of the *Margaret*, of about 150 tons. Haswell, captain of Gray's *Adventure*, said, "she was as fine a vessel as I ever saw for her size, and appeared exceedingly well fitted out for his voyage." Bostonians Joseph Barrell and Thomas Perkins were among her backers. While in Parry Sound, Magee in 1792 suffered from debilitating cholera that was to undermine him for months. He again rested ashore at Friendly Cove in quarters supplied by Bodega. There he manufactured a poisonous brand of spiritous liquors at four dollars per gallon, until Vancouver intervened.

Returning from Macao in 1793 Magee began trading in the Queen Charlottes. A tender built for him at Friendly Cove was launched in December 1792. It is possible that this is the "longboat" course, which we see here in Bacstrom's chart. When *Margaret* meets the new vessel in Nootka on 10 June, she has collected 1,000 skins. Important to us however is the fact that *Margaret* returned again to Canton and then home to Boston in August 1794. She brought a large collection of

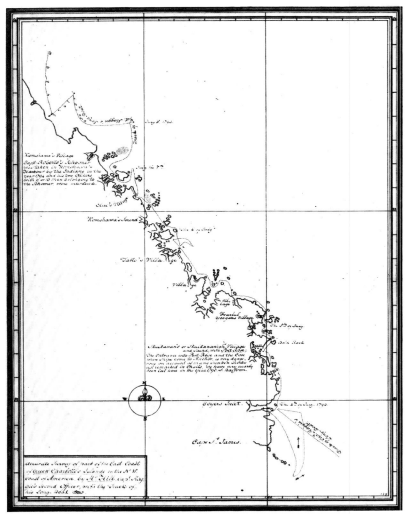

Indian artifacts, which were given to the Massachusetts Historical Society and eventually to the Peabody Museum, Harvard University. (S. Bacstrom, Private collection)

Under the influence of the vigorous and saintly Father Ivan Veniaminov (who became Metropolitan Innokentii, head of the Orthodox Church for all the Russias), Russian Orthodox missionaries learned to communicate with the natives of Russian America in their own languages, and then taught them to read and write. This Aleutian-Kodiak primer was compiled by Father Ilia Tyzhnov and printed at the Synod Press in St. Petersburg. It included the words for the days of the week, the months, and numbers from 1 to 400. (OHS Library)

75

IV
BOOK
CHAPTER
VIII

Having by information and every appearance purchased all the furs commanshisses a my of his Aistes, productse di it, prudent I determine to leave them and try my fortune on the south-west as - I had on board several articles of trade which I had from Boston for that part only besides I hop in over to purchase some more their a new garments and shided which I made number of 5? out Mart 35 page 1853 here I knew were so generally plently and of no great value to the S? but at their Indianum appeared to every thing else exceedingly at C? in the Evening with a fine breeze from the West? on weigh and sent to most of the sailend Commanshisses with shorty and dismissile of the lade remain to on board till we were well out I led them, I should be with them again in 10 days and desired them to examine what stores they could collect till my return the they commanced, I made use of them a present and they took their leave, so on the Evening we were about of Wanna villay but as they had nothing worth shopping for when we boarded them last I did not see any much inclione for so you and at daylight next morning we saw a sail to the East? of us which I immediaun to be the Lucheta -

Cap?

232

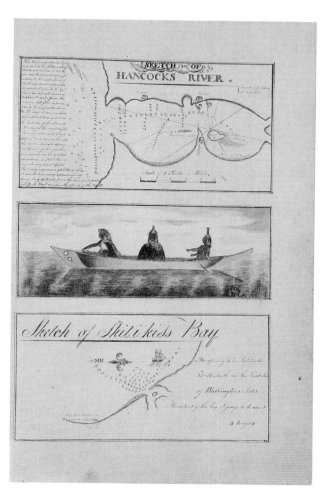

Ingraham was one of the vigorous, sometimes perhaps improper Bostonians. We are very much obligated for his accounts while on the *Columbia* with Gray, and certainly later while captain of the merchant-trader *Hope*. His employers thought highly of him and much regretted his later decision to join the United States Navy, which service he entered as lieutenant in 1799. In 1800 he left Wilmington in the USS *Pickering*, which that autumn vanished in a seasonal gale.

This journal (shown this page and opposite) reveals an extremely bright, able and energetic young man filled with pride in the new Republic. It is he who named the Washington Islands in Polynesia, for Knox, Hancock, General Lincoln and others. (Library of Congress, Washington, D.C.)

233

234

In detail (right) we see why Ingraham referred to the "land of the lob-lips." Many natives of both sexes slit their under lips, although the men did not always adorn the aperture with labrets. The Tlingit women were given a slit bottom lip into which (at age 13 or 14) larger and larger oval or elliptical pieces were gradually inserted. Those of great distinction might have a large lip three by five inches thick, indicating noble rank. (von Langsdorff, The Bancroft Library)

George von Langsdorff, the close observer, said the Tlingits seem to have little "affinity with the Mongol tribes." They plucked their hair, the men leaving few or no whiskers, taking them as they appear in the Aleut manner. They prized red and blue, wearing woolen trade cloths. As we see here the men danced during bartering sessions. Designs are painted on their faces with cinnabar, chalk, ochres and coal dust. Down feathers taken from sea eagles cover their heads.

They scarcely moved as they danced (opposite), clutching the tail or wing of an eagle, or ermine skins. The women sang "a not inharmonious melody" and here the leader on the left stamps time with a staff studded with sea otter teeth. On the ground appear to be native boxes and a European chest. The babes are described as scarcely clothed, while the men favor blankets of mountain goat hair, bird skins and sailors' clothes with brass buttons. The women always wear a garment, usually of simple design. (von Langsdorff, The Bancroft Library)

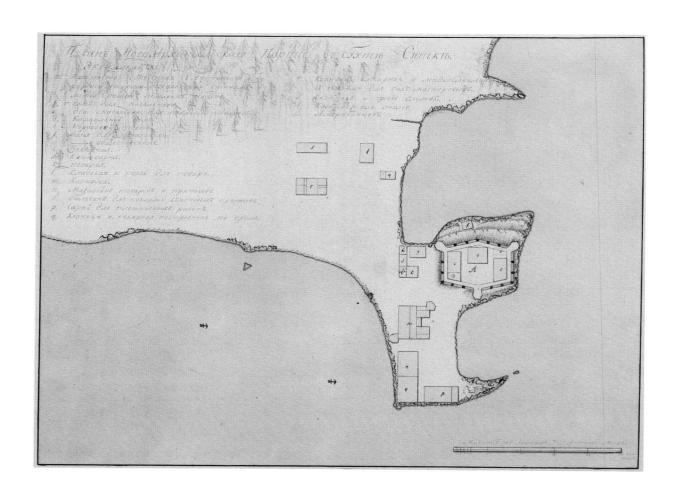

236

In August, 1804 Aleksandr Baranov landed and "took possession of an eminence" next to what the commander thought to be an abandoned Tlingit village. We are so fortunate to have this obscure map of New Arkhangel (Sitka) in its infancy, drawn by George von Langsdorff, who arrived from Japan in 1805 in the train of Court Chamberlain, Count Rezanov, an unexpected visitor.

Looking from the anchorages in this foreground harbor the explanation (as translated by E.A.P. Crownhart-Vaughan):

a. Fortress, constructed of inner and outer walls of wood with earthen fill between.
b. Administrator's [Baranov's] quarters.
c. Two storage warehouses.
d. Sentry box [which was manned on a 24-hour basis].
e. Powder magazine.
f. Baranov's bathhouse [in executive solitude].
g. General bathhouse.
h. Bakehouse.
j. Kvass or brew house.
k. Kitchen.
l. Larder and cook's quarters.
m. Barracks for men.
n. Storehouses.
o. Balagan for baggage and food.
p. Carpentry shed.
q. Forge and bakehouse.
r. Forge, metal workshop and smeltry, wtih quarters.
s. Livestock herders and other workers.
t. Barracks for Americans [i.e., Aleuts and other natives].

The "Gilbraltar of the North" has begun to take form next to the Tlingit settlement, a settlement that plagued two generations of Colonial administrators. The cathedral of St. Michael appropriately located in the settlement of New Arkhangel does not yet appear, nor does one sense the rocky grandeur and tide sluices surrounding the town shown in this rare drawing. (von Langsdorff, The Bancroft Library)

This relatively somber scene was drawn by von Langsdorff near the island of St. George, on the way from Japan to Sitka via Petropavlovsk. Rezanov wished to visit the remote Pribilov Islands discovered by Russian sea hunters in 1786. The almost surrealistic precision of these painted ships on a painted ocean scarcely conveys how wild and furious are the storms that annually break on these rocky shores. The sea was alive with birds, including pelicans, gulls and albatross. (von Langsdorff, The Bancroft Library)

238

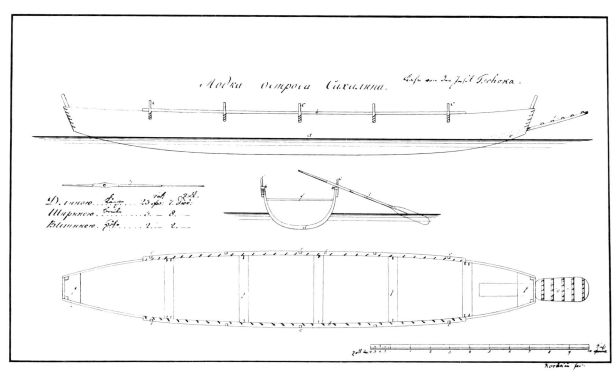

This beautifully executed plan shows the very familiar *lodka* used by the Russians as they followed the Siberian river systems using sails and oars. Because of their shallow draft these craft moved over rough water in easily maneuvererd flotillas. Such a dependable craft was naturally carried to Alaska, as was the Siberian sled, so unlike that used in the French Canadian north. This boat was 7.18 meters long, 1.12 meters in width and had a 66 cm draft. (von Langsdorff, The Bancroft Library)

This stylized print is interesting in what it does and does not reveal about Tlingit culture. The blanket is faithful enough and to some degree the chieftan's hat (*see*, respectively, ethnographic artifacts Nos. 74 and 12). His apron suggests more that he is in a fraternal lodge rather than his own more loosely constructed habitation. One might rather want to see him in wooden armor so dramatic in appearance, or that made of elkskin. The wife and daughter (?) wearing labrets and single garments are faithful enough, as is the north raven rattle (*see* No. 85) and rather freely translated mask (*see* No. 52) of red and blue (those favorite colors), walrus whiskers and ermine. The hatchet by its shape reveals Russian trade associations. A more detailed picture would show an American musket or two and perhaps a flintlock pistol. (OHS Library)

240

Tab. XVII.

The fur seal was an important part of the ocean trade; it was sometimes called the sea-bear, as the otter was called the sea-beaver. George von Langsdorff in May of 1805 observed many thousands of seals swimming in a shoal extending in a line two sea miles in length. At first glance this appears to be a ledge of seals on the Pribilov Islands, but in fact they must be sea otters with their peculiar flattened and flipper-like rear limbs, and with a 12-inch tail which is used as a rudder. (von Langsdorff, The Bancroft Library)

This wonderful drawing, "Sunday on Unalaska Island," reveals a four-post hut with a shaggy roof of earth and grass in front of which 12 Aleuts or "creoles" stand. Some are holding bottles and one has a kettle, perhaps a tea pot (*see* illustration, p. 18). This could be the native church, where the Aleuts gathered to attend the Russian Orthodox service at which time, once inside the door, they would be given a *charka* or cup of vodka. (The barrel may provide a clue.) Captain Pavel Golovin suggested natives would proclaim Islam for a ladle of vodka, but then so would the Russian American Company promyshlenniks (fur trappers or traders).

Ilia Gavrilovich Voznesenskii (1816-1871) came to Russian possessions in Alaska in the 1840s sailing from St. Petersburg (Kronstadt) in 1839, via Brazil and Cape Horn. He reached Sitka 1 May 1840 and he travelled throughout the colony until May 1845. He sketched and drew constantly. The Museum of Anthropology and Ethnography, the grand old institution on the Neva founded by Peter the Great, owns 50 of his drawings. The zoologist was not a great artist but his scenes are of enormous historical and ethnographic value. (I. Voznesenskii, Museum of Anthropology and Ethnography, Leningrad)

242

A view of the Illiliuk settlement on Unalaska Island with the typical church facing a number of Russian American Company houses with four-post roofs. Voznesenskii observed the village of Gavanskoe recorded by Cook and Webber and in the Fox Island group. Here were centered all trapping and trading activity in the Unalaska Department. The Russians referred to the Aleut underground dwellings as "iurts." Gardens are in evidence. Veniaminov in the late 1830s wrote that there were 27 iurts in the settlement.

Golovin, who was reasonably detached, reported in 1861: "Thanks to the organization of schools . . . a large part of the Aleuts know how to read and write and in some places, for example on the islands of St. Paul and St. George, there is not a single illiterate person." (I. Voznesenskii, Museum of Anthropology and Ethnography, Leningrad)

This drawing shows Little and Big Iablochnye islands in a background of rain sweeping Sitka Bay. The Tlingits are paddling a *bata* made of cedar. The forward paddler has a woven cedar rain hat familiar to the area, while the one at the stern wears his hair pulled back in an old-fashioned style. While they are wearing cloaks, one also observes the wool trade clothing, which had at that time almost replaced the old garments of cedar, goat and dog hair. Labrets and nose rings are in evidence, as are many boxes and two dogs. (I. Voznesenskii, Museum of Anthropology and Ethnography, Leningrad)

244

Pavlovsk Harbor on Kodiak Island shows the general settlement with houses perched randomly in suitable places. To the right of the three-man baidarka (carrying a company official or priest) once can see the edge of the treeless island that protects the anchorage even today. Just over the canoe the Russian Orthodox church can be seen. The company buildings including the warehouse are marked by the company flag, a tricolor of the Russian Empire with a double-headed eagle on the upper white quarter. The Erskine House is still there on the shore as it was in 1793.

The brig *Promysel* (?) built at Sitka is anchored in the channel facing off toward Cook Inlet. A gun battery overlooks the vessel, protecting the narrow passage. (I. Voznesenskii, Museum of Anthropology and Ethnography, Leningrad)

There is some confusion about this Tlingit settlement. The village next to Baranov's proposed headquarters site was first thought to be abandoned. Baranov did not wish Indians living anywhere near his headquarters, including the nearby islands, although he wished Aleuts placed on some of these. It was M.I. Muravev, (chief administrator 1821-26) who decided it would be best to have the Tlingits settled next to the fortress walls, right under the cannon barrels. Around 1843 when this fine view was taken there were about 1,350 Tlingits settled here, which number included their nearly 100 slaves.

Behind the plank and timbered buildings, typical of northern Indian design, a chapel is being built for native worship. The American explorer, Lt. W. Elliott, described this in 1874 as "an old Indian Chapel or Greek Catholic Church." Square little Tlingit huts with steep roofs hold cremated Tlingit ashes and favored objects of the dead.

A gate in the palisade opened into a protected market place. The Tlingits might trade there under supervision of armed guards. They brought fish, potatoes, wild sheep and birds, berries and elk. They traded with the Russians and their Aleut and "creole" clerks for axes, knives, kettles, tobacco and manufactured goods often brought in by American merchants. The market closed at 4:00 P.M. each day, and the natives were then sent back through the gates. (I. Voznesenskii, Museum of Anthropology and Ethnography, Leningrad)

246

This Tlingit elder's funeral ceremony inside a large log dwelling is rich in ethnographic information and anthropology. The body of the chieftain is wrapped in a Tlingit ceremonial blanket of complex design, and he wears a headpiece of exceptional design, a man's face perhaps, crowned with walrus whiskers. As Leningrad scholar E.E. Blomquist observed: "All his best belongings are spread around him including a decorated copper shield, all manner of boxes filled with woolen clothes, a fine woven hat and other beautiful blankets." It appears that this is the Wolf clan, and the deceased (injured in a fracas) is Kukhan-Tan. He may have been one of three leaders with whom Baranov first negotiated when he came to Sitka. In the flickering firelight they are singing and dancing to the sound of drums and pounded staffs." (I. Voznesenskii, Museum of Anthropology and Ethnography, Leningrad)

247

It would appear that one of the gentlemen Sykes has drawn lounging on the shore through a spacious Georgian afternoon is Thomas Manby and another is Lt. Peter Pugett (*sic*), for whom *the lower end* of the vast body of water would be named by Captain Vancouver. Later his name would encompass the entire Sound. (J. Sykes, The Bancroft Library)

248

Thomas Manby notes about 2 May 1792, "both Vessels weighed and stood for Port Discovery [near Port Townsend] with a day peculiarly fine and clear.

"By noon we arrived at our intended situation and moored in 34 fathoms about two cables lengths from a murmuring transparent stream. . . . Without loss of time two tents were pitched and the Observatory erected. My fondness for employment procured me the charge of a party to carry on various operations. I took up my abode in one of the Tents and set the Artificers to work. The Carpenters felling timbers for Planks, Armorers, Sailmakers and Coopers in their respective stations. Every morning and evening the Seine was hauled in [as in this drawing] with pretty good success: it brought in large Flounders, Bream, Crabs and very fine Trout." (J. Sykes, The Bancroft Library)

249

View of Volcano Mount. Cooks River. S 32 W. Mount St Augustine S 11 W. nearest shore 2½ Miles. taken at Anchor   John Sykes

20

Mount St Augustine, bea.g S 4 W with Cape Douglas   John Sykes

21

Mount St. Augustin (these two views) near the north shore of Cook Inlet was one of several volcanoes noted by Vancouver while he was in Alaskan waters, particularly around Cook Inlet (then called Cook's River). Another, Illiamna, was noted by many through the years; the Spanish perhaps noted it as Miranda on their charts.

Puget's journal reported, "a compact, connected body of very high mountainous land binds the western shore of this inlet, at no great distance from the water side, all the way from cape Douglas to the volcano; from whence the same lofty range mountains that, from the upper part of the inlet, bore the appearance of being detached. The sound, whole waters appeared to us on the 15th of April to wash the base of the volcano mountain." (J. Sykes, The Bancroft Library).

250

View in the Gulf of new Georgia, the distant land being the S° side of the straits of Juan de Fuca — 13.

W. Humphries

Gulf of New Georgia looking across the southerly end of Vancouver Island toward the Olympics. These rolling foreground hills are easily recognizable today even though they are now covered with homes, even as Captain Vancouver had long ago envisioned. This drawing may have some provenance problems attached to it since W. supplants the initial H. in the usual Humphrys signature.

Henry Humphrys was born in America in 1773. A nephew of Vancouver's West Indies superior, Sir Alan Gardner, he came to the *Discovery* at age 19 probably through that influence. Sykes had also served with Captain Gardner in the *Courageaux*. Humphrys moved up during the expedition, but in the unfortunate Camelford Affair he sided with "the half mad lord." He was court martialed for disrespect in 1798 and his career subsequently floundered. In October 1799 he died of smallpox. It is possible that he and José Cardero (or other members of the second unit of Malaspina's Expedition) could have met anywhere between Vancouver Island and Monterey. These persons doing the sketching would have had much in common to discuss or exchange. (W. Humphrys, The Bancroft Library)

View of the Entrance into Port Quadra   John Sykes

23.

View of Mount Olympus, bear.ᵈ E N E. 4 leag.ᵗ off shore   John Sykes —

10

"On the 15th [of October 1792] the day being clear we had a fine view of Mount Olympus [lower illustration], as we passed close under its foot: it was covered half way down with snow where the warmth of the Sun produced many copious streams & beautiful Cascades which greatly enriched the scene." So recorded Thomas Manby in his journal, now part of the Oregon Historical Society Library collection.

Sykes joined the navy as a captain's servant in 1783. He came to Vancouver as a midshipman and left as a master's mate. In 1795 he was a lieutenant and was promoted through the years eventually rising to the rank of vice admiral in 1848. Top illustration is Sykes' rendering of Port Quadra. (J. Sykes, The Bancroft Library)

252

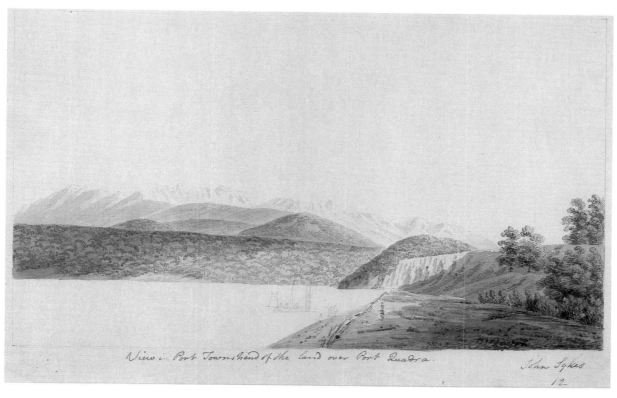

View in Port Townshend of the land over Port Quadra.

John Sykes

12

Manby may really have had a view like this in mind when he said: "Few parks in England could equal this Natural Landscape only inhabited by Indians and wild beasts." It is interesting too that in making his entries the young man does not fail to note that Sir Francis Drake was on this coast "in the reign of Queen Elizabeth. . . ." The small exploring cutter is the type used by Puget and Lt. W. Broughton on the Columbia River (see also the shore of Humphrys' Nootka). Today his 110-mile upriver journey is marked by Broughton's Reach, Chatham Island and Point Vancouver. This area of the "Streights" was also surveyed by Joseph Whidbey, master of the *Discovery,* for whom the large island in the Sound is named. Today we refer to the competent Peruvian-born naval officer as Bodega, rather than Quadra. (J. Sykes, The Bancroft Library)

253

Thomas Manby's journal, the original of which is housed in the collections of the Oregon Historical Society. (OHS Library)

254

rise to about eleven feet perpendicular height. the springs about 3 feet higher. When we had approached within twenty miles of its termination. we often saw a Canoe. and sometimes two or three: all our endeavours would not bring them near us. as they paddled away with all possible speed. When first seen they were generally fishing or hunting the Seal. — In rowing along shore we popp'd on a small party digging Clams at low water: the whole flew to the Woods, and would not return whilst we remained there. To convince them of our amicable intentions. their Clams and property were left untouched, and a few Buttons. Hawkes bells and other trinkets deposited in their Canoe which was constructed in a similar way to those we saw on entering the Straits. About six miles from the head we stopped at a small Village. every inhabitant expressed their consternation by an immediate flight. We could plainly hear them in the interior part of the forest. shrieking loud. and their dogs yelling to a very great degree. — The Huts were constructed by broad plank resting on Rafters: a large fire was burning in the middle. a number of Salmon were extended on Sticks. and hung in the smoke for the purpose of drying and some Clams were roasting. most likely for present use. Two baskets full of these testacious fish. with part of a Seal fresh killed. lay by the fire. and bladders of oil were suspended round the habitation. Two elderly men came and peeped at us; observing them we made every friendly salutation for them to advance: with cautious fear they did sufficiently near to see their dwellings stand unspoiled. This gave them confidence. they came to us without fear perfectly naked. By signs we asked for Salmon and Clams: our request was instantly understood and granted. In return they were presented with a piece of Copper. and each a pair of brass bracelets. — On obtaining this finery their countenances brightened up. Our dress a good deal excited their attention. they expressed by signs the soles of their feet were as hard as our shoes. We plainly heard the fugitives talking in the Woods. one of our new friends went to them. subsided their fears. and made them desirous of metal decorations. A good many men and some boys instantly came out and placed themselves near us without any apprehensions.

This favored view of Mount Baker shows the peak just named by Vancouver to honor his special map-making associate, Joseph Baker. In 1790 Quimper had named the peak "Gran Montaña del Carmelo," but Baker's name eventually prevailed. While in Bellingham Bay in the summer of 1792, *Sutil* and *Mexicana* observers noted rumblings and flashes of fire in the east. Although from time to time reported as dormant, the towering North Cascade volcano is today sporadically active.

There is particular interest in the fact that T. Manby's father, Matthew, a former officer in the Welsh Fusiliers, was aide-de-camp to Lord Townshend during his rule in Ireland as lord lieutenant. From a genuine relationship, Manby could write not only about the ability of Baker, for whom this "extinct volcano" on the mainland was named, but also his noble friends. "A clump formed by fine prodigious Cypress Trees: on the most stately of the number I carved with my knife Ann Marie Townshend and under it T.M. 1792. . . . On joining my party I found them all preparing to depart; I therefore only waited a moment to mix a jorum of Grog which I passed round with some honest fellows to the Health of all my dear and respected Townshend Friends." The "h" was officially dropped in 1851. (J. Sykes, The Bancroft Library)

View in Port Townshend of Mount Baker

Warre and Vavasour were given a six-hour passage across the Strait of Juan de Fuca in Captain Gordon's sailing barge, "the strong tides and currents which cross and recross one another in every direction retarded our progress." Warre has here included what must be a Hudson's Bay Company express canoe moving south along the Sound: "The Views Eastward across the Straits are very beautiful—High broken land extending far into the blue distance and above all Mount Baker standing in milky whiteness." (H. Warre, American Antiquarian Society, Worcester, Mass.)

256

This 1845 waterside view from the Warre and Vavasour journey points
up again the special qualities of the elegant "trolling canoe." Its raised
bow provided excellent lift in the choppy waters of the sounds for the
two or three passengers in the narrow dugout hull of cedar or fir (inevitably
referred to as pine). In the foreground is the so-called "freight canoe" or
perhaps a small version of the war canoe or ocean-going craft, which
would carry more paddlers as well as passengers.

Along the sounds and the inland waters much attention had to be
given beach encampments which could be quickly flooded by 8- to 12-
foot tides. (H. Warre, American Antiquarian Society, Worcester, Mass.)

Thomas Manby in the *Discovery* noted that Protection Island (Juan de Fuca) was half-a-mile long and lay athwart the entrance to Port Discovery, "which is commodiously situated for any vessel requiring a place of safety to recruit her crew after a long Voyage." This same site was being used by sailors and traders whom Warre observed in 1846, and is a favored spot today as a recently established federal bird sanctuary actually about two miles in length. (H. Warre, American Antiquarian Society, Worcester, Mass.)

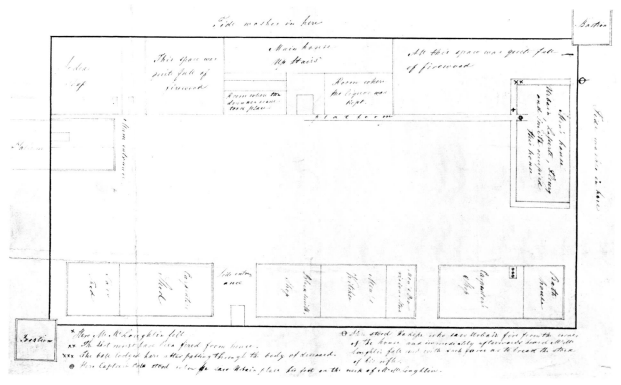

Fort Stikine on the mainland above the Russian settlements was founded by John McLoughlin, operating from Fort Vancouver. It was in this remote site up the Stikine River that the Chief Factor sent his sometimes wayward son. John, Jr., did a very good job in this tide-lapped fur bastion, but as often happened, he had been sent some of the Company's dregs to man this advance post.

This interesting 1842 document (above) might have been secured as evidence during Simpson's cursory, on-the-spot investigation just after young McLoughlin's murder and prior to Simpson's departure for Siberia and St. Petersburg by Russian ship. It might be part of the record gathered by Dr. John McLoughlin to prove overwhelmingly that his son had been shot down by a mutinous staff who were much in contempt of the Bay's regulations for acceptable conduct at such posts. In accordance with Simpson's 1841 analysis of profitable trade, this and other north coast posts were abandoned and replaced by boat traders such as the *Beaver*. (Published by permission of the Hudson's Bay Company Archives, Winnipeg, Manitoba, Canada)

H. Warre and M. Vavasour were most acute observers. By now the sea fur trade had dropped and the two British army lieutenants noted that whalers, especially Americans, had become troublesome.

In 1846 the officers crossed from Port Discovery on the south shore of the Strait of Juan de Fuca to the newly built Hudson's Bay Company post Fort Victoria (above). Off to the side is a roughly sketched Indian village, which impressed the reconnoitering pair no more than the fort. Warre wrote: "The position has been chosen solely for its agricultural advantages, and is ill adapted either as a place of refuge for shipping, or as a position of defense." Vavasour drew fine sketch maps, including Esquimalt harbor. (H. Warre, American Antiquarian Society, Worcester, Mass.)

Joseph Drayton's 1841 view from the west bank of the north-flowing Willamette River beneath Willamette Falls, shows Indians fishing the whirlpools for salmon as they had done for centuries. This observer from the Charles Wilkes United States Exploring Expedition notes suckers and lamprey eels taken by net. While fishing, hours were whiled away with nocturnal gambling games played by both sexes.

Within ten years of Drayton's visit, these falls had become an important trade and waterpower site known as "the American settlement" (Oregon City), to which the towering Hudson's Bay Company leader John McLoughlin retired with his family. (OHS Library)

As elsewhere noted, the Russian traders of the Northwest Coast had to cross westward the North Pacific Ocean and thence go overland to the border town of Kiakhta to conduct their Chinese fur trade. By 1785 a regular supply of sea otter skins plus other less desirable pelts were being carried by sea traders other than Russians, traders who had access to the Chinese market through Portuguese Macao or Canton. It was not easy. The market was unpredictable and what a dramatic change from the fog and rain-driven islands and Northwest coves, were the humid, fetid and complex labyrinths of the Pearl River. Hong Kong was not yet a consideration, but Macao (see p. 265) was jammed with ships that faced the vast Praia Grande. Canton had been made the sole port of entry to China in 1757. Prior to that it had been the great south China commercial port, the meeting place of river and sea trade for the rich Kwantung Province and much more.

The Great West Channel (see p. 266) of the Pearl River was northerly. Two days upriver with a pilot came Lintin Island. The islands were infested with pirates descended from generations of pirates. From this anchorage the fur trader sailed two more days to anchorage at Second Bar, identified by Edmund Hayes as the last stop before anchoring the following day at Whampoa (see p. 268). By then one had with luck passed several sprawling river islands, seen several great towers and pagodas, passed the Anumgnoy Forts, Tiger Island and other challenges. At Whampoa (the Pagoda Anchorage) the cargoes were unloaded. The distance to European and American factories in Canton was still twelve miles upstream by Chinese lighterage. These factories were the only place the Chinese allowed the Westerners to trade.

These details were cared for by a surety man (fiador), a Chinese merchant or his agent who handled all aspects of the transaction. There were thirteen controlling companies in the trading monopoly which was called Co-Hong. Their control was complete. Aside from the compradore (or middleman provisioner) assigned, the fur trader had to work with the hoppo-man, the all-important agent from the Hoppo, the Chinese customs office. The Chinese had been doing business this way on that river for thousands of years. The hoppo-man expected many gifts. Eventually, with the help of an assigned linguist, the sampans reached the factory where furs and other goods were to be stored below the Forbidden City of Rams.

The procedures were vexing and attention to detail was imperative. Captain Gray had a few bad moments on his second voyage when he left his "grand chop" behind in Boston. Happily it caught up with him for his Pearl River transactions. In general the traders felt that the hongs were scrupulously fair, but the Treaty of Nanking in 1832 destroyed the hong system, allowing the establishment of Hong Kong almost 80 miles away. The cession of that vast, empty harbor of Kowloon and Stonecutter's Island assured the success of Hong Kong. That port became the deepwater anchorage for Canton and Macao.

French, Danes, Swedes, British, Americans, Dutch and Portuguese all had factories (*see* pp. 269, 270) and participated in this trade. Their factories were jammed into a small waterfront space. Drawings and paintings on paper, canvas and metal trays reveal how imposing and organized the frenetic scene actually was. Young John Boit, Jr., of Boston had great hopes for his cargo in the *Union,* but in early December 1795, the 20-year-old captain noted a sharp fall in the price for otter skins. "However, as fortune is fickle it's no use to repine our ill luck."

How smart he was to learn this and so much else so early. But in the meantime there was the whole broad stream of Chinese culture all about. While there was little social contact between the elegant Chinese and the "round eyes," there was everything to see: temples, castles, ferryboats (*see* p. 267), floral boats (with warm and welcoming occupants), extensive Chinese gardens and even a small space for western churches, plantings and amenities, reminiscent of an English square (*see* p. 269).

This truly wonderful series of drawings (*see* pp. 264-70, 272) of the period luxuriantly reveals the ways of life during this middle Manchu period. Tinqua has given us a masterful insight into the Chinese tenor of life. But in fact the river swarmed with traders interested in the exchange of goods, not culture. Morison reports Russell Sturgis saying "he never knew better gentlemen than the Hong merchants." (Tinqua, Peabody Museum, Salem, Mass.)

Decorated Chinese junk in the Pearl River estuary. (Tinqua, Peabody
Museum, Salem, Mass.)

The harbor and city of Macao. (Tinqua, Peabody Museum, Salem, Mass.)

Chinese and Western ships in the Pearl River. (Tinqua, Peabody Museum, Salem, Mass.)

Chinese ferry. (Tinqua, Peabody Museum, Salem, Mass.)

Ships of five nations stand in the harbor at Whampoa, surrounded by sampans. (Tinqua, Peabody Museum, Salem, Mass.)

Western factories (left) and church at Canton. (Tinqua, Peabody
Museum, Salem, Mass.)

A Western factory at Canton. (Tinqua, Peabody Museum, Salem, Mass.)

SHIPPED in good Order and well conditioned, by *Joseph Ingraham* in and upon the *good Ship* called the *Columbia* ————— whereof is Master, for this present Voyage, *Robert Gray* ————— now riding at Anchor in the River of *Canton* and bound for *Boston North America* — To say;

Seventeen whole and one Half Chest of Bohea Teas

B N° 1 a 17 Chest
SC N° 21 —½ Chest

being marked and numbered as in the Margin, and are to be delivered, in the like good Order and well conditioned, at the aforesaid Port of *Boston* ————— (the Danger of the Seas only excepted) unto *Thomas H. Perkins* ————— or to *His Order* ————— Assigns, he or they paying Freight for the said Goods *either to Joseph Ingraham or the Owners of the Ship Columbia as customary* — with Primage and Average accustomed. In Witness whereof the Master or Purser of the said *Ship* ————— hath affirmed to *three* — Bills of Lading, all of this Tenor and Date ; the One of which *three* Bills being accomplished, the other *two* ————— to stand void. Dated in *Canton 6 February 1790* —

Robert Gray

Robert Gray's bill of lading through mate Joseph Ingraham for "the good ship called *Columbia* . . . now riding at anchor in the River of Canton and bound for Boston, North America," to be delivered to Thomas Perkins mentions 17 and 14 chests of tea. This from Canton on 6 February 1790.

On the second great voyage it would seem that mate John Box Hoskins was on occasion acting as Joseph Barrell's confidential agent. On 13 December 1792 he dashed off a note to Boston to go on the *Hannibal* departing Whampoa. "Furs are very cheap and almost impossible to get rid of for money, however shall see in a few days what can be done." (OHS Library)

The Red Fort. (Tinqua, Peabody Museum, Salem, Mass.)

The superb pen and ink drawing by an unknown Chinese artist shows
Shanghai in 1860 located on the west bank of the Whangpoo in the
vast Yangtse River system, which has already grown rapidly since its
opening as one of the five Treaty Ports by the 1842 Treaty of Nanking.
The shallow port is already filling with factories and steam vessels fol-
lowing on the first British settlement of 1843. Canton declined as Hong
Kong flourished and Shanghai became supreme. (Peabody Museum,
Salem, Mass.)

273

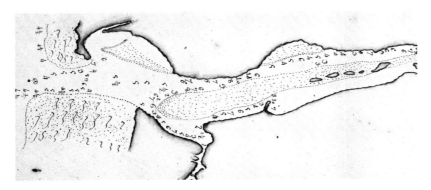

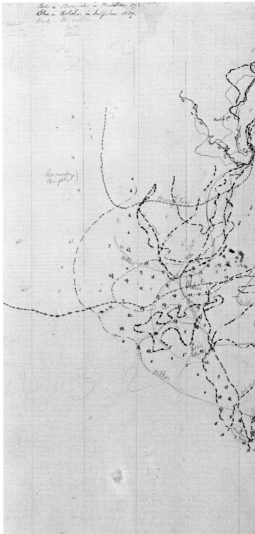

This is a detail (above) from a superb manuscript map (69x47.5 cm) of the Columbia River, which must have been made during negotiations in Monterey, California, in 1792 or early 1793. The *Chatham* had rejoined *Discovery* after the precipitous separation off the turbulent river mouth, and Bodega and Vancouver were getting on very well personally. Important exchanges of geographical information took place. This accurate Spanish copy of the map made by Lt. Broughton and his crew during their eight-day exploration up the Columbia in the *Chatham* fails to note his impressions of the dangerous south shore breakers. (OHS Library)

This splendid manuscript map (63x100 cm) was compiled by the great George Davidson (1825-1911) about 1858 (right). He was working up materials for the *American Coast Pilot* and his research, shown in complex detail, embraces the track and sounding of Lt. Broughton, RN, of the skilled and fiery Belcher in HMS *Sulphur* (which grounded, as did *Chatham*). The survey of Captain Wilkes is noted and other Americans, especially Davidson's associates in the U.S. Geodetic Survey, Wm. Alden and Lt. W.P. McArthur who led the 1849-50 survey in the *Ewing*.

Davidson's engrossment in historical detail is illuminated as he notes the survey points, anchorages and the tiny territorial settlement of Astoria. Warre's survey, those of Hudson's Bay Company (Scarborrough and others) are not noted because they were held secret at this time. (OHS Library)

274

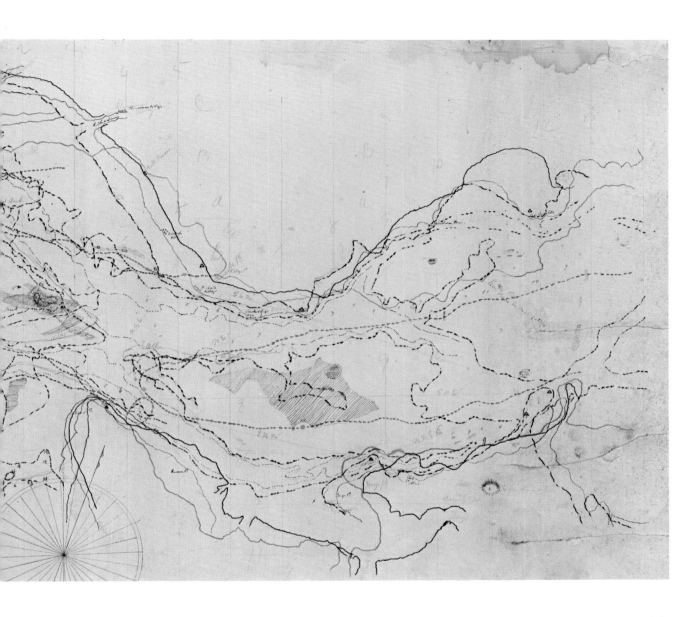

275

The HMS *Hecate*'s principal assignment was "to keep the Indians in awe" on Vancouver Island.

There is something odd if not incongruous about a surveying ship running aground, but this six-gun British paddle-sloop managed it near Neah Bay, Strait of Juan de Fuca, in 1861. The native appears less awed than bemused.

Furthermore, after preliminary repairs at Esquimault the ship had to be towed down to San Francisco Bay and the Mare Island Navy Yard for more substantial repairs. This at the height of the famous "Trent Affair" in which Commodore Wilkes was the principal actor. Had Britain and the Northern states gone to war over this episode the capture of the *Hecate* stuck in a United States drydock would have been assured. (National Maritime Museum, Greenwich)

The fur trade has vanished. Fort Vancouver, which served it so critically, stands like a deserted set (ca. 1856). Dr. John McLoughlin has moved to Oregon City and the new Bay Company leaders have reestablished themselves with Chief Factor James Douglas at Fort Victoria headquarters.

Attention is now directed to the new army post rising along the hill where U.S. Grant and other young officers of pre-Civil War days are stationed. All is peaceful beneath the gaze of Mt. Hood and the outsized American flag now riding triumphant over the newly acquired territory north of the Columbia River, the "St. Lawrence of the West." (John W. Hopkins, OHS Museum)

Soft Gold

Bibliography

Bibliography

Abbott, Donald N., ed. *The World is as Sharp as a Knife: An Anthology in Honour of Wilson Duff*. Victoria, 1981.

Adams, Henry. *The United States in 1800*. Ithaca, 1955.

Akrigg, G.P.V. and Helen B. Akrigg. *British Columbia Chronicle 1778-1846: Adventures by Sea and Land*. Vancouver, 1975.

Anderson, Bern. *The Life and Voyage of Captain George Vancouver, Surveyor of the Sea*. Seattle, 1960.

Andreev, Aleksandr, ed. *Russkie Otkrytiia V Tikhom Okeane I Severnoi Amerike v XVIII Veke*. Moscow-Leningrad, 1948. Translated by Carl Ginsburg: *Russian Discoveries in the Pacific and in North America in the 18th and 19th Centuries*. Ann Arbor, 1952.

Bagrow, Leo. *History of Cartography*. Revised and enlarged by R.A. Skelton. London, 1964.

Bancroft, Hubert H. *History of Alaska, 1730-1855*. San Francisco, 1886.

———— *History of British Columbia, 1792-1887*. San Francisco, 1887.

———— *History of the Northwest Coast*. 2 vols. San Francisco, 1884-86.

Barratt, Glynn. *Russia in Pacific Waters, 1715-1825*. Vancouver, 1981.

Beaglehole, John C. *The Exploration of the Pacific*. Stanford, 1966.

———— *The Life of Captain James Cook*. Stanford, 1974.

Beals, Herbert K., ed. *For Honor and Country: The Diary of Bruno de Hezeta and the Voyage of the Santiago*. To be published by OHS, Portland, 1983.

Belcher, Sir Edward. *Narrative of a Voyage Round the World, Performed in Her Majesty's Ship* Sulpher, *During the Years 1836-1842.* London, 1843.

Blomkvist, E.E. "Risunki I. G. Voznesenskogo (ekspeditisiia 1839-1849 godov)." *Sbornik Muzeia Antropologii I Etnografii,* t. 13 (1951). Translated by Basil Dmytryshyn and E.A.P. Crownhart-Vaughan: "A Russian Scientific Expedition to California and Alaska, 1839-1849." *Oregon Historical Quarterly* 73 (1972).

Boas, Franz. "The Religion of the Kwakiutl Inidans." *Columbia University Contributions to Anthropology,* vol. 10. New York, 1930.

Bodega y Quadra, Juan Francisco de la. "Primer Viaje hasta la altura de 58° . . . 1775." *Anuario de la Direccion de Hidrografia 3.* Madrid, 1865.

————— "Segunda Salida hasta los 61 grados en la fragata Nuestra Senora de los Temedios (a) la Favorita . . . 1779," *Anuario de la Direccion de Hidrografia 3.* Madrid, 1865.

Bolkhovitinov, Nikolai N. *Russko-Amerikanskie Otnosheniia, 1815-1832.* Moscow, 1975.

————— *Stanovlenie Russko-Amerikanskikh Otnoshenii, 1775-1815.* Moscow, 1966. Translated by Elena Levin: *The Beginnings of Russian-American Relations, 1775-1815.* Cambridge, Mass., 1975.

British Columbia Coast (Sailing Directions). 10th ed., vol. 1. Victoria, 1976.

Broughton, William R. *A Voyage of Discovery to the North Pacific Ocean . . . in the Years 1795, 1796, 1797, 1798.* London, 1804.

Brown, Jennifer S.H. *Strangers in Blood: Fur Trade Company Families in Indian Country.* Vancouver, 1980.

Carey, Charles H. "Some Early Maps and Myths." *Oregon Historical Quarterly* 30 (1929).

Chinard, Gilbert. *Le Voyage de La Perouse sur les Cotes de l'Alaska et de Californie, 1786.* Baltimore, 1937.

Clowes, G.S. Laird, *Sailing Ships: Their History and Development.* 4th ed., part 2. London, 1952.

Cobbe, Hugh, ed. *Cook's Voyages and Peoples of the Pacific.* London, 1979.

Cole, Douglas. "Sigismund Bacstrom's Northwest Coast Drawings and an Account of his Curious Career." *BC Studies*, no. 46 (1980).

Colnett, James. *The Journal of Captain James Colnett Aboard the Argonaut From April 26, 1789 to November 3, 1791.* Edited by F.W. Howay. Toronto, 1940.

———— *A Voyage to the South Atlantic and Round Cape Horn into the Pacific Ocean.* London, 1798.

Cook, James. *A Voyage to the Pacific Ocean.* 3 vols. and atlas. London, 1784.

Cook, Warren L. *Flood Tide of Empire.* New Haven and London, 1973.

Cordes, Frederick, C., trans. "Letters of A. Rotchev, Last Commandant at Fort Ross, and the Resumé of the Report of the Russian-American Company for the Year 1850-51." *California Historical Society Quarterly* 39 (1960).

Coxe, William, *Account of the Russian Discoveries Between Asia and America.* London, 1780.

Crownhart-Vaughan, E.A.P. "Clerke in Kamchatka, 1779: New Information for an Anniversary Note," *Oregon Historical Quarterly* 80 (1979).

Cutter, Donald C., ed. *Journal of Tomas de Suria of His Voyage With Malaspina to the Northwest Coast of America in 1791.* Fairfield, Wash., 1980.

De Wolf, John. *A Voyage to the North Pacific and a Journey Through Siberia more than a Century ago.* Cambridge, 1861.

Dixon, George. *Letter and Memorandum from Capt. George Dixon to Sir Joseph Banks Regarding the Fur Trade on the Northwest Coast, A.D. 1789.* San Francisco, 1941.

———— *A Voyage Round the World, But More Particularly to the North West Coast of America.* London, 1789.

Dmytryshyn, Basil and E.A.P. Crownhart-Vaughan, trans. and eds. *The End of Russian America: Captain P.N. Golovin's Last Report 1862.* Portland, 1979.

Drucker, Philip. *Cultures of the North Pacific Coast.* San Francisco, 1969.

Duflot de Mofras, Eugene. *Exploration du Territoire de l'Oregon, des Californies et de la Mer Vermeille.* 2 vols. and atlas. Paris, 1844.

DuFour, Clarence John. "The Russian Withdrawal from California." *Quarterly of the California Historical Society* 13 (1933).

Dunn, John. *History of the Oregon Territory.* London, 1846.

Elliott, T.C., ed. *Captain Cook's Approach to Oregon.* Portland, 1974.

Ellis, William. *An Authentic Narrative of a Voyage Performed by Captain Cook.* 2 vols. London, 1782.

Emmons, George T. "The Basketry of the Tlingit." *American Museum of Natural Memoirs,* vol. 3, pt. 2. Leiden, 1905.

Ernst, Alice H. *The Wolf Ritual of the Northwest Coast.* Eugene, 1952.

Espinoza y Tello, Jose. *A Spanish Voyage to Vancouver Island and the Northwest Coast of America.* Translated by Cecil Jane. London, 1930.

Essig, E.O. "The Russian Settlement at Ross." *Quarterly of the California Historical Society* 13 (1933).

Fedorova, Svetlana G. *Russkoe Naselenie Aliaski I Kalifornii.* Moscow, 1971. Translated by Richard Pierce and Alton Donnelly: *The Russian Population in Alaska and California, Late 18th Century-1867.* Ontario, 1973.

Forbes, Esther. *Paul Revere & the World He Lived In.* Boston, 1942.

Franchere, Gabriel. *Journal of a Voyage on the Northwest Coast of North America During the Years 1811, 1812, 1813, 1814.* Toronto, 1969.

Friendly, Alfred. *Beaufort of the Admiralty: The Life of Sir Francis Beaufort 1774-1857.* New York, 1977.

Ganiushknina, Tamara I., Rita S. Razumovskaia, Irina F. Shavrina. *Museum of Anthropology of Ethnography.* Leningrad, 1973.

Gassner, J.S. *Voyages and Adventures of La Perouse.* Honolulu, 1969.

Gibson, James R. "Bostonians and Muscovites on the Northwest Coast, 1788-1841." In *The Western Shore: Oregon Country Essays Honoring the American Revolution,* edited by Thomas Vaughan. Portland, 1975.

———— *Imperial Russia in Frontier America: The Changing Geography of Supply of Russian America, 1784-1867.* New York, 1976.

Godwin, George S. *Vancouver, A Life, 1757-1798.* New York, 1931.

Golder, Frank A. *Bering's Voyages.* New York, 1922-25.

Gough, Barry M. *Distant Dominion: Britain and the Northwest Coast of*

America, 1579-1809. Vancouver and London, 1980.

———— *The Royal Navy and the Northwest Coast of North America, 1810-1814.* Vancouver, 1971.

Gunther, Erna. *Indian Life on the Northwest Coast of North America, As Seen by the Early Explorers and Fur Traders During the Last Decades of the Eighteenth Century.* Chicago, 1972.

Gutierrez, Camarena Marcial. *San Blas y las Californias. Estudio Historico del Puerto.* Mexico City, 1956.

Halpin, Marjorie. "Masks as Metaphors of Anti-Structure." Unpublished paper. 1975.

Hanson, Charles E., Jr. *The Northwest Gun.* Lincoln, 1955.

Haring, C.H. *The Spanish Empire in America.* New York, 1947.

Hayes, Edmund, Sr., ed. *Log of the Union: John Boit's Remarkable Voyage.* Portland, 1981.

Holm, Bill. *The Crooked Beak of Heaven: Masks and Other Ceremonial Art of the Northwest Coast.* Seattle, 1975.

———— *Northwest Coast Indian Art: An Analysis of Form.* Seattle, 1965.

———— "The Trade Gun as a Factor in Northwest Coast Indian Art," Paper presented at the 23rd Annual Meeting, Northwest Anthropological Conference, Victoria. 1969.

Holm, Bill and George I. Quimby. *Edward S. Curtis in the Land of the War Canoes: A Pioneer Cinematographer in the Pacific Northwest.* Seattle, 1980.

Holmberg, J.H. "Ethnographische Skizzen über die Völker des Russischen Amerika." *Acta Societalis Scientiarum Fennucaem,* vol. 4. Helsingfors, 1856.

Hoskins, John. "Narrative of the Second Voyage of the *Columbia,* 1790-1792." *Proceedings of the Massachusetts Historical Society,* vol. 79. Boston, 1941.

Hough, Walter. "Primitive American Armor." *United States National Museum Report for 1893.* Washington, D.C., 1894.

Howay, Frederick W. *A List of Trading Vessels in the Maritime Fur Trade, 1785-1825.* Reprint. Kingston, Ontario, 1973.

————— *Voyages of the* Columbia *to the Northwest Coast, 1787-1790 &* *1790-1793.* Boston, 1941.

————— ed. *The Dixon-Meares Controversy.* Toronto, [1929].

Humboldt, Alexander von. *Essai Politique sur le Royaume de la Nouvelle Espagne.* 4 vols. and atlas. Paris, 1811.

Hussey, John A., ed. *The Voyage of the* Racoon: *A "Secret" Journal of a Visit to Oregon, California, and Hawaii, 1813-1814.* San Francisco, 1858.

Ingraham, Joseph. "Log of the Brigantine Hope from Boston to the Northwest Coast of America, and Journal of Events, 1790-1792." MS, OHS Library.

Jackman, S.W. *The Journal of William Sturgis.* Victoria, 1978.

Johansen, Dorothy O. *Empire of the Columbia: A History of the Pacific Northwest.* New York, 1967.

Johansen, Dorothy O., ed. *Voyage of the* Columbia *Around the World with John Boit, 1790-1793.* Portland, 1960.

Jonaitis, Aldona. "Land Otters and Shamans: Some Interpretations of Tlingit Charms." *American Indian Art Magazine,* vol. 4, no. 1. Scottsdale, 1978.

————— *The Relationship Between the Social and Shamanic Art of The Tlingit Indians of the Northwest Coast of America.* Ann Arbor, 1977.

Joppien, Rüdiger. "The Artistic Bequest of Captain Cook's Voyages: Popular Imagery in European Costume Books of the Late Eighteenth and Early Nineteenth Centuries." *In Captain James Cook and His Times,* edited by Robin Fisher and Hugh Johnston. Vancouver, 1979.

————— "Die Bildillustrationem zum Atlas der *Voyage de LaPerouse* Zur Dokumentation ihrer Entstehung." In *Die Buchillustration im 18 Jahrhundert.* Heidelberg, 1980.

Kaeppler, Adrienne L. *Artificial Curiosities: Being an Exposition of Native Manufactures Collected on the Three Pacific Voyages of Captain James Cook, R.N.* Honolulu, 1978.

Khlebnikov, Kyrill T. *Colonial Russian America: Kyrill T. Khlebnikov's Reports, 1817-1832.* Translated by Basil Dmytryshyn and E.A.P. Crownhart-Vaughan. Portland, 1976.

King, J.C.H. *Artificial Curiosities from the Northwest Coast of America.* London, 1981.

———— *Portrait Masks from the Northwest Coast of America.* London, 1979.

Krasheninnikov, Stepan P. *Opisanie Zemli Kamchatki.* Translated and edited by E.A.P. Crownhart-Vaughan: *Explorations of Kamchatka: North Pacific Scimitar.* Portland, 1972.

Krause, A. *The Tlingit Indians.* Translated by Erna Gunther. Seattle, 1956.

Langle, Paul Fleuriot de. *La Tragique Expedition de La Perouse et de Langle.* Paris, 1954.

Langsdorff, Georg Heinrich von. *Voyages and Travels in the Various Parts of the World, During the Years 1803, 1804, 1805, 1806 and 1807.* 2 vols. London, 1813-14.

Laguna, Frederica de. "Under Mount Saint Elias: The History and Culture of the Yakutat Tlingit." *Smithsonian Contributions to Anthropology,* vol. 17, parts 1-3. Washington, D.C., 1972.

La Perouse, Jean-Francois de. *Voyage Autour de Monde sur l'Astrolabe et la Boussole (1785-1788).* Paris, 1980.

———— *Voyage de la Perouse Autour du Monde.* 4 vols. and atlas. Paris, 1797.

———— *A Voyage Round the World.* London, 1798.

Lavender, David S. *Land of the Giants: The Drive to the Pacific Northwest, 1750-1950.* New York, 1958.

Ledyard, John. *A Journal of Captain Cook's Last Voyage to the Pacific Ocean.* Hartford, 1783.

Leonard, H.L.W. *Oregon Territory: Containing a Brief Account of Spanish, English, Russian and American Discoveries on the North-West Coast of America. Also, the Different Treaty Stipulations Confirming the Claim of the United States, and Overlands Expeditions to the Columbia River.* Cleveland, 1846.

Liapunova, Roza G. *Ocherki Po Etnografii Aleutov, Konets XVIII – Pervaia XIX v* [Essays on the Ethnography of the Aleuts from the Late 18th Century to the First Half of the 19th]. Leningrad, 1975.

286

Lisianskii, Iurii F. *A Voyage Round the World, in the Years 1803, 4, 5, & 6: Performed, by an Order of His Imperial Majesty Alexander the First, Emperor of Russia, in the Ship Neva.* London, 1814.

Macnair, Peter, Alan Hoover and Kevin Neary. *The Legacy: Continuing Traditions of Northwest Coast Indian Art.* Victoria, 1980.

Malaspina, Alejandro. *Viaje Politico Cientifico Alrededor del Mundo por las Corbetas Descubierta y Atrevida.* Madrid, 1885.

Manby, Thomas. "Journal." MS, OHS Library.

Massachusetts Historical Society. *Proceedings of the Massachusetts Historical Society,* vol. 1, 1791-1835. Boston.

Meares, John. *Voyages Made in he Years 1788 and 1789, From China to the North West Coast of America.* London, 1790.

Merk, Frederick, ed. *Fur Trade and Empire: George Simpson's Journal.* Cambridge, Mass., 1960.

Morison, Samuel Eliot. "The *Columbia*'s Winter Quarters of 1791-1792 Located," *Oregon Historical Quarterly* 39 (1938).

————— *Maritime History of Massachusetts, 1783-1860.* Boston, 1921.

Müller, Gerhard F. *Voyages From Asia to America, for Completing the Discoveries of the North West Coast of America. To Which is Prefixed, a Summary of the Voyages Made by the Russians on the Frozen Sea, in Search of a North East Passage.* London, 1761.

Munro, Wilfred H. *Tales of an Old Sea Port.* Princeton, 1917.

Murray-Oliver, A.A. St. C.M. *Captain Cook's Hawaii as Seen by His Artists.* Wellington, New Zealand, 1975.

Museum National d'Histoire Naturelle. *Voyages et Decouvertes des Voyageurs Naturalistes aux Chercheurs Scientifiques.* Paris, 1981.

Ogden, Adele, *The California Sea Otter Trade, 1784-1848.* Berkeley, 1941.

————— "Russian Sea-Otter and Seal Hunting on the California Coast, 1803-1841," *Quarterly of the California Historical Society* 13 (1933).

Okun, Semen B. *Rossiisko-Amerikanskaia Kompaniia.* Moscow-Leningrad, 1939. Translated by Carl Ginsburg: *The Russian American Company.* Cambridge, Mass., 1951.

The Pacific: Russian Scientific Investigations. Leningrad, 1926.

Pethick, Derek. *First Approaches to the Northwest Coast*. Vancouver, 1976.

————— *The Nootka Connection: Europe and the Northwest Coast, 1790-1795*. Vancouver, 1980.

Portlock, Nathaniel. *A Voyage Round the World: But More Particularly to the North West Coast of America; Performed in 1785, 1786, 1787, and 1788 in the* King George *and* Queen Charlotte, *Captains Portlock and Dixon*. London, 1789.

Quimper, Manuel. "Diario, 1790." Translated by H.R. Wagner in: *Spanish Explorations in the Strait of Juan de Fuca*. Santa Ana, 1933.

Rasmussen, Louise. "Artists with Explorations on the Northwest Coast." *Oregon Historical Quarterly* 42 (1941).

Ratner-Shternberg. "Muzeinye Materialy po Tlingitam," *Akademiia Nauk SSSR. Muzei Antropologii i Etnografii Sbornik* 6. Moscow, 1927-1930.

Samuel, Cherly. *The Dancing Blanket*. In press.

Saum, Lewis O. *The Fur Trader and the Indian*. Seattle, [1965].

Schafer, Joseph, ed. "Documents Relative to Warre and Vavasour's Military Reconnoissance in Oregon," *Oregon Historical Quarterly* 10 (1909).

Schur, L.A. and R.A. Pierce. "Artists in Russian America: Mikhail Tikhanov (1818)," *The Alaska Journal* 6 (1976).

Seafaring in Colonial Massachusetts. Papers from a Conference held by The Colonial Society of Massachusetts November 21 and 22, 1975. Boston, 1980.

"Secret Mission of Warre and Vavasour" [Documents]. *The Washington Historical Quarterly* [now *Pacific Northwest Quarterly*] 3 (1912).

Sheehan, Carol. *Pipes that Won't Smoke, Coal that Won't Burn*. Calgary, 1981.

Shotridge, Louis. "Ghost of Courageous Adventurer." *The Museum Journal* vol. 11, pt. 1. Philadelphia, 1920.

Simpson, Sir George. *Narrative of A Journey Round the World During the Years 1841 and 1842*. 2 vols. London, 1847.

Spaulding, Kenneth A. *The Fur Hunters of the Far West*. Norman, [1956].

Stejneger, Leonhard. *Georg Wilhelm Stellar, the Pioneer of Alaskan Natural History.* Cambridge, Mass., 1936.

Stenzel, Franz. *Cleveland Rockwell, Scientist and Artist, 1837-1907.* Portland, 1972.

Stewart, Hilary. *Indian Artifacts of the Northwest Coast.* Seattle, 1973.

Sturgis, William. *The Northwest Fur Trade.* Old South Leaflets No. 219.

Sturtevant, William, ed. *Boxes and Bowls: Decorated Containers by Nineteenth Century Haida, Tlingit, Bella Bella and Tsimshian Indians.* Washington, D.C., 1976.

Swanton, John R. "Contributions to the Ethnology of the Haida." *American Museum of Natural History Memoirs,* vol. 5, pt. 1. 1905.

——— "Haida Texts and Myths." *Bureau of American Ethnology Bulletin,* no. 29. Washington, D.C., 1905.

——— "Tlingit Texts and Myths." *Bureau of American Ethnology Bulletin,* no. 39. Washington, D.C., 1909.

Taylor, E.G.R. *Navigation in the Days of Captain Cook.* London, 1975.

Tebenkov, Mikhail D. *Atlas Severozapadnykh Beregov Ameriki.* St. Petersburg, 1852.

Tikhmenev, P.A. *A History of the Russian-American Company.* St. Petersburg, 1861-63. Translated and edited by Richard A. Pierce and Alton S. Donnelly. Seattle, 1978.

Tolstoy, Nikolai. *The Half-Mad Lord: Thomas Pitt 2nd Baron Camelford (1775-1804).* New York, 1978.

Torre Revello, Jose. *Los Artistas Pintores de la Expedicion Malaspina.* Buenos Aires, 1944.

Vancouver, George. *A Voyage of Discovery to the North Pacific Ocean and Round the World.* 3 vols. and atlas. London, 1789.

Vaughan, Thomas, ed. *The Western Shore: Oregon Country Essays Honoring the American Revolution.* Portland, 1975.

Vaughan, Thomas and A.A. St. C.M. Murray-Oliver. *Captain Cook, R.N., the Resolute Mariner: An International Record of Oceanic Discovery.* Portland, 1974.

Vaughan, Thomas, E.A.P. Crownhart-Vaughan and Mercedes Palau de Iglesias. *Voyages of Enlightenment: Malaspina on the Northwest Coast, 1791/92.* Portland, 1977.

Viana, Francisco Xavier de. *Diario del Teniente de Navio D. Francisco Xavier de Viana, Trabajado en el Viaje de las Corbetas de S.M.C. Descubierta y Atrevida en los Años de 1789, 1790, 1791, 1792, y 1793.* Cerrito de la Victoria, Uruguay, 1849.

Vilar, E. Vila. *Los Rusos en America.* Sevilla, 1966.

Wagner, Henry R. *Cartography of the Northwest Coast of America to the Year 1800.* Berkeley, 1937.

———— *Spanish Explorations in the Strait of Juan de Fuca.* Santa Ana, 1933.

Warre, H.J. *Overland to Oregon in 1845: Impressions of a Journey Across North America.* Edited and with an introduction by Madeleine Major-Fregeau. Ottawa, 1976.

Waterman, T.T. and Geraldine Coffin. *Types of Canoes on Puget Sound* (Indian Notes and Monographs). New York, 1920.

Wilkes, Charles; *Narrative of the United States Exploring Expedition During the Years 1831, 1839, 1840, 1841, 1842.* 5 vols. Philadelphia, 1849.

Williams, Glyndwr. *The British Search for the Northwest Passage in the Eighteenth Century.* London, 1962.

Wing, Robert C. with Gordon Newell. *Peter Puget.* Seattle, 1979.

Wright, Robin. "Haida Argillite Pipes." MA Thesis, University of Washington, 1977.

Soft Gold
Afterword & Acknowledgements

Afterword

As the fur trade developed along the Northwest Coast of America during the eighteenth and nineteenth centuries, it exposed the Indians of the region and their culture to the world, and the world quickly noted the extraordinary and sophisticated cultures that existed in this far corner of the globe. The exhibition and this publication, both entitled *Soft Gold: The Fur Trade and Cultural Exchange on the Northwest Coast of America*, have charted a similar course of exposure and influence.

Initiated by the Oregon Historical Society interest in the Collection Sharing Program of the Peabody Museum of Archaeology and Ethnography at Harvard University, the concept for the exhibition and publication grew to one of international stature during a three-year period. Loaned for the duration of the exhibition, the 142 Peabody artifacts give an interpretive core of the ethnographic portion of this international exhibition. These artifacts are of great importance because of their intrinsic aesthetic value and because of their documented lineage (so rare with early Northwest Coast objects).

Paintings, drawings, maps and additional historic materials have been generously loaned from institutions throughout North America and around the world. These special materials illustrate vividly the impact of the fur trade based on the pelts and hides from the Northwest Coast. A number of significant trade related items from the collections of the Oregon Historical Society add luster to *Soft Gold*.

The fur trade was a grand scheme of merchandising. Mariners from

Europe and the United States came to the Northwest Coast to trade for pelts, which they shipped to the Far East and around the world. For furs from the Indians, the Westerners traded metal, cloth, beads and other items. As the process evolved, the artisans along the Northwest Coast began to cater to the traders. They not only created traditional objects using materials brought by the foreigners, but objects of Western design. As a result, the Indian artisans imposed western designs on traditional objects, and produced objects whose design origins were Western.

A little recognized facet of the trading process was the involvement of Indian women. Merchants in their own right, women gained both great material wealth and high social status. In many instances, women were directly responsible for the great accumulation of wealth dispersed during potlatches.

The Oregon Historical Society continues the Northwest potlatch tradition by sharing this accumulation of priceless materials.

Many dedicated persons and learned institutions helped gather and present *Soft Gold*. The following is a list of those responsible for helping disperse the wealth of visual and factual information.

Robert Stark
Museums Administrator
Oregon Historical Society

Acknowledgements

Academy of Fine Arts
  Moscow
  Petr M. Sysoev
Alaska State Museum
  Juneau
  Alan R. Munro, Director
  Dan Monroe, Deputy Director
American Antiquarian Society
  Worcester, Massachusetts
  Marcus A. McCorison, Director
Anchorage Historical and Fine Arts Museum
  R. L. Shalkop, Director
  M. Diane Brenner, Archivist
Archivo General de Indias
  Sevilla
  Rosario Parra Cala, Director
Archivo General de la Nacion
  Mexico City
  Alejandra Moreno Toscano, Director
  Sra. Monasterio, Exhibits Coordinator
  Silvia Galicia, Maps & Plans
The Bancroft Library
  Berkeley
  James D. Hart, Director
Bibliotheque Historique de la Marine
  Paris
  Gabriel Labar
Bibliotheque Nationale
  Paris
  Mlle. Pelletier, Chief Conservator, Maps & Plans
Roswell S. Bosworth, Jr.

294

The British Library
   London
      Helen Wallis, Keeper of Maps
      Derek Turner, Manuscripts Exhibitions
The British Museum
   London
      David Wilson, Director
Mrs. Milton Brunkow
E. W. Caswell, Jr.
Central Naval Museum
   Leningrad
      M. A. Fateev, Director
      A. A. Shapovalov, Associate Director
      L. S. Zolotorev, Chief Curator
      E. G. Kushnarev, Academic Secretary (retired)
Dixson Library, State Library of New South Wales
   Sydney
      R. F. Doust, State Librarian
      Dianne Rhodes, Dixson Librarian
Geographical Society of the Academy of Sciences
   Leningrad
      Sergei Lavrev, President
      Tamara P. Matveeva
      Lidiia I. Iarkova
Glenbow Museum, Calgary
   Alberta
      Duncan Cameron, Director
      Hugh Dempsey, Chief Curator
Hawaii State Archives
   Honolulu
Hudson's Bay Company
   Winnipeg
      Shirlee Anne Smith, Archivist
      Gayle Holcomb

Hydrographic Service, Ministry of Defence
  Taunton, Somerset, England
  Rear Admiral D. W. Halsam, Hydrographer of the Navy
  Lt. Cmdr. A. C. F. David
  Margaret Perry, Curator
Institute of Ethnography of the Academy of Sciences
  Moscow
  Acad. Iu. V. Bromley, Director
  Svetlana G. Fedorova
  Leningrad
  Rostislav V. Kinzhalov
  Roza G. Liapunova
  Avraam D. Dridzo
  Galina Dzeniskevich
Institute of General History of the Academy of Sciences
  Moscow
  Aleksei L. Narochnitskii
  Nikolai N. Bolkhovitinov
  A. I. Alekseev
Kodiak Historical Society
  Marian Johnson, Director
Makah Cultural and Research Center
  Neah Bay, Washington
  Cherl Verna Parton, Museum Secretary
Mariners' Museum
  Newport News
Massachusetts Historical Society
  Boston
  Louis L. Tucker, Director
Ministry of Culture
  Moscow
  Hon. Petr N. Demichev, Minister

296

Musees de France
    Paris
    Hubert Landais, Director
Ministere des Affaires Etrangeres
    Paris
    Marie Hamon, Diplomatic Archives
Musee de la Marine
    Paris
    Le Commandant Bellec, Director
Museo de Americas
    Madrid
    Juan Gonzalez Navarrette, Director
    Maria Concepcion Garcia Saiz, Conservator
Museo Naval
    Madrid
    Jose Maria Zumalacarregui Calvo, Director
Museum National d'Histoire Naturelle
    Paris
    Yves Laissus, Chief Conservator
Museum of the Academy of Fine Arts
    Leningrad
    Ekaterina V. Grishina
National Board of Antiquities and Historical Monuments
    Helsinki
    Raimo Fagerström, Curator
National Endowment for the Humanities
    Washington, D.C.
    William Bennett, Chairman
    Joseph Duffey, Past Chairman
    Cheryl McClenney, Program Director
National Library of Australia
    Office of Museums and Historical Agencies
    Canberra
    Catherine Santamaria, Director, Australian Studies

National Maritime Museum
   Greenwich
     Basil Greenhill, CMG, Director
     John Morrison, Board of Directors
     Anthony Cayser, Chairman of Board
     W. B. Mansell, MC, Secretary
     Elizabeth Warren
     Percival Prescott
     Roger Quarm
National Museum of Finland
   Helsinki
   Osmo Vuoristo, Director
The Peabody Museum
   Salem, Massachusetts
   Peter Fetchko, Director
   Lucy J. Batchelder, Registrar
   Geraldine Byers
State History Museum
   Moscow
   Konstantin G. Levykin, Director
United States Coast Guard Academy Museum
   New London, Connecticut
   Paul H. Johnson, Curator
United States Embassy
   Mexico City
   Diane Stanley
United States Library of Congress
   Washington, D.C.
   Paul E. Edlund, Division Chief
   Christopher Wright, Interlibrary loans
United States Senate
   Hon. Mark O. Hatfield
University of Leningrad
   Boris N. Komissarov

HONORARY COMMITTEE

*Mrs. Harold A. Miller	Oregon, Chairman
Academician Anatolii P. Aleksandrov	USSR
The Honorable Victor Atiyeh	Governor of the State of Oregon
Academician Iu. V. Bromley	USSR
*C. Howard Burnett, President	Oregon Historical Society
David L. Davies	Oregon
The Right Reverend Gregory	Bishop of Sitka and Alaska
*Edmund Hayes, Sr.	Oregon
*Nils B. Hult	Oregon
*Samuel S. Johnson	Oregon
W. Kaye Lamb	Canada
Sir Charles Madden, Bt., GCB	Great Britain
Sir James McDonald, KBE	Oregon
*Donald H. McGraw	Oregon
*Aubrey N. Morgan, CMG	Washington
Amelia Peabody	Massachusetts
Mrs. Francis B. Sanborn	Arizona
The Honorable John Sharpe	Canada
*Moe M. Tonkin	Oregon
*Mrs. John Youell	Oregon
*Thomas Vaughan	Oregon Historical Society Corresponding Secretary

*Members of the Planning Committee

299

SOFT GOLD SCHOLAR ADVISORY COMMITTEE

Nikolai N. Bolkhovitinov	USSR
Georgia Bumgardner	Massachusetts
Douglas Cole	Canada
E.A.P. Crownhart-Vaughan	Oregon
Donald Cutter	New Mexico
Jane Dacey	England
Andrew C.F. David	England
Lawrence Dinnean	California
Basil Dmytryshyn	Oregon
Jean Dorst	France
Raymond H. Fisher	California
Jon Freshour	Washington, D.C.
James R. Gibson	Canada
Barry Gough	Canada
Bruce Taylor Hamilton	Oregon
James D. Hart	California
Edmund Hayes	Oregon
Bill Holm	Washington
Maxwell Hope	New Zealand
Rüdiger Joppien	West Germany
Rostislav V. Kinzhalov	USSR
Priscilla Knuth	Oregon
Hubert Landais	France
Gordon Manning	Oregon
Aleksei L. Narochnitskii	USSR
Tove Olsoni-Nilsson	Finland
Mercedes Palau de Iglesias	Spain
Edmund Pognon	France
Harley Preston	England
Dianne Rhodes	Australia
Catherine Santamaria	Australia
the late Erna V. Siebert	USSR
Fran Silverman	Massachusetts
Jane Silverman	Hawaii

Shirlee A. Smith	Canada
Robert Stark	Oregon
John Steelquist, M.D.	California
Alejandra Moreno Toscano	Mexico
Stephen S.P. Vaughan	Oregon
Thomas Vaughan	Oregon
Helen Wallis	England
A. Paul Winfisky	Massachusetts

Colophon

Soft Gold is typeset in 10 pt. Goudy Old Style, Frederic W. Goudy's classic and elegantly straightforward roman face, less Venetian in influence, but based on capitals designed by Hans Holbein, first used in 1915. The display typography, Cancelleresca Bastarda, is a derivation of the italic writing hand that so influenced the first Italic type designs at the beginning of the sixteenth century. This volume was printed on 100-pound Wedgewood Offset Gloss, and the paperbound cover is Kromekote. The clothbound edition is bound in Crown Linen.

All objects from the Peabody Museum of Archaeology and Ethnology at Harvard University were photographed by Hillel Burger, except the details of objects Nos. 24 and 67, which were photographed by George Champlin of the Oregon Historical Society. All other photographs were taken by Mr. Champlin, Durham & Downey and Trade Litho. All illustrations have been reproduced in 200-line screens.

The production of *Soft Gold* was accomplished through the cooperation and professional skills of the following firms:

Typesetting:	Precision Graphics (text)
	Spartan Typography (display)
Color Transparencies:	SpectraChrome
Color Separations:	Trade Litho
Paper:	Western Paper
Printing:	Durham & Downey
Binding:	Lincoln & Allen

Special acknowledgement is made to Colleen Campbell.
Soft Gold was designed and produced by Bruce Taylor Hamilton.

COUNTY LIBRARY

TILLAMOOK, ORE.